My Daily Eucharist

Compiled & Edited by

Joan Carter McHugh
Lake Forest, Illinois

Nihil Obstat
James P. Campbell, D.Min.
Censor Deputatus
February 29, 1996

Imprimatur
Most Reverend Raymond E. Goedert, M.A., S.T.L, J.C.L.
Vicar General
Archdiocese of Chicago
March 1, 1996

Published by:
Witness Ministries
825 S. Waukegan Road. PMB 200
Lake Forest, IL 60045
Tel: 847-735-0556 or 866-WITNESS (948-6377) FAX: 847-735-0911
www.witnessministries.org
E-mail: witnessm@aol.com

© Joan Carter McHugh, 2002

Sixth printing
November 2002

ISBN: 0-9640417-3-1

About the Cover

My Daily Eucharist needed a special cover which I was at a loss to find. So I asked the Lord to help me find a beautiful cover which would do justice to the contents of this work.

Needing more research material, I asked and received permission to borrow books from the library of the Franciscan Friars at Marytown. While rummaging through the shelves, I found an oversize Eucharistic anthology of quotations and excerpts on devotion, adoration and reparation to the Eucharistic Heart of Jesus by Fr. Albert Kretschmer, SVD. While flipping through it, one page took my breath away—a black and white photocopy of this cover—which, as soon as I saw it, I knew to be the answer to my prayer.

The copyright owner was the Convent of the Sacred Heart in Sault, Montreal. Warm feelings of delight and gratitude washed over me. I spent twelve years at the Convent of the Sacred Heart in New York City— twelve wonderful years. I phoned Montreal and Sr. Jo McCarthy, RSCJ, told me a little about St. Margaret Mary Nealis, the artist, who died in 1958. Sr. Jo referred me to Sr. Margery Lanigan RSCJ in Halifax, Nova Scotia, who might possibly have a color reproduction of the painting.

"Yes, I certainly do have a color print," she said, "and you are welcome to it. Sr. Margaret Mary will be happy in heaven to know that her painting will be on the cover of a book on the Eucharist!" Sr. Margaret Mary painted it in response to a request from a commercial photographer in Montreal, Mr. F.J. Topp, whose sideline was publishing religious pictures. He asked her to paint a picture of Our Lord saving the world. "This was her inspiration," Sr. Lanigan said, "Our Lord saving the world through the Cross, the Mass and the Eucharist."

Amen, Amen, I say to you, whoever believes has eternal life. I am the bread of life. Your ancestors ate the manna in the desert, but they died; this is the bread that comes down from heaven so that one may eat it and not die. I am the living bread that came down from heaven; whoever eats this bread will live forever; and the bread that I will give is my flesh for the life of the world.

The Jews quarreled among themselves, saying, "How can this man give us his flesh to eat?" Jesus said to them, "Amen, amen, I say to you, unless you eat the flesh of the Son of Man and drink his blood, you do not have life within you. Whoever eats my flesh and drinks my blood has eternal life, and I will raise him on the last day. For my flesh is true food, and my blood is true drink. Whoever eats my flesh and drinks my blood remains in me and I in him. Just as the living Father sent me and I have life because of the Father, so also the one who feeds on me will have life because of me. This is the bread that came down from heaven. Unlike your ancestors who ate and still died, whoever eats this bread will live forever."

Then many of his disciples who were listening said, "This saying is hard; who can accept it . . . ?"

As a result of this, many of his disciples returned to their former way of life and no longer accompanied him. Jesus then said to the Twelve, "Do you also want to leave?" Simon Peter answered him, "Master, to whom shall we go? You have the words of eternal life."

John 6: 53-60, 66-69

Catechism Of The Catholic Church

The mode of Christ's presence under the Eucharistic elements is unique. It raises the Eucharist above all the sacraments as "the perfection of the spiritual life and the end to which all the sacraments tend." In the most Blessed Sacrament of the Eucharist "the Body and Blood, together with the soul and divinity, of our Lord Jesus Christ and, therefore, the *whole Christ is truly, really and substantially* contained. We call this presence "real" not in an exclusive way, as if his other modes of being present were not real, but "because it is a presence par excellence, since it is substantial, in the sense that Christ, whole and entire, God and man, becomes present (no. 1374).

The Council of Trent summarizes the Catholic Faith by declaring "Because Christ our Redeemer said that it was truly His Body that He was offering under the species of bread, it has always been the conviction of the Church, and this Holy Council declares it again that: by the consecration of the bread and wine there takes place a change of the whole substance of the bread into the substance of the Body of Christ our Lord and of the whole substance of the wine into the substance of His Blood. The Catholic Church fittingly and properly called this change *transubstantiation* (no. 1376).

The Documents Of Vatican II

The other sacraments, as well as every ministry of the Church and every work of the apostolate, are linked with the holy Eucharist and are directed toward it. For the most blessed Eucharist contains the Church's entire spiritual wealth, that is, Christ Himself, our Passover and living bread. Through His very flesh, made vital and vitalizing by the Holy Spirit, He offers life to men. They are thereby invited and led to offer themselves, their labors, and all created things together with Him.

Hence the Eucharist shows itself to be the source and the apex of the whole work of preaching the gospel. Those under instruction are introduced by stages to a sharing in the Eucharist. The faithful, already marked with the sacred seal of baptism and confirmation, are through the reception of the Eucharist fully joined to the Body of Christ (no. 5).

Decree on the Ministry and Life of Priests

Author's Preface

My Daily Eucharist is for hearty appetites—that is to say for people who are hungry for God. If you are empty and looking for nourishment, you have found the right book. If you desire to deepen your faith in our Eucharistic Lord, you have found the right book. If you are questioning and searching for Gospel truth, especially as it relates to the Eucharist, you have found the right book. If you want to enrich your prayer life and add grist for the mill of your meditations, you have found the right book.

Like a gourmet dinner, this book should be savored slowly. Each day serves up a special read which will nourish your heart and mind with love for Our Lord in the Blessed Sacrament. Altogether it is a feast for your soul, prepared by hundreds of disciples who have labored in the vineyard of the Church since the time of Christ.

My Daily Eucharist includes testimony on the Real Presence of Christ in the Eucharist from the Fathers of the Church up to modern, twentieth century theologians, with a wide variety of authors in between. There are treasured excerpts from diaries of Saints and Popes, special revelations from Our Lord and Our Lady, stories of apparitions and miracles related to the Eucharist, testimonies of personal conversions and healing, and historical and biographical entries which add continuity to the work.

I felt the need to include some reflections on the prefigurement of the Eucharist in the Old Testament, because as our Holy Father, Pope John Paul II said when speaking about Holy Thursday, "the mysterious reality of the Eucharist introduces us into the 'plan' of God, Creator and Redeemer. God wanted His only son to be incarnate and ever present among us as our traveling

vii

companion on the arduous journey toward eternity." The Eucharist is not something that Christ all of a sudden decided to do for us. He came to fulfill the New Law, with His "blood of the new and everlasting covenant."

In the Old Testament salvation "came from the Jews," whereas in the New Testament salvation comes from the cross of Christ. The Holy Sacrifice of the Mass is the means by which the Lord's Supper and His sacrifice of the cross are perpetuated and made present in our midst. Through the words of Consecration during Mass, Jesus is made present on our altars, offering Himself to the Father on our behalf, in an unbloody manner for our salvation.

> During the meal Jesus took bread, blessed it, broke it, and gave it to his disciples. "Take this and eat it," he said, "this is my body." Then he took a cup, gave thanks, and gave it to them. "All of you must drink from it," he said, "for this is my blood, the blood of the covenant, to be poured out in behalf of many for the forgiveness of sins." (Mt 26: 26-28)

There is no greater gift on earth than to attend Mass at the altar of the cross where we are united to Jesus in His offering and in His Real Presence hidden under the appearance of bread and wine. St. Teresa appeared to one of her religious after her death and said to her, "You should adore god on the altar just as we adore Him in Heaven, for He is the same God."

While researching this book, it would have been easy to organize another book around the historical evidence for belief in the Real Presence which was passed on from the Apostles and continued in an unbroken line from the institution of the Sacrament at the Last Supper. Despite heresies, wars and persecutions of all kinds, the doctrine of the Eucharist remains intact. Yet, it has suffered. Results of a 1992 Gallup survey on U.S. Catholic understanding of Holy Communion reveal that only 30 percent of

Catholics believe they are receiving the Body, Blood, Soul and Divinity of our Lord Jesus Christ under the appearance of bread and wine. This caused Bishop James Griffin of Columbus, Ohio, to speak out during the annual chrism Mass, "from now until the millennium" about the primacy of the Eucharist in the faith lives of Catholics. "One of the deepest concerns that I have for the church today," Bishop Griffin said, is that without the Real Presence, we "would lose the biblical rootedness of our faith . . . we would be sorely tempted, in every age, to fall down in worship of the gods of reason, the gods of the Enlightenment, the gods of what our Holy Father has named the culture of death—in truth the golden calves of human history."

Perhaps that is why I have compiled this book. I feel a sense of urgency to awaken people to the awesome gift of God's Real Presence. "If you only recognized God's gift, and who it is that is asking you for a drink, you would have asked Him instead and He would have given you living water" (Jn 4: 10-11), Jesus said to the Samaritan woman. "If we only knew the gift of our Eucharistic Jesus in our midst, we need never hunger or thirst again!" I have attempted to show this gift to you through *My Daily Eucharist.* My goal was to find the most spiritually nourishing excerpts on the Eucharist from significant people throughout Church history who have recognized the value of the Mass and the Real Presence of Jesus in the Eucharist and put them in one place. Taken together, these writings form a convincing body of "evidence" for belief in the Real Presence and present a veritable feast of great variety and abundance. May your faith be strengthened through theirs, and may you be filled to the brim with new awareness and gratitude for our Savior's love for you in the Blessed Sacrament.

Joan Carter McHugh
Lake Forest, Illinois
September 1995

Acknowledgements

It is fitting in a book about the Eucharist to acknowledge my gratitude to people who have been "living Eucharists," to family and friends who have "been there" to help launch this work. Publishing *My Daily Eucharist* has been a joy and that's because I had so much help—with editorial and spiritual guidance from Fr. Anselm Romb, OFM CONV., with typing from Judy Kozak, with "whatever needs to be done" from Velma Murphy, with the use of the library of the Franciscan Friars at Marytown, with prayer support from Marge Lukacs, with the extra hands of Marge Galiene, with the computer expertise of Peter Ptak, with the help of Sister Margery Lanigan, RSCJ in obtaining a photo of the original painting for the cover, with countless hours of proofreading by my husband, Tom, and Dan Gallio, and, last but not least, with encouragement from my son, Danny, whose enthusiasm for the concept of this book was the spark that ignited my fire to begin *My Daily Eucharist*. I want to thank them publicly because this book is the result of their love and support.

Solemnity of Mary, Mother of God

Cana is a delightful story of loving concern. Mary's maternal solicitude moved her to intercede with her Son even though his hour had not yet come. The loving heart of Jesus could not turn a deaf ear to his Mother's intercession.

Jesus used this occasion to reveal to us the power of his Mother's intercession; also, to teach us Mary's role as Mother of the Church and intercessor for her children. Changing water into wine is a symbolic sign and a remote preparation for the Eucharist.

At the very first Mass offered on Calvary's heights, Mary again fulfilled her role of intercessor. John gives us this brief account without adjective or adverb, yet so descriptive: "Near the cross of Jesus there stood his Mother (Jn 19:25) . . ."

The Church has always incorporated Mary's role into the Mass. Mary is the channel through which Jesus came to us. She is also the channel through which we go to Jesus.

As Queen-Mother of our eternal High Priest, Mary continues to intercede in heaven as she did on earth. Her intercession at Nazareth drew down our Redeemer. Her intercession on Calvary opened the floodgates of God's mercy. Her intercession in the Upper Room called down the Holy Spirit upon the disciples, and the Church was born.

David E. Rosage
The Bread of Life

The sacrifice of the Cross is so decisive for the future of man that Christ did not carry it out and did not return to the Father until he had left us the means to take part in it as if we had been present. Christ's offering on the Cross—which is the real Bread of Life broken—is the first value that must be communicated and shared. The Mass and the Cross are but one and the same sacrifice. Nevertheless the eucharistic breaking of bread has an essential function, that of putting at our disposal the original offering of the Cross. It makes it actual today for our generation. By making the Body and Blood of Christ really present under the species of bread and wine, it makes—simultaneously—the Sacrifice of the Cross actual and accessible to our generation, this Sacrifice which remains in its uniqueness, the turning point of the history of salvation, the essential link between time and eternity.

Pope John Paul II
Message to the Eucharistic Congress at Lourdes
July 21, 1981

The references of St. Ignatius of Antioch (d. 107) to the Eucharist in the seven authentic letters he wrote while on his way to Rome to suffer martyrdom are sufficient to indicate that the Mystery of the Lord's Body and Blood was a most significant aspect in his thought and in his own spiritual life. In his letter to the Christians of Tralles, for example, he apparently compares the virtues of faith and love to the Eucharistic Mystery when he writes: "Therefore, arming yourselves with gentleness, renew yourselves in faith, which is the Flesh of the Lord, and in charity, which is the Blood of Jesus Christ. Hold nothing against your neighbor." His letter to the Romans is almost mystical in its Eucharistic allusions. He compares his own coming tortures to the process that the wheat must undergo. In facing death, Ignatius states that his only remaining desire is to encounter him who has made himself the food and drink of Christians. *I am God's grain, and I am being ground by the teeth of wild beasts in order that I may be found [to be] pure bread for Christ. My [earthly] love has been crucified, and there is in me no fire of material love, but rather a living water, speaking in me and saying within me, "Come to the Father." I take no pleasure in corruptible food or in the delights of this life. I want the Bread of God, which is the Flesh of Jesus Christ, who is of the seed of David; and as drink I want his Blood, which is incorruptible love.*

Rev. James T. O'Connor
The Hidden Manna,
A Theology of the Eucharist

Feast of St. Elizabeth Ann Seton
1774-1821

As a young Episcopalian widow visiting Italy, Elizabeth Bayley Seton attended Mass with Italian friends and heard an Englishman mutter at the elevation of the Host, "This is what they call their Real Presence." She was deeply disturbed by the remark and later wrote in her diary of the "unfeeling interruption."

Shortly afterward she wrote her sister-in-law: "How happy we would be if we believed what these dear souls believe, that they possess God in the Sacrament and that He remains in their churches and is carried to them when they are sick! Oh, my! When they carry the Blessed Sacrament under my windows, while I feel the loneliness and sadness of my case, I cannot stop my tears at the thought: My God, how happy I would be, even so far away from all so dear, if I could find You in the Church as they do . . . The other day, in a moment of excessive distress, I fell on my knees without thinking when the Blessed Sacrament passed by and cried in an agony to God to bless me if He was there, that my whole soul desired only Him."

John M. Haffert
The World's Greatest Secret

Feast of St. John Neumann
1811-1860

Loving his Eucharistic Lord and wishing to dramatize the Blessed Sacrament and to center spiritual life in his diocese around It, Saint John Neumann dreamed of bringing the Forty Hours Devotion to the United States.

At first the idea was received coldly: "You can't do that! If you left the Blessed Sacrament exposed in churches for forty long hours, don't you know what would happen? The ignorant and the impious would profane and dishonor It."

The idea might have died there except for what happened one night. The Bishop had been writing letters for hours and he grew so weary that he fell asleep at his desk. When he awoke an hour or so later his papers were a charred mass. Whether a puff of wind had blown a letter into the flames of a candle, or whether the candle had overturned, he could not tell. Only one letter remained intact, except for charred edges. Picking it up he saw that it was the only letter that he had written that evening about the Forty Hours Devotion.

At this discovery he dropped to his knees. It seemed to him that a voice was telling him: "As this writing was saved from the flames, so shall I preserve My Son, present in the Blessed Sacrament, from profanation and dishonor. Wait no longer. Carry out your plan."

The Bishop again eagerly took up his pen. Letter after letter he wrote on through the night, ordering the celebration of the Forty Hours Devotion in every church of his Philadelphia Diocese.

John M. Haffert
The World's Greatest Secret

Now he was at the altar, in his white vestments, opening the book. I was kneeling right at the altar rail. The bright sanctuary was all mine. I could hear the murmur of the priest's voice, and the responses of the server, and it did not matter that I had no one to look at, so that I could tell when to stand up and kneel down again, for I was still not very sure of these ordinary ceremonies. But when the little bells were rung I knew what was happening. And I saw the raised Host—the silence and simplicity with which Christ once again triumphed, raised up, drawing all things to Himself—drawing me to Himself.

Presently the priest's voice was louder, saying the *Pater Noster*. Then, soon, the server was running through the *Confiteor* in a rapid murmur. That was for me. Father Moore turned around and made a big cross in absolution, and held up the little Host.

"Behold the Lamb of God: behold Him Who taketh away the sins of the world."

And my First Communion began to come towards me, down the steps. I was the only one at the altar rail. Heaven was entirely mine—that Heaven in which sharing makes no division or diminution. But this solitariness was a kind of reminder of the singleness with which this Christ, hidden in the small Host, was giving Himself for me, and to me, and, with Himself, the entire Godhead and Trinity—a great new increase of the power and grasp of their indwelling that had begun only a few minutes before at the font.

I left the altar rail and went back to the pew where the others were kneeling like four shadows, four unrealities, and I hid my face in my hands.

Thomas Merton
The Seven Storey Mountain

Christ is present in his church and through it proclaims the Gospel, worships the Father, shows concern for the world and its problems. Caring for our neighbor and working for peace and justice follow upon the celebration of the Eucharist. Pope John Paul II, in his encyclical *On Social Concerns*, brings this out: "The kingdom of God (salvation) becomes present above all in the sacrament of the Eucharist, which is the Lord's sacrifice. All who take part in the Eucharist are called to discover through this sacrament the profound meaning of our actions in the world in favor of development and peace and to receive from it strength to commit ourselves ever more generously, following the example of Christ who in this sacrament lays down his life for his friends."

To love the eucharistic Christ means to love our neighbor. There is only one Christ, present in the Eucharist and in his church. John Chrysostom admonished his congregations: "Do not honor Christ here in church clothed in silk vestments and then pass him by untouched and frozen outside. . . . God does not need golden chalices but golden hearts." The same Christ is in the Eucharist as in the poor and needy.

Fr. Thomas McKeon, sss
Emmanuel Magazine, April 1994

Imagine the Pope inviting you to Rome to spend an hour with him; you would feel like the most important person in the world. Who would not see this as a great honor and do anything to get there? Yet it is a much greater honor to spend an hour with Jesus Himself.

Those who kept company with Jesus in the gospel stand out as men and women of great faith—they were His chosen friends who really believed in Him. They were ridiculed then, but are admired now. Those who keep company with Jesus in the Blessed Sacrament are His friends today who will stand out for all eternity for their faith in His Real Presence.

Jesus hides His glory in the Blessed Sacrament that you may give Him glory by coming to Him in faith, and that you may love Him for Himself!

He could fill every Catholic church 7 days a week, 24 hours a day by letting a single ray of His glory shine out. People would come from all over the world to see the miracle. But the miracle He wants us to see is the miracle of His divine love and humility where He Who created the whole world and Whom the whole world cannot contain, contains Himself in the Blessed Sacrament for love of us, to be Our Divine Companion during our pilgrimage through life, to be Our Good Shepherd who leads us to life-giving waters, to be Our Divine Physician who comes to heal the lonely and the broken-hearted.

Fr. Martin Lucia, MSS
Rosary Meditations from Mother Teresa of Calcutta

The Fourth General Council of the Lateran, in 1215, defined that "the Body and Blood of Christ are truly contained in the Sacrament of the Altar by Transubstantiation." Transubstantiation is a changing across from one substance to another. A transcontinental railroad will take a person from New York to San Francisco but it does not change New York into San Francisco. Take the word "transformation." A carpenter can transform a log of wood into all kinds of furniture. He gives the wood another form or shape. In Transubstantiation it is a question not of another form or shape, but of another substance. Hydrogen and oxygen are two gaseous substances, but we know that they can be changed into the substance of water. So also, Transubstantiation changes the substance of bread into the Substance of the Body of Christ. When hydrogen and oxygen are changed into water they lose their previous form or gaseous appearance whereas the bread retains its previous appearance, the substance alone being changed. The word "Transubstantiation," therefore, is used by the Catholic Church to show that the substance of bread, which was present before the consecration, has been changed into the Substance of Our Lord's Body, although the appearance of bread still remains.

Fr. Charles M. Carty and Dr. L. Rumble, MSC,
Q. A. Eucharist, Quizzes to a Street Preacher

The Lord Jesus came among us to share in all our miseries and humanity. By His love, He transformed suffering into sacrifice, bringing salvation to all of us. Now He invites you and me to unite our sufferings with His, with even the little love we can muster up, to be a sacrifice bringing His salvation to those in need. He invites all of us to be partners in His continued work of redemption.

The teaching about offering our own selves along with the Immaculate Victim is made even more explicit in the main document of Vatican II, the *Dogmatic Constitution on the Church*, which spells out the many aspects of our lives we should offer, exercising our baptismal priesthood:

[As for the lay faithful] *all their works, prayers, and apostolic endeavors, their ordinary married and family life, their daily labor, their mental and physical relaxation, if carried out in the Spirit, and even the hardships of life, if patiently borne— all of these become spiritual sacrifices acceptable to God through Christ Jesus (see I Pt. 2:5). During the celebration of the Eucharist, these sacrifices are most lovingly offered to the Father along with the Lord's Body. Thus, as worshippers whose every deed is holy, laity consecrate the world itself to God.* (Lumen Gentium, no. 34).

Rev. George W. Kosicki, CSB
*Living Eucharist, Counter-Sign to Our Age
and Answer to Crisis*

"I want to tell them of the poignant sorrows which filled My Heart at the Last Supper. If it was bliss for Me to think of all those to whom I should be both Companion and Heavenly Food, of all who would surround Me to the End of Time with adoration, reparation, and love . . . this in no wise diminished My grief at the many who would leave Me deserted in My tabernacle and who would not even believe in My Real Presence.

"Into how many hearts defiled by sin would I not have to enter . . . and how often this profanation of My Body and Blood would serve for their ultimate condemnation.

"Sacrileges and outrages, and all the nameless abominations to be committed against Me, passed before My eyes . . . the long, lonely hours of the day and of the night in which I would remain alone on the altars . . . and the multitudes who would not heed the appeals of My Heart . . .

"Ah! Josefa, let the thoughts of My Heart sink deep into yours.

"It is love for souls that keeps Me a Prisoner in the Blessed Sacrament. I stay there that all may come and find the comfort they need in the tenderest of Hearts, the best of Fathers, the most faithful of Friends, who will never abandon them.

"The Holy Eucharist is the invention of Love . . . Yet how few souls correspond to that love which spends and consumes itself for them!"

Words of Our Lord to Sr. Josefa Menendez
The Way of Divine Love

It is this intense desire of God to enter into the most intimate relationship with us that forms the core of the Eucharistic celebration and the Eucharistic life. God not only wants to enter human history by becoming a person who lives in a specific epoch and a specific country, but God wants to become our daily food and drink at any time and any place.

Henri Nouwen
With Burning Hearts,
A Meditation on the Eucharistic Life

The secret of Therese Neumann's abundant life despite her complete abstinence from all earthly food is revealed in her statement that she is sustained by a heavenly food, the Body of her Eucharistic Lord.

On Palm Sunday evening, 1930, the third year of absolute fast, Father Hartl asked Resl if she was hungry. "You know very well that I do not eat," she answered. The curate of the village church then asked, "Do you wish to be greater than the Saviour? He ate when He was on earth." Therese smiled and said: "The Saviour can do all things. Or do you not think He is all-powerful?" Turning to the other priest present, Father Helmut Fahsel of Berlin, she declared with great earnestness: "The Saviour sustains me. He said, 'My body is food indeed,' so why shouldn't it be actually true for once, if He wills it?"

Albert Paul Schimberg
The Story of Therese Neumann

Did you know that every Sunday, at all the masses in all the Catholic churches in the world, millions of people join in prayers for healing?

The fact that most people are surprised by that statement merely shows our lack of attention to the words we pray. For every Catholic immediately recognizes the prayer I am talking about, which the priest and congregation recite together just before Communion: "Lord, I am not worthy to receive you. But only say the word, and *I shall be healed*."

As even that one prayer indicates, the Eucharist is truly a sacrament of healing. The Eucharist celebrates our covenant with God—the covenant that frees us from sin and from all the effects of sin, including affliction and death. Through the Eucharist we take part in Jesus' sacrifice of his very life, the sacrifice that has become life and healing for us.

The Eucharist brings us into the most intimate possible contact with Jesus himself. His Blood flows through our veins; his Body becomes one with ours. His mind touches our mind; his very being touches our being. When we enter this moment with real awareness of what is happening and with genuine faith in the Lord's presence, how can it help but be a moment of healing? "With faith in your love and mercy I eat your body and drink your blood. Let it not bring me condemnation, but *health in mind and body*."

John Bertolucci
Healing: God's Work Among Us

A young priest phoned me, very anxious and afraid. He had just found out he had cancer of the vocal chords and he had to have his voice box removed in three weeks. He was telling me he was desperate. He had been ordained only about six years.

As I prayed with him, I felt the Lord wanted me to tell him about the Eucharist. I said, "Father, I can pray with you now on the phone, and I will, but this morning, didn't you meet Jesus? Don't you meet him every day?"

What I didn't know was that this priest didn't celebrate Mass daily.

I told him, "Father, every single day when you go to Mass, when you take that sacred Host, when you eat it, you meet Jesus. The woman only touched the hem of Jesus' cloak. But you touch Jesus and receive him into your body. You have him as food. Do you realize that Jesus is actually going down through your throat? There is no better one to go to than Jesus. You ask Jesus to heal you."

I heard him crying over the phone. He kept saying to me, "Oh, Sister, thank you. Thank you."

Three weeks later, he went in for his surgery. He phoned me later to tell me that he didn't have the surgery. The doctors discovered the cancer was gone and he had brand new vocal chords.

Sister Briege McKenna, osc
Miracles Do Happen

Dearest daughter, contemplate the marvelous state of the soul who receives this bread of life, this food of angels, as she ought. When she receives this sacrament she lives in me and I in her. Just as the fish is in the sea and the sea in the fish, so am I in the soul and the soul in me, the sea of peace. Grace lives in such a soul because, having received this bread of life in grace, she lives in grace. When this appearance of bread has been consumed, I leave behind the imprint of my grace, just as a seal that is pressed into warm wax leaves its imprint when it is lifted off. Thus does the power of this sacrament remain there in the soul; that is, the warmth of my divine charity, the mercy of the Holy Spirit, remains there. The light of my only-begotten Son's wisdom remains there, enlightening the mind's eye. [The soul] is left strong, sharing in my strength and power, which make her strong and powerful against her selfish sensuality and against the devil and the world.

Words of God the Father
Catherine of Siena, The Dialogue

Saint Maximilian was deeply touched by the real presence of Jesus, the God-Man, under the eucharistic species. Before the Blessed Sacrament altar, he acted as though he saw the Savior. "God dwells in our midst," he exclaimed, "in the Blessed Sacrament of the altar." "He remains among us until the end of the world. He dwells on so many altars, though so often offended and profaned." But even more, the founder of the MI was fascinated by the fact that Jesus in the sacrament gives Himself to us as food. Once he went so far as to say: "The culmination of the Mass is not the consecration, but Communion." With his heart full of gratitude, he said to Jesus: "You come to me and unite yourself intimately to me under the form of nourishment. Your blood now runs in mine, your soul, Incarnate God, compenetrates mine, giving it courage and support. What miracles! Who would ever have imagined such!". "If angels could be jealous of men," Father Kolbe was in the habit of saying, "they would be so for one reason: Holy Communion."

Jerzy Domanski, OFM CONV.
For The Life of the World,
Saint Maximilian and the Eucharist

Noah, a good man (Gen 6: 9), is said to have worked a hundred years to build the ark, so that he and a few others might be saved (I Pet 3: 20). How, then, can I in one short hour prepare myself to receive with reverence the Creator of the world? Moses, Your great servant and especial friend, constructed an Ark of imperishable wood (Exod 25: 10), and covered it with purest gold, in order to house the Tablets of the Law: and how shall I, a corruptible creature, dare so lightly to receive You, the Maker of the Law and Giver of life? Solomon, wisest of Israel's kings (I Kings 5: 7), spent seven years in building a splendid Temple in praise of Your name. For eight days he kept the Feast of its Dedication, and offered a thousand peace-offerings. To the sound of trumpets, he solemnly and joyfully bore the Ark of the Covenant to its appointed resting-place. How, then, shall I, unworthiest and poorest of men, welcome You into my house (Luke 7: 6), when I can hardly spend half an hour devoutly? If only I could spend even half an hour as I ought!

O my God, how earnestly did all these strive to please You! And how little, alas, can I do! How short is the time that I employ in preparing myself for Communion! Seldom am I entirely recollected, and very seldom free from all distraction. Yet in Your saving presence, O God, no unbecoming thought should enter my mind, for it is not an Angel, but the Lord of Angels who comes to be my guest.

Words of the Disciple
The Imitation of Christ
Thomas à Kempis

After Communion today, Jesus told me how much He desires to come to human hearts. "I desire to unite Myself with human souls; **My great delight is to unite Myself with souls**. Know, My daughter, that when I come to a human heart in Holy Communion, My hands are full of all kinds of graces which I want to give to the soul. But souls do not even pay any attention to Me; they leave Me to Myself and busy themselves with other things. Oh, how sad I am that souls do not recognize Love! They treat Me as a dead object." (Diary 1385)

"Oh, how painful it is to Me that souls so seldom unite themselves to Me in Holy Communion. I wait for souls, and they are indifferent toward Me. I love them tenderly and sincerely, and they distrust Me. **I want to lavish My graces on them, and they do not want to accept them.** They treat Me as a dead object, whereas My Heart is full of love and mercy. In order that you may know at least some of My pain, imagine the most tender of mothers who has great love for her children, while those children spurn her love. Consider her pain. No one is in a position to console her. This is but a feeble image and likeness of My love." (Diary 1447)

Rev. George W. Kosicki, CSB
Tell My Priests, The Words of Our Lord to Priests about His Mercy as Revealed to Sr. Faustina Kowalska

At last the most wonderful of all days arrived. Every little detail of those heavenly hours is with me still. I remember how joyfully we woke at dawn, the grave and tender kisses of the nuns, the dressing room where we were all clothed, and, above all, our entering the chapel and singing the morning hymn: "O blessed altar, ringed with angels."

Oh, how sweet the first kiss of Jesus was! It was a kiss of love. I knew that I was loved and I declared: "I love You and I give myself to You for ever!" Jesus made no demand on me; He asked for no sacrifices. For a long time Jesus and little Therese had gazed at each other and they understood each other. On that day it was no longer a matter of gazing: it was a union. There were no longer two of us. Therese had disappeared like a drop of water lost in the depth of the ocean. Only Jesus remained— as Master and King. For had not Therese begged Him to take away her freedom? Freedom frightened her, for she knew herself to be so weak and feeble that she wished to be united with the divine Power for ever.

St. Therese of Lisieux
The Story of a Soul

January 21

Feast of St. Agnes
Fourth Century

On the Feast of St. Augustine, as God showed Gertrude the merits of many saints, she desired to know something of the merits of St. Agnes, whom she had loved from her very infancy with the greatest tenderness and devotion. Our Lord yielded to her desire and prayer and showed her that great Saint, so united to His Heart as to indicate her extraordinary innocence and to manifest the truth of what has been said by the Wise Man, that "Incorruption bringeth near to God" (Wis 6: 20). She seemed so near God, that it appeared as if no one in heaven could equal her innocence and love.

From this she learned that there is not an instant in which God does not place before Him the devotion and joy which holy souls either have felt or will yet feel from the sweet words of St. Agnes which are recited by the Church and that He causes the pleasure which He finds therein to pour forth from His Heart into that of this holy virgin, which is so intimately united to His, while she becomes marvelously adorned thereby with new jewels, casting rays of light every moment into those souls who rejoice in her devotion.

Monsignor William J. Doheny, CSC
The Revelations of Saint Gertrude

Her meditation over, Mother joined her clear, melodious voice with those of the sisters who were reciting the Office. When she thus recited the Office with them all the sisters felt exhilarated in their devotion. The penetrating accentuation with which she recited the psalms manifested audibly how deeply she felt the meaning of these inspired hymns. Who of her daughters does not remember, as they heard it exemplified, the special emphasis with which she used to pronounce the words: "*Si iniquitatis observaveris, Domine, Domine, quis sustinebit*"? When pronounced in this manner, the Office was an excellent preparation for receiving Jesus in the Blessed Sacrament. This was her Beloved! Mother had yearned for Him the whole day before; every action of the afternoon had been offered in anticipation of the coming of the Divine Guest. Her last thought before retiring was of the tabernacle; and her first on rising was of her strong desire to receive Jesus. After saying the *Confiteor*, which she inspired the sisters also to recite in a loud voice, she would rise and go to the holy table. As she moved, she seemed to fly rather than to walk, so light and so swift was her step. For the children, it was always a fresh and joyful sight to watch Mother Cabrini going to and coming from Holy Communion, because the raptures of her soul were delineated on her countenance from which radiated supernal expression.

Mother Saverio De Maria, MSC
Mother Frances Xavier Cabrini

January 23

Feast of St. Clement of Ancyra
Fourth Century

O ne of the earliest reports of a mystical reception of the
Eucharist is that of St. Clement, Bishop of Ancyra, who
suffered a long imprisonment and torture for the Faith during
the fourth century persecution of Diocletian. After being persecuted elsewhere, he was imprisoned in Rome, where he so impressed his fellow prisoners with his patience, his inspired words
and his compliance with the will of God, that many asked for
Baptism at his hands. Instructions in the Faith and Baptisms
took place during the late hours of the night so as not to arouse
the fury of the guards.

During one of these nights the assembled group saw the cell
become illuminated by an extraordinary light. Through this light
stepped a handsome young man clothed in shining garments.
Walking toward the bishop, the heavenly being gave him a chalice and a large Host, and then disappeared. St. Clement divided
the Host among the astonished witnesses and shared the contents of the chalice. History relates that the following day all
went joyfully to their execution except St. Clement, who suffered still more before he was eventually beheaded.

Joan Carroll Cruz
Eucharistic Miracles

Feast of St. Francis de Sales
1567-1622

When the bee has gathered the dew of heaven and the earth's sweetest nectar from the flowers, it turns it into honey, then hastens to its hive. In the same way, the priest, having taken from the altar the Son of God (who is as the dew from heaven, and true son of Mary, flower of our humanity), gives him to you as delicious food. When you have received him, stir up your heart to do him homage; speak to him about your spiritual life, gazing upon him in your soul where he is present for your happiness; welcome him as warmly as possible, and behave outwardly in such a way that your actions may give proof to all of his presence. If it is impossible to go to Communion, at least unite yourself to him spiritually by a fervent desire for the life-giving flesh of your Savior. Your principal motive in going to Communion should be to advance, strengthen and console yourself in the love of God, receiving for love alone what is given for love alone. At no other time is our Lord more loving and more tender than when he, as it were, humbles himself and comes to us in the form of food that he may enter our soul and enter into intimate union with us. If you are asked why you go to Communion so often say it is to learn to love God, to be purified from your imperfections, delivered from your miseries, consoled in your troubles and strengthened in your weaknesses.

As mountain hares become white in winter because they neither see nor eat anything but snow, so by adoring and feeding on beauty, purity and goodness itself in the Eucharist you will become altogether beautiful, pure, and good.

St. Francis de Sales
Introduction to the Devout Life

When I was vested, the name of Jesus impressed itself upon me more and more; I felt fortified against all attacks. I wept and sobbed afresh . . . When I had begun the Holy Sacrifice, I received many graces and pious emotions and gentle tears, which lasted long. As the Mass continued, many inspirations confirmed what I had resolved; and when I raised the Sacred Host, I felt as it were an inward suggestion, and a powerful impulse never to abandon Our Lord, in spite of all obstacles; and this was accompanied by a new delight, and fresh impressions. This . . . lasted the whole time, even after Mass, and throughout the day. Whenever I thought of Jesus this pious feeling and this fixed purpose returned to my mind.

St. Ignatius of Loyola
The Spiritual Journal of St. Ignatius of Loyola

The great evil of the times is that people do not go to Jesus Christ as their Savior and their God. The sole basis, law, and grace of salvation is set aside. The malaise of sterile piety is that it does not share or draw its vitality from Jesus Christ; it stops short along the way; it distracts itself with externals. But divine love has its life, its center uniquely in the sacrament of the Eucharist . . .

What must be done? Return to the source of life: not merely to Jesus of history in Judea or to Jesus glorified in heaven, but to Jesus in the Eucharist. He must not long be neglected but placed again at the head of Christian society, which he will direct and save . . . He must have faithful servants, a family of friends, an adoring people.

Thus, this is the mission and glory of our century, which will come to rank as great among the greatest ages and as holiest among the most holy. It is a fact that an age waxes or wanes in proportion to the worship of the divine Eucharist. It is there that is found the life and the measure of its faith, its charity, and its vitality. May the reign of the Eucharist come about more and more. For too long impiety and ingratitude have been allowed to hold sway over the world! *Adveniat regnum tuum.* Thy kingdom come. (St. Peter Julian Eymard, *Le Tres Saint Sacrement*, June 1864)

Fr. Michael L. Gaudoin-Parker
The Real Presence through the Ages

The Holy Mass of Padre Pio in the little chapel was his life, his calvary, his crucifixion, his paradise. It lasted about three hours. I would follow him with great attention and emotion in the various phases of the celebration. At the Memento for the Living, his meditation was deep, lengthy, interminable, and interrupted only by some painful sighs. He proceeded slowly in the painful ascent of his mystical calvary, and he arrived exhausted to his crucifixion. The moment of Consecration was the climax of his passion, it was the crucifixion with Jesus. As he pronounced the words of the Consecration, one noted on his pale and exhausted face, the signs of indescribable internal suffering, the horrible martyrdom of the tortured one on the cross.

He looked like Jesus Crucified.

Padre Alberto D'Apolito
Padre Pio of Pietrelcina

Feast of St. Thomas Aquinas
1225-1274

When he was stationed at Paris, the other Doctors of the Sorbonne put before him a problem about the nature of the mystical change in the elements of the Blessed Sacrament, and he proceeded to write, in his customary manner, a very careful and elaborately lucid statement of his own solution. Needless to say, he felt with hearty simplicity the heavy responsibility and gravity of such a judicial decision; and not unnaturally seems to have worried about it more than he commonly did over his work. He sought for guidance in more than usually prolonged prayer and intercession; and finally, with one of those few but striking bodily gestures that mark the turning points of his life, he threw down his thesis at the foot of the crucifix on the altar, and left it lying there; as if awaiting judgment. Then he turned and came down the altar steps and buried himself once more in prayer; but the other Friars, it is said, were watching; and well they might be. For they declared afterwards that the figure of Christ had come down from the cross before their mortal eyes; and stood upon the scroll, saying "Thomas, thou has written well concerning the Sacrament of My Body." It was after this vision that the incident is said to have happened, of his being borne up miraculously in mid-air.

G. K. Chesterton
Saint Thomas Aquinas,
"The Dumb Ox"

A man who lived near the church wondered what the new Cure was doing in there so very early each morning. One morning, long before dawn, when the man saw a tiny candle making its way from the rectory through the darkness across the cemetery, he sneaked over to the church and peeked in to find out for himself. There was the pastor, pouring out his heart to Jesus hidden in the Blessed Sacrament! "Ah," said the man, "he is not like other men!" What did the Cure say to his blessed Jesus? Henri Gheon has given us his version of the Cure's prayer. Prostate on the floor or kneeling with outstretched hands, the Cure thus prayed or groaned or wept out his heart:

My God, my all, You see how I love You, and I do not love you enough.

My God, You have given me all; behold the little that I give You. Give me the strength to give more.

My God, here is all—take all; but convert my parish. If You do not convert it, will be because I have not deserved it.

My God, I count my merits as nothing, but Yours are infinite. May they win for me the grace of suffering.

My God, I consent to suffer all that You may wish for all my life . . . for a hundred years . . . and the most bitter suffering, but convert them . . . " (St. John Vianney, The Cure of Ars).

Fr. Bartholomew O'Brien
The Cure of Ars, Patron Saint of Parish Priests

One time, during the celebration of Holy Mass in the Church of St. Paul at the Three Fountains in Rome, St. Bernard saw an unending stairway which went up to Heaven. Very many angels went up and down on it, carrying from Purgatory to Paradise the souls freed by the Sacrifice of Jesus, renewed by priests on the altars all over the world.

Thus, at the death of one of our relatives, let us take much more care about having celebrated, and assisting at, Holy Masses for him, rather than about the flowers, the dark clothes and the funeral procession . . .

There are recounted many apparitions of souls being purified in Purgatory who came to ask Padre Pio to offer Holy Mass for their intentions so that they would be able to leave Purgatory. One day he celebrated Holy Mass for the father of one of his fellow Franciscan brothers. At the end of the Holy Sacrifice, Padre Pio said to his brother, "This morning the soul of your father has entered into Heaven." The brother was very happy to hear that, yet he said to Padre Pio, "But, Father, my good father died thirty-two years ago." "My son," Padre Pio replied, "before God everything is paid for." And it is Holy Mass which obtains for us a price of infinite value: The Body and the Blood of Jesus, the "Immaculate Lamb" (Apoc. 5:12).

Father Stefano Manelli, OFM CONV.
Jesus Our Eucharistic Love

Feast of St. John Bosco
1815-1888

On May 30, 1862, Don Bosco recounted that, in a dream, he had seen an immense sea, on which a great many ships were arranged for battle, against a larger and taller ship. He also saw others which were defending the tall ship.

"In the midst of this endless sea, two solid columns, a short distance apart, soar high into the sky. One is surmounted by a statue of the Immaculate Virgin, at whose feet a large inscription reads: **'Help of Christians.'** The other, far loftier and sturdier, supports a Host of proportionate size, and bears beneath it the inscription: **'Salvation of believers.'**

"The flagship commander—the Roman Pontiff—standing at the helm, strains every muscle to steer his ship between the two columns, from whose summit hang many anchors, and strong hooks linked to chains. The entire enemy fleet closes in, to intercept and sink the flagship at all costs. They bombard it with everything they have: books and pamphlets, incendiary bombs, firearms, cannons. Beaked prows ram the flagship again and again, but to no avail, as, unscathed and undaunted, it keeps on its course. At times a formidable ram splinters a gaping hole in its hull, but, immediately, a breeze from the two columns instantly seals the gash . . .

Suddenly the Pope falls, seriously wounded. He is instantly helped up, but, struck a second time, dies. A shout of victory rises from the enemy; wild rejoicing sweeps their ships. But no sooner is the Pope dead, than another takes his place . . . "Breaking through all resistance, the new Pope steers his ships safely between the two columns; first, to the one surmounted by the Host, and then to the other, topped by the statue of the Virgin . . . The enemy ships panic and disperse, colliding and scuttling each other.

To Jesus Through Mary
Perpetual Eucharistic Adoration Society

My dear child, today I wish to speak further on the Eucharist, My Presence in the host you receive.

My dear one, how I long for My people to come and receive Me openly and sincerely. I wish for them to tell Me their most intimate feelings, thoughts and worries. I wish for them to share their joyful events, their sorrows and their struggles. I long to advise them, counsel them and comfort them. Oh, if only they would realize **it is I** they receive and not a piece of man-made host. **It is I, in My true presence, Who dwells in you each time you receive Me.**

So many of My people and My priests simply, routinely go through the motions. So many of My people, who are My beloved ones, are so entangled and afflicted with self issues! They do not come to share with Me or allow Me to comfort or counsel with My love. They complain of their own afflictions.

It is time My people know the truth, and listen to Me!

I am here for them.

It is I Who humbles Myself to be consecrated to them!

Could they give Me the moment to receive My consecration, and allow My Presence to absorb their being?

Words of Our Lord
I Am Your Jesus Of Mercy
The Riehle Foundation

A nonbeliever in the Real Presence said: "If I could believe that God is really there on the altar, I think I would fall on my knees and stay there forever." Jesus is probably not demanding this of us, because we also have duties to charity and service to our brothers and sisters. He is probably not asking us to stay kneeling physically, but spiritually he is asking us to do so. In our hearts we can stay in adoration of the Blessed Sacrament while our hands are working, writing, absolving. A Christian's life, particularly where religious and priests are concerned, must be oriented to the tabernacle. By an ancient tradition, churches have always been "oriented," that is, they look towards the "Orient," because it was in Jerusalem, in the Orient, that Christ died and rose again. So the temple of our hearts must look towards the Orient, towards the Sun of Justice shining on the Church from the Eucharist. Jesus said that where our treasure is, there will our hearts be also (cf. Matt 6:21). Our greatest treasure in this world ("the treasure hidden in the field") is Jesus in the Eucharist, and none other. May our hearts be there, may they return there after our night's rest, may their dwelling place be the tabernacle. It is possible to spend, in spirit, hours and hours on our knees before the Most Holy Sacrament while still working or traveling.

Fr. Raniero Cantalamessa
The Eucharist, Our Sanctification

Almost invariably the Lord showed Himself to me in His resurrected body, and it was thus, too, that I saw Him in the Host. Only occasionally, to strengthen me when I was in tribulation, did He show me His wounds, and then He would appear sometimes as He was on the Cross and sometimes as in the Garden. On a few occasions I saw Him wearing the crown of thorns and sometimes He would also be carrying the Cross—because of my necessities, as I say, and those of others—but always in His glorified flesh. Many are the affronts and trials that I have suffered through telling this and many are the fears and persecutions that it has brought me. So sure were those whom I told of it that I had a devil that some of them wanted to exorcize me. This troubled me very little, but I was sorry when I found that my confessors were afraid to hear my confessions or when I heard that people were saying things to them against me. Nonetheless, I could never regret having seen these heavenly visions and I would not exchange them for all the good things and delights of this world. I always considered them a great favour from the Lord, and I think they were the greatest of treasures; often the Lord Himself would reassure me about them. I found my love for Him growing exceedingly: I used to go to Him and tell Him about all these trials and I always came away from prayer comforted and with new strength. I did not dare to argue with my critics, because I saw that made things worse, as they thought me lacking in humility. With my confessor, however, I did discuss these matters; and whenever he saw that I was troubled he would comfort me greatly.

St. Teresa of Avila
The Autobiography of St. Teresa of Avila
E. Allison Peers

The Old Testament predicts that Christ will offer a true sacrifice to God in bread and wine—that He will use those elements. And this prediction is every bit as clear as the prediction that He will also offer Himself upon the Cross. Thus Gen XIV: 18, tells us that Melchisedech, King of Salem, was a priest, and that he offered sacrifice under the form of bread and wine. Now Ps. 109 predicts most clearly that Christ will be a priest according to the order of Melchisedech, i.e., offering a sacrifice under the forms of bread and wine. You may say that Christ fulfilled the prediction at the Last Supper, but that the rite was not to be continued. However, that admits that the rite was truly sacrificial—and the fact is that it has been continued in exactly the same sense. It was predicted that it would continue. After foretelling the rejection of the Jewish priesthood, the Prophet Malachy predicts a new sacrifice to be offered in every place. "From the rising of the sun even to the going down my name is great among the Gentiles: and in every place there is sacrifice and there is offered to my name a clean oblation." Mal I: 11. The Sacrifice of Calvary took place in one place only. We must look for a sacrifice apart from Calvary, one offered in every place under the forms of bread and wine. The Mass is that Sacrifice.

Fr. Charles M. Carty and Rev. Dr. L. Rumble, MSC
Q. A. Eucharist, Quizzes to a Street Preacher

The attitude of those who heard Christ's promise and His reaction furnish an argument for the Real Presence. It is very evident that they understood Our Lord to be referring to His own body and blood, and not to a mere symbol. Now, from Christ's manner of acting on other occasions we can conclude that if they had interpreted Him wrongly He would have set them right. Thus, when the disciples understood literally His announcement: "Lazarus sleepeth," He told them plainly: "Lazarus is dead." Again, when He spoke of meat which He had to eat, and they thought He referred to material food, He told them: "My meat is to do the will of Him that sent Me" (John 11: 11-14; 4: 32-34). But on the present occasion, when it was evident that His followers were accepting His words literally, He did not say: "I intend merely to give you bread and wine as a symbol of My body and blood." On the contrary, He repeated His promise even more explicitly; and though He saw many departing from His company, He uttered not a single word implying that He had been speaking in figurative language.

Rev. Francis J. Connell, CSSR
The Seven Sacraments

The term "covenant" refers to the historic event at Mount Sinai when the tribes of Israel were formed into one people (Exodus 24:1-11). That covenant was in blood, the blood of animals that were offered in sacrifice. For Israelites and other ancient peoples, blood was the symbol of life. Sprinkling the blood of the sacrificial animals on the altar and on the people symbolized the union of God and people, now sharing in the one life that was offered to God. So it is that the covenant at Sinai formed the people of Israel into a people of God.

The cup of the Lord's Supper was not just a renewal of the Sinai covenant. It was "the new covenant," a reference to Jeremiah 31:31-34, which announced "a new covenant" with the law inscribed not on tablets of stone but on people's hearts and with God forgiving the people's sins. The "new covenant" established by Christ would not be in the blood of animals, but in his own blood, "which would be shed for you." It would be established in the sacrificial blood of Christ, the Passover Lamb (see 22:7).

When at the Lord's Supper Christians do what Christ did— namely, take the cup, give thanks and give it to one another— they join Christ in offering their own blood for others. They renew the new covenant in Christ's blood. They forgive one another, extend peace to one another and strengthen the covenant relationship that makes them one people of God.

Eugene LaVerdiere, sss
Dining in the Kingdom of God

But after lots of prayer and study, I realized that Jesus could not have been speaking figuratively when he taught us to eat his flesh and drink his blood. The Jews in his audience would not have been outraged and scandalized by a mere symbol. Besides, if they had misunderstood Jesus to be speaking literally—when he meant his words to be taken figuratively—he could have easily clarified his point. In fact, since many disciples stopped following Jesus because of this teaching (v. 60), he would have been morally obliged to explain the saying in purely symbolic terms.

But he never did. Nor did any Christian, for over one thousand years, ever deny the Real Presence of Christ in the Eucharist. No wonder. So I did what any (Protestant) pastor or seminary professor would do if he wanted to keep his job. I promptly stopped my sermon series on the Gospel of John at the end of chapter 5 and basically skipped over chapter 6 in my classroom lectures.

Scott Hahn
Rome Sweet Home, Our Journey to Catholicism

Every time I hear anyone speak of the Sacred Heart of Jesus or of the Blessed Sacrament I feel an indescribable joy. It is as if a wave of precious memories, sweet affections and joyful hopes swept over my poor person, making me tremble with happiness and filling my soul with tenderness. These are loving appeals from Jesus who wants me whole-heartedly there, at the source of all goodness, his Sacred Heart, throbbing mysteriously behind the Eucharistic veils. The devotion to the Sacred Heart has grown with me all my life. Hardly had that good old man, my uncle Zaverio, presented me, a new-born babe, at the baptismal font, than he consecrated me there in the little church of my own village to the Sacred Heart, so that I should grow up under its protection, a good Christian. I remember that among the first prayers I learnt at the knee of that good soul was the beautiful prayer that I love to repeat today: "Sweet Heart of my Jesus, make me love you more and more."

My parents and my uncle intended me to become a good peasant, like themselves. But the Sacred Heart wanted me among its own elect, and to that end used that other good soul, my parish priest Rebuzzini, of blessed memory. He also was a lover of the Sacred Heart, and had worked very hard for its triumph during his youth. I cannot forget the Eucharistic Congress of Milan of 1895, the year in which I received the first tonsure which left me with such a strong attachment to the Blessed Sacrament. I cannot forget the little discourses to the clergy in the seminary, and the evening visits to my humble church at Sotto il Monte during the endless autumn holidays. Later on came my repeated consecrations to the Sacred Heart of Jesus . . . and the reading of so many books and writings about this beloved devotion.

Pope John XXIII
Journal of a Soul

Happy is he who, back at his seat after Communion, does not need any words, but adores and is silent. On the evening of Holy Thursday, the beloved apostle had rested his head on the breast of Christ; since Holy Thursday, Christ has been resting in the breasts of His friends, not only once but every morning, if they are pure of heart.

The faithful must refrain from giving too much importance to sensible favors received in Communion. Often, a person who suffers from aridity at the Holy Table will recognize suddenly the blessing of this Presence when he least expects it, during the day, when performing some task. Or else, at the moment of a violent temptation he may experience the inner certitude of not being alone, an impression of heavenly security, as if he actually heard the words: "It is I; do not be afraid." What is almost always obtained through frequent Communion is a grace which surpasses all perceptible favors; an increased light and, better still, a new strength in God.

Francois Mauriac
Holy Thursday, an Intimate Remembrance

"It has been decided that I am to settle at a French garrison named Beni Abbes. This is an important oasis in the Sahara, located on the Moroccan border. A wonderfully fine assignment has been entrusted to your child: to bring the Blessed Sacrament farther into the Sahara, both south and west, than it probably ever has been, farther anyway than it has been since the time of Saint Augustine, to bring the aids of religion to our dying soldiers. It is a great mission, a beautiful one, but which requires much virtue. The good Lord never fails, and I am sure of always having His help; but I fear I shall fail Him and I mistrust myself. Pray very, very much that I be faithful! . . .

"My trip goes on blessed by God. . . . I wanted to travel on foot like a poor monk; I had to accept a horse and an escort. At every post I am so kindly treated that I am filled with gratitude to God and to these kind souls. I said Mass (at Taghit) this morning before the officers of the garrison. It is the first Mass celebrated here since the French occupation. Probably no priest has ever been here. It affects me to be the first priest to bring Jesus down in these parts where He probably never has been corporally. It is a great grace for your child; pray much that he might not be too unworthy of it."

Msgr. Leon Cristiani
Charles De Foucauld, Life and Spirit

(Fr. Charles was later killed by the Berber tribesmen. Ed.)

February 11

Feast of Our Lady of Lourdes

The crypt of the new church was blessed for divine service on May 21st, 1866. Thousands of pilgrims thronged to the solemnity. "No sooner did anyone arrive in the town than he found himself already in an atmosphere of rejoicing. Triumphal arches spanned the main streets; the houses disappeared beneath masses of garlands and trophies, on every side the eye encountered inscriptions in honour of Mary."

The cortege formed in the parish church, and an endless procession wound its way to the Grotto, to the accompaniment of choirs posted at intervals along the route. The Bishop appeared on the heights preceded by the Canons. An immense crowd followed him and surrounded the Grotto on all sides, covered the rocks above, and filled every inch of space available.

Pontifical High Mass was sung at an altar facing the statue of the Grotto. At the elevation the silence of the multitude was impressive; it was the supreme moment of a supreme solemnity, a moment comparable to that of the Apparitions. The Son of Mary came down to the spot that His Mother's feet had trod; He came at her bidding. It was for Him that the Virgin had desired a sanctuary. He was about to take possession of it and make it His dwelling-place; and in doing so He bore eternal witness to His Mother's prerogative. Jesus Christ, Himself a pilgrim like themselves for that day, descended for the first time in their midst, in order to honour His most Holy Mother and give the Grotto His divine consecration.

J. H. Gregory
Bernadette of Lourdes

Once, when Gertrude heard the bell which called her to Communion and the chant had already commenced, as she felt that she was not sufficiently prepared, she said to our Lord: "Behold, Lord, Thou art coming to me. Why hast Thou not granted me the grace of devotion, so that I might present myself before Thee with a better preparation?" He replied: "A bridegroom admires the personal beauty of his bride more than her ornaments. In like manner I prefer the virtue of humility to the grace of devotion."

Once, when many of the religious had abstained from Communion, Gertrude returned thanks to God, saying, "I thank Thee, O Lord, that Thou hast invited me to Thy sacred Banquet." To which our Lord replied, with words full of sweetness and tenderness: "Know that I have desired thee with My whole heart." "Alas, Lord," she exclaimed, "what glory can accrue to Thy Divinity when I touch this Sacrament with my unworthy lips?" He replied: "Even as the love which we have for a friend makes us take pleasure in hearing him speak, so also the charity which I have for My elect makes Me sometimes find satisfaction in that in which they find none."

Once, as the Saint ardently desired to see the sacred Host as the priest communicated the people, but could not do so on account of the crowd, she heard our Lord saying to her: "A sweet secret shall be between us, which is unknown to those who absent themselves from Me. Thou, if thou wouldst enjoy it, approach. Thou shalt not see, but taste and prove the sweetness of this hidden manna."

Monsignor William J. Doheny, csc
The Revelations of Saint Gertrude

Hence, we can say that at the first step the Church takes, at the moment when Jesus celebrates Mass for us, our own Mass begins, as does our sacrifice for others. Our sacrifice grows as a result of Christ's sacrifice, and it is the highest result we can reach, a point of departure and of arrival.

So our lives can be a Mass, a Eucharist for others. This fulfills us, unites us and becomes something concrete in the world. We are linked with Christ in the true unification of life, and we become a living sacrifice to render glory to the Father. We become His presence in the world, continuing the work of Redemption, having been ourselves the result of this Redemption.

For this reason, in the sense that it is a life of love, the Christian life is essentially Eucharistic, giving itself willingly and joyously to others. In this way, the Eucharist becomes a source of peace. Every path to peace is the way of the Eucharist. The more unselfish the love we show to others, the more easily peace can be made with God and with man.

Fr. Slavko Barbaric, OFM
Celebrate Mass with Your Heart

In order to enliven our faith in His Real Presence, Our Lord has frequently manifested Himself in a sensible manner in the Holy Eucharist. Church history abounds in instances of the kind. The first that I shall relate is that of a miracle which occurred in the church of St. Denis in Douay and is recorded by Thomas Cantipratensis, an eye-witness. A certain priest, after having distributed Holy Communion to the faithful, found one of the Sacred Hosts lying on the floor. Full of consternation he knelt down to take it up, when the Host arose of its own accord and placed itself on the purifier. The priest immediately called those who were present, and when they came near the altar, they all saw in the Sacred Host Jesus Christ under the form of a child of exquisite beauty. "On hearing the news," says our author, "I too went to Douay. After I had declared to the dean the object of my visit, we went together to the church, and no sooner had he opened the ciborium wherein the miraculous Host was contained than we both beheld our Divine Saviour." "I saw," says Thomas, "the head of Jesus Christ, like that of a full grown man. It was crowned with thorns. Two drops of blood trickled down His forehead and fell on His cheek. With tearful eyes I fell prostrate before Him. When I arose again, I no longer saw either the crown of thorns or the drops of blood, but only the face of a man whose aspect inspired great veneration." This miracle gave rise to a confraternity in honor of the Most Holy Eucharist, to which several popes, especially Paul IV and Clement XIV, granted numerous indulgences. (P. Favre, *Le Ciel Ouvert.*)

Fr. Michael Muller, CSSR
The Blessed Eucharist, Our Greatest Treasure

There are still thirteen days left of my vacation. Oh may I behave like the seminarist I have always wanted to be, and have never been! May I be strengthened by the example of my beloved and deeply mourned parish priest, for whom I implore eternal peace and glory. May I have the grace to do two things well: the visit and the rosary. All the rest will follow.

O Jesus in the Blessed Sacrament, I would like to be filled with love for you; keep me closely united with you, may my heart be near to yours. I want to be to you like the apostle John. O Mary of the rosary, keep me recollected when I say these prayers of yours; bind me forever, with your rosary, to Jesus of the Blessed Sacrament. Blessed be Jesus, my love, blessed be the Immaculate Virgin Mary.

Pope John XXIII
Journal of a Soul

Naked I hung on the Cross with arms outstretched, offering Myself freely to God the Father for your sins (Isa 53: 7; Heb 9: 28), My whole Person a sacrifice of divine propitiation: you, too, must willingly offer yourself daily to Me in the Eucharist with all your powers and affections as a pure and holy offering. I require nothing less of you than that you should strive to yield yourself wholly to Me. Whatever you offer to Me besides yourself, I account as nothing; I seek not your gift, but yourself (Phil 4: 17).

Were you to possess everything in the world except Me, it could not satisfy you; so neither can anything you give Me be acceptable without the gift of yourself. Offer yourself to Me, and give yourself wholly to God; so shall your offering be acceptable (Eccl 35: 7). I offered Myself wholly to the Father for you: I have given My very Body and Blood to be your food, that I may be all yours, and that you may be mine forever. But if you trust in yourself and do not offer yourself freely to My will, your offering is not complete, nor can our union be perfect. A free offering of yourself into the hands of God must therefore precede all your doings if you desire to obtain freedom and grace. The reason why so few receive inward light and freedom is that they cannot wholly renounce self. My words remain unalterable: whoever does not renounce everything cannot be My disciple (Luke14: 33). Therefore if you wish to be My disciple, offer yourself to Me with all your heart.

Words of Christ
The Imitation of Christ
Thomas à Kempis

Jesus made himself the Bread of Life
to make sure we understand what he is saying
to satisfy our hunger for him
to satisfy our love for him.
Even that is not enough for him
so he makes himself the hungry one
so we can satisfy his hunger for our love.
And by doing to the poor what we are doing
we are satisfying his hunger for our love.

Mother Teresa
Words to Love By

I did not even know who Christ was, that He was God. I had not the faintest idea that there existed such a thing as the Blessed Sacrament. I thought churches were simply places where people got together and sang a few hymns. And yet now I tell you, you who are now what I once was, unbelievers, it is that Sacrament, and that alone, the Christ living in our midst, and sacrificed by us, and for us and with us, in the clean and perpetual Sacrifice, it is He alone who holds our world together, and keeps us all from being poured headlong and immediately into the pit of our eternal destruction. And I tell you there is a power that goes forth from that Sacrament, a power of light and truth, even into the hearts of those who have heard nothing of Him and seem to be incapable of belief.

Thomas Merton
The Seven Storey Mountain

Sister Briege (McKenna) tells of a healing involving an eighteen-year-old girl who had been abandoned on the streets when she was seven. The girl was a prostitute, a heroin addict, and was going blind. She was as hard and bitter a young person as you can possibly imagine.

Some people who wanted to help this girl brought her to a Mass where Sister Briege would be speaking.

"She didn't want to be in the church," says Sister Briege. "She thought we were a pack of hypocrites. She didn't listen to a word I said or a word the priest said. But suddenly she began crying—the first time she had cried since she was thirteen—and she couldn't stop.

"When she was walking out the door she said, 'O God, I wish I could believe.' At that moment she had her sight back. She was freed from the heroin as well and never had a moment's withdrawal.

"When I saw her later she said, 'I know what happened. At the moment Christ came, when the bread and wine changed into Jesus, I was changed.'"

This is the power, the reality, the healing love, that is offered to each one of us every time we take part in the Eucharist. A priest who is a friend of mine once told me about a woman who had said to him, "I am not a Catholic. But if I believed what you Catholics say you believe about the Mass, I would *crawl on my knees* to be there every day."

John Bertolucci
Healing: God's Work Among Us

It naturally follows from all that has been said, that the Blessed Sacrament is the magnet of souls. There is a mutual attraction between Jesus and the souls of men. Mary drew Him down from heaven. Our nature attracted Him rather than the nature of angels. Our misery caused Him to stoop to our lowness. Even our sins had a sort of attraction for the abundance of His mercy and the predilection of His grace. Our repentance wins Him to us. Our love makes earth a paradise to Him; and our souls lure Him as gold lures the miser, with irresistible fascination. This is the attraction on our side. On the other hand, He draws us to Himself by grace, by example, by power, by lovingness, by beauty, by pardon, and above all by the Blessed Sacrament. Every one who has had anything to do with ministering to souls has seen the power which Jesus has. Talent is not needed. Eloquence is comparatively unattractive. Learning is often beside the mark. Controversy simply repels. But the simple preaching of Jesus Christ and Him Crucified will collect a congregation, fill a Church, crowd the confessionals, furnish the altar rail, and solemnize a feast, when nothing else will do so. There is not a power on earth to be compared to the simple and unadorned preaching of the Gospel. Sermons on Jesus, and affectionate expositions of His mysteries, will make men perform their ordinary actions and relative duties more perfectly than direct instructions on those very things. All the attraction of the Church is in Jesus, and His chief attraction is the Blessed Sacrament.

Fr. Frederick William Faber
The Blessed Sacrament

The testimony of the Fathers of the Church follows . . . upon that of the apostles. The earliest witness is St. Ignatius, who was a disciple of two of the apostles—St. Peter and St. John— and who saw Our Lord Himself after the Resurrection . . . eight of his epistles are still extant . . . "I desire no perishable food. I desire the divine Bread, the Bread of Heaven, the Bread of Life, which is the flesh of Jesus Christ, the Son of God. I desire His blood, the celestial drink, which is never failing charity, life eternal."

St. Irenaeus, bishop of Smyrna, was a disciple of St. Polycarp, who in his turn was a scholar of St. John the Evangelist . . . "We offer to God the bread we have blessed and the chalice we have blessed and call upon the Holy Ghost, that He may cause this oblation of bread to become the body of Christ, this wine His blood, in order that he who receives these gifts may obtain re- mission of sin and everlasting life."

. . . the Fathers who assembled, to the number of three hun- dred, at the first Council of Nicea . . . solemnly declared: "We must not confine our attention to the bread and the chalice of- fered upon the altar, but raise our hearts upward and perceive by faith the Lamb of God, who taketh away the sins of the world, who is sacrificed upon that altar in an unbloody manner by the priest; and when we truly receive His precious body and blood we must firmly believe that this is the actual pledge of our res- urrection."

. . . the beliefs of the early Church differed in no respect from the truths which she now teaches and which we hold stead- fastly.

Rev. H. Rolfus
An Explanation of the Holy Sacraments

Arminda dos Campos had been ill for nine years and had undergone seven major operations. She had a greatly distended abdomen, total paralysis and an opening in her side cut by a surgeon's scalpel to drain purulent matter. I was standing directly in front of her at the moment of her cure and saw the blankets flatten on her body, saw her sit up, and within two hours *I saw the scars which had instantaneously formed in the place of the incisions.*

This cure also took place immediately after the young woman was blessed by the Holy Eucharist.

"As I stood near the side of the table opposite the Bishop, the cured girl was introduced by one of the nurses. The Bishop of Fatima listened patiently. "Then I heard the nurse saying: 'Show the Bishop the scars where the fistulas were.'

"After staring at the healed tissue . . . I saw the face of the nurse. Tears were streaming down her cheeks. With an open-arm gesture and trembling hands, suddenly she exclaimed: 'And Your Excellency, to think that this morning I put bandages there on large running openings!'

"It was only in the final moment . . . looking into the tear-stained face of that nurse . . . that the miracle made its full impact. In that moment I believed with all my heart that we in that room were experiencing the same wonder experienced when Christ healed the nine lepers, or when the blind man shouted out that he could suddenly see. We were . . . seeing it with our own eyes—not two thousand years ago, but *now.* We were objectively experiencing the reality of the Eucharist, the reality of Christ among us."

John M. Haffert
The World's Greatest Secret

What Christ gives us is quite *explicit* in his own words if interpreted according to their Aramaic meaning. The expression *"This is my body"* means *"This is MY SELF"*; for this reason John 6:57 has replaced the words "body" and "blood" simply by the phrase "whoever eats ME." Indeed, He gives himself as nourishment as a whole. This is the reason adoration is utterly legitimate, because one finds oneself before not any kind of food, which one takes as a thing, but face to face with Him, himself. Also that manner of treating the Eucharist as a thing—such as is found in antiquity—cannot pretend to be an authentic and complete interpretation of the biblical data. The "Medieval" attitude of discovering in the Sacrament the living person of Jesus Christ is perfectly in accord with the Bible. Thus, this is the reason all endeavors to meet a person, or rather *this* Person are entirely legitimate (Karl Rahner, sj, "Uber die Besuchung des Allerheiligsten" in Geist und Leben, 1959).

Fr. Michael L. Gaudoin-Parker

The Real Presence through the Ages

Our Lord knew well that we were too weak to walk courageously along the road of life that is often very difficult. So His prophet who saw from afar all the treasures hidden in the Church of Jesus Christ said: "Thou hast prepared a table before me, against them that afflict me." The food of this table is Jesus Christ Himself; His Divine Flesh, His Precious Blood. It is He who prepares the feast and invites us to it. How is it that after many Communions we still have so few victories over ourselves? We receive the God of Strength and we are without courage! It is because we have not enough faith. With a little faith, trust, and fidelity to duty, we should obtain from Our Lord all that we ask of Him. What greater gift could He give us than Himself? A soul who is simple, faithful, who sees only Our Lord, does with Him, so to speak, what she wills; He lends Himself to her least desires; she has all power over His Divine Heart.

Saint Madeleine Sophie Barat talks to the children
Saint Madeleine Sophie Barat,
Foundress of the Society of the Sacred Heart
A. M. Barry, RSCJ

I realized that it appeared more or less incongruous when we arrived in town for a game, for the general public to see my boys rushing off to church as soon as they got off the train, while their coach rode to the hotel and took his ease. So for the sake of appearances, if nothing else, I made it a point to go to church with the boys on the morning of a game.

Along about five or six o'clock in the morning I started pacing the lobby of the hotel; when suddenly I ran into two of my players hurrying out. I asked them where they were going at such an hour, although I had a good idea. Then I retired to a chair in the corner of the lobby where I couldn't be seen, but where I could see everyone who went in or out of the door.

Within the next few minutes, my players kept hurrying out of the door in pairs and groups until the last members of the squad hurried out of an elevator and made for the door. I asked them if they, too, were going to Mass, and they replied that they were. I decided to go along with them.

These youngsters were making a powerful impression on me with their piety and devotion, and when I saw them walking up to the communion rail to receive, and realized the sleep they had sacrificed in order to do this, I understood for the first time what a powerful ally their religion was to them. This was when I really began to see the light, to know what was missing in my life, and, later on, I had the great pleasure of being able to join my boys at the Communion rail.

Knute Rockne
Hidden Treasure, The Riches of the Eucharist
Louis Kaczmarek

God continues to reveal His desire for deeper devotion to the Eucharist. The last word God shared with me happened while I was preparing this booklet. God has given me the gift of being responsible for the Portiuncula, the chapel on campus that is set aside for adoration. I believe, as caretaker of this chapel, God is calling me to Perpetual Adoration. This means that I am to adore Jesus in the Eucharist whether I am in the Portiuncula or not. I have been doing this by adoring Him in Spirit from wherever I am.

I think that God desires to speak a new word to everyone concerning Eucharistic Adoration. I believe that God wants to bless each and every person with deeper faith in our Eucharistic Lord. My reason for writing this booklet is to encourage others to a deeper faith in Jesus truly present in the Sacrament of the altar. I encourage you to do what I personally have done in the past four years. Seek to grow in faith in the Eucharist. I believe that Jesus—Emmanuel— "God with us" was first veiled in humanity. I further believe that Jesus is now veiled in bread and wine. It took faith to believe in the historic Jesus. It took faith to recognize Jesus clothed in humanity. It takes faith for us to recognize Jesus in bread and wine. Pray for that faith; pursue that faith. I personally believe that Eucharistic Adoration should become our highest priority. If we can remove the veil that hides Jesus in the Eucharist, we will more easily find Him in all the other ways He desires to be present with us.

Fr. Sam Tiesi, TOR
Remain with Me

There is another life above the life of the body; namely, the life of the soul. Just as the life of the body is the soul, so, too, the life of the soul is God. This Divine life we receive in Communion. If the sunlight and moisture and the chemicals of the earth could speak they would say to the plants: "Unless you eat me you shall not have life in you;" if the plants and the herbs of the field could speak, they would say to the animals: "Unless you eat me you shall not have life in you;" if the animals and plants and the chemicals of the universe could speak they would say to man: "Unless you eat me you shall not have life in you." So, too, the Son of God says to us that unless we receive of Him we shall not have Divine life in us. The law of transformation holds sway, the lower is transformed into the higher; chemicals into plants, plants into animals, animals into man and man into God without, however, man ever losing his personal identity. Hence the word that is used for Communion is "to receive" Our Lord, for literally we do receive the Divine life, more significantly than a babe receives human life as it is nursed by the mother, for in this latter case, the human is being nourished by the human, but in Communion the human receives Divine life from God. But like all words, even this one has some imperfection for in communion it is not so much we who receive Christ as Christ who receives us, incorporating us into Himself.

Bishop Fulton Sheen
This Is the Mass

My Jesus, I wish I had been in the Upper room the night before You suffered for the redemption of those You loved so much. Again I entertain vain desires for am I not really present at the Last Supper at every Mass? My faith is weak and my love lukewarm, Yes, I am there—that awe-inspiring moment when Your Apostles understood Your previous revelation of Your Body and Blood as food, is totally mine at every Mass. I can offer God to God in reparation for my sins. I can receive God into my soul so His Precious Blood, shed for me, begins to run its course in my heart.

I can see Your Face at the Last Supper, Lord Jesus, as You looked up to heaven to the Father who sent You and gave Him thanks and praise. I wish I had the courage to praise the Father before every sacrifice that His Wisdom asks of me. Give me that total consecration to the Father's Will, that union with the Father's Love.

Did the Apostles gasp in wonder as they heard You say, "Take this, all of you, and eat it: this is My Body which will be given up for you"?

I look upon the Host whenever I am at Mass, speechless and struck with awe at such humility. My life is so full of me—so full of pride—so full of the need to keep my identity. You are willing to hide Your Glory and Majesty behind this wafer, so I may gaze at my God and not die. You want me to be comfortable in Your Presence—to speak to You unencumbered by the difference in our natures. Oh Love, that is not loved, how can I return Your love? Wash me clean, dear Jesus, clean of every sin and weakness. Cover me over with mercy and forgiveness.

Mother Angelica
The Mass in My Life

On 22nd January 1854, in Besancon, in the chapel of the Hospital of St. James, a eucharistic soul "whose perfect self-abnegation had led to a close intimacy with the heart of the Master, was in profound adoration before the Most Blessed Sacrament. All of a sudden, Jesus appeared to him abegging love: "My heart asks for love, as a poor man asks for bread . . . I thirst to be loved by men in the Most Blessed Sacrament . . . How many souls surround me and do not console me . . . I AM THE EUCHARISTIC HEART . . . Make me known, make me loved . . . spread this devotion" (P. Garenaux, "La Devotion au Coeur Eucaristique de Jesus" Paris).

Fr. Albert Kretschmer, SVD
Eucharistic Heart Anthology

Devotion to the Blessed Sacrament was at the center of his heart; he spoke of it over and over again, and we feel how he felt the insufficiency of his words. "Kissing your feet, I implore you all my brothers, and with the utmost affection I beseech you to show the greatest possible reverence and honor to the most holy Body and Blood of our Lord Jesus Christ . . . Consider your dignity O Brothers who are priests, and be holy because He is holy . . . It is a great misfortune and a miserable fault to have Him thus near you, and to be thinking of anything else. Let the whole man be seized with dread; let the whole world tremble; let the heavens exult when Christ, the Son of the living God, is on the altar in the hands of the priest. O amazing splendor and astounding condescension! O sublime humility! O humble sublimity! The Master of the universe, God Himself and Son of God humbles Himself so far as to hide Himself for our salvation under the feeble appearance of bread! See brothers the humility of God . . . keep nothing of yourselves for yourselves, so that He may possess you entirely, who has given Himself wholly for you."

Nesta de Robeck
The Life of St. Francis of Assisi

I betake myself to one of our altars to receive the Blessed Eucharist; I have no doubt whatever on my mind about the Gift which that Sacrament contains; I confess to myself my belief, and I go through the steps on which it is assured to me. "The Presence of Christ is here, for It follows upon Consecration; and Consecration is the prerogative of Priests; and Priests are made by Ordination; and Ordination comes in direct line from the Apostles. Whatever be our other misfortunes, every link in our chain is safe; we have the Apostolic Succession, we have a right form of Consecration; therefore we are blessed with the great Gift." Here the question rises in me, "Who told you about that Gift?" I answer, "I have learned it from the Fathers: I believe the Real Presence because they witness to it. St. Ignatius calls it "the medicine of immortality"; St. Irenaeus says that "our flesh becomes incorrupt, and partakes of life, and has the hope of the resurrection," as "being nourished from the Lord's Body and Blood"; that the Eucharist "is made up of two things, an earthly and an heavenly"; perhaps Origen, and perhaps Magnes, after him, say that It is not a type of our Lord's Body, but His Body; and St. Cyprian uses language as fearful as can be spoken, of those who profane it. I cast my lot with them. I believe as they.

John Henry Cardinal Newman
An Essay on the Development of Christian Doctrine

In the Eucharist, Jesus gives all. The bread is not simply a sign of his desire to become our food; the cup is not just a sign of his willingness to be our drink. Bread and wine *become* his body and blood in the giving. The bread, indeed, is his body given for us; the wine his blood poured out for us. As God becomes fully present for us in Jesus, so Jesus becomes fully present to us in the bread and the wine of the Eucharist. God not only became flesh for us years ago in a country far away. God also becomes food and drink for us now at this moment of the Eucharistic celebration, right where we are together around the table. God does not hold back; God gives all. That is the mystery of the Incarnation. That too is the mystery of the Eucharist. Incarnation and Eucharist are two expressions of the immense, self-giving love of God. And so the sacrifice on the cross and the sacrifice at the table are one sacrifice, one complete, divine self-giving that reaches out to all humanity in time and space.

Henri Nouwen
With Burning Hearts,
A Meditation on the Eucharistic Life

L ike the Resurrection, the Real Presence matters only inso-
far as it is a thing "out there" and not a mere psychological
projection originating in the mind of the believer. In other words,
the Eucharist is either changed or it is not, just as Christ is either risen or He is not. And if the Eucharistic change is a fact,
then it is a fact not just in our hearts but even for those who
disbelieve it. Similarly, if the Eucharist is *not* the Body and
Blood, then no amount of self-willed "faith" on my part could
make it otherwise. Thus, much as I would have liked to, I realized I could not rush off to my local Evangelical church and
"consecrate in my heart" the unconsecrated bread and grape
juice I received there any more than I could privately write my
own Scriptures or declare myself an Apostle.

For the change in the bread and wine can only be accomplished by the authority and power of the Lord Christ Himself.
And this authority, according to Scripture and Catholic teaching, has been delegated by Christ to the Church solely through
His apostles. As Justin Martyr writes: "The apostles in the mem-
oirs, which are called Gospels, have handed down what Jesus
ordered them to do; that He took bread and, after giving thanks,
said: "Do this in remembrance of me; this is My Body." In like
manner He took also the chalice, gave thanks, and said, "This is
My Blood." And to them only did He give it *(First Apology)*.

Mark Shea
This Is My Body:
An Evangelical Discovers the Real Presence

Only one thing remains to be done: I cannot fight against God who calls me to His Church: if I were to delay and die in the meantime I should have no plea why my soul was not forfeit. I have no power in fact to stir a finger: it is God Who makes the decision and not I.

But you do not understand what is involved in asking me to delay and how little good you would get from it. I shall hold as a Catholic what I have long held as an Anglican, that literal truth of our Lord's words by which I learn that the least fragment of the consecrated elements in the Blessed Sacrament of the Altar is the whole Body of Christ born of the Virgin Mary, before which the whole host of saints and angels as it lies on the altar trembles with adoration. This belief once got is the life of the soul and when I doubted it I should become an atheist the next day. But, as Monsignor Eyre says, it is a gross superstition unless guaranteed by infallibility. I cannot hold this doctrine confessedly except as a Tractarian or a Catholic: the Tractarian ground I have seen broken to pieces under my feet. What end then can be served by a delay in whether I should go on believing this doctrine as long as I believed in God and should be by the fact of my belief drawn by a lasting strain towards the Catholic Church?

Gerard Manley Hopkins, SJ, in a letter to his father
The Real Presence through the Ages
Fr. Michael L. Gaudoin-Parker

Feast of St. Colette
1381-1447

Bollandus relates of St. Coletta that one day, when she was hearing the Mass of her confessor, she suddenly exclaimed at the Elevation: "My God! O Jesus! O ye Angels and Saints! O ye men and sinners, behold the great marvels!" After the Mass her confessor asked her why she had wept so bitterly and uttered such pitiable cries. "What was it that you saw?" asked her confessor further. "Although that which I heard and saw," she replied, "is so sublime and so divine that no man can ever find words to express it in a becoming manner, yet I will endeavor to describe it to Your Reverence as well as my feeble language will permit."

"When Your Reverence was raising the Sacred Host, I saw Our Lord Jesus Christ as if hanging on the cross, shedding His blood, and praying to His heavenly Father in most lamentable accents: 'Behold, O My Father, in what condition I was once hanging on the cross and suffering for the redemption of the world. Behold My wounds, My sufferings, My death; I have suffered all this in order that poor sinners might not be lost. But now Thou wilt send them to Hell for their sins. What good, then, will result from my sufferings and cruel death? Those damned souls, when in Hell, instead of thanking Me for My passion, will only curse Me for it; but should they be saved, they would bless Me for all eternity. I beseech Thee, My Father, to spare poor sinners and to forgive them for My sake; and for the sake of My passion, preserve them from being damned forever.'"

Fr. Michael Muller, CSSR
The Blessed Eucharist, Our Greatest Treasure

Father Hartl was present again in Resl's room after the Midnight Mass on Christmas of 1930. "She felt . . . in a manner that cannot be explained naturally, the nearness of the Eucharist before It was brought to her . . . While lying in bed, she described exactly how the pastor (Father Naber) was taking the Blessed Sacrament from the tabernacle to bring her Communion. She described vividly his coming to her home. The road was icy and she saw how carefully he walked and made a little detour." Father Naber tells how, because he stopped enroute to visit a parishioner who was sick, he was delayed in arriving at Resl's home. She knew of this delay and suffered because of it. When the pastor finally reached her room, she said in her childlike manner to her Eucharistic Lord, "Oh, Saviour, you treated me unkindly today!"

When Therese travels to places where there are both Catholic and Protestant churches, she can perceive at once in which ones the Real Presence abides. Once, passing through a strange town, she stopped suddenly and cried out, "The dear Saviour is here!" The building before which she stopped was not a church, but upon inquiry it was found to be a house chapel in which the Blessed Sacrament was reserved. She perceives the presence of the Sacred Species in those who have received Holy Communion a short time before, and recognizes priests though they come in the attire of laymen, because their consecrated hands have held the host which is her only sustenance. She is keenly conscious also of the continuing Eucharistic presence within herself.

Albert Paul Schimberg
The Story of Therese Neumann

" They recognized him." This "recognizing him" is offered to us today if we keep our eyes open at the eucharist and see the eucharistic bread and wine, the body and blood of Christ, broken and shared with those coming up the communion line. Look at what is going on. Look at all the people coming up to communion. With our eyes open we can see Jesus giving over his very self to everyone . . . This is who Jesus is. He invites all to his table to enjoy a meal with him. At this meal he gives himself over in love totally to everyone present. This is love. This is real food to see Christ in action. This is real food to see Christ giving himself lovingly to everyone.

If we see this, can we not be called and impelled to do the same? As we see Jesus' attitude toward people we know coming up to receive the person of Jesus, the body and blood of Christ, are we not drawn to have the same attitude as Jesus toward them? Are we not attracted to the freedom of loving with that same love of Jesus? Are we not empowered by what we see here to have the attitude Jesus has toward those we know who are coming up the communion line to receive the presence of God? This is real food. To be nurtured by what we see here is real food. This is why Jesus came: to feed us, to feed us on who he is, to feed us on who God is, and to feed us on the image and the actions of God. Jesus' gift is to show us God, and to have us feast our eyes on who God is. Here we have such a feast. Here we have such a sight each day at the eucharist.

Robert Fabing, SJ
Real Food

Christianity is more than a doctrine. It is Christ Himself, living in those whom He has united to Himself in one Mystical body. It is the mystery by which the Incarnation of the Word of God continues and extends itself throughout the history of the world, reaching into the souls and lives of all men, until the final completion of God's plan. Christianity is the "re-establishment of all things in Christ" (Ephesians 1:10).

Now Christ lives and acts in men by faith and by the sacraments of faith. The greatest of all the sacraments, the crown of the whole Christian life on earth, is the Sacrament of charity, the Blessed Eucharist, in which Christ not only gives us grace but actually gives us Himself. For in this most Holy Sacrament Jesus Christ Himself is truly and substantially present, and remains present as long as the consecrated species of bread and wine continue in existence. The Blessed Eucharist is therefore the very heart of Christianity since it contains Christ Himself, and since it is the chief means by which Christ mystically unites the faithful to Himself in one Body.

Thomas Merton
The Living Bread

February 2, 1937. Today, from early morning, Divine absorption penetrates my soul. During Mass, I thought I would see the little Jesus, as I often do; however, today during Holy Mass I saw the Crucified Jesus. Jesus was nailed to the cross and was in great agony. His suffering pierced me, soul and body, in a manner which was invisible, but nevertheless most painful. (Diary 913)

Oh, what awesome mysteries take place during Mass! A great mystery is accomplished in the Holy Mass. With what great devotion should we listen to and take part in this death of Jesus. **One day we will know what God is doing for us in each Mass**, and what sort of gift He is preparing in it for us. Only His divine love could permit that such a gift be provided for us. O Jesus, my Jesus, with what great pain is my soul pierced when I see this fountain of life gushing forth with such sweetness and power for each soul, while at the same time I see souls withering away and drying up through their own fault. O Jesus, grant that the power of mercy embrace these souls. (Diary 914)

Rev. George W. Kosicki, CSB
Tell My Priests,
The Words of Our Lord to Priests about His Mercy
as Revealed to Sr. Faustina Kowalska

The great joy of the Saharan novitiate is the solitude, and the joy of solitude—silence, true silence, which penetrates everywhere and invades one's whole being, speaking to the soul with wonderful new strength unknown to men to whom this silence means nothing. Here, living in perpetual silence, one learns to distinguish its different shades: silence of the church, silence in one's cell, silence at work, interior silence, silence of the soul, God's silence.

To learn to live these silences, the novice-master lets us go away for a few days' "desert." A hamper of bread, a few dates, some water, the Bible. A day's march: a cave.

A priest celebrates Mass; then goes away, leaving in the cave, on an altar of stones, the Eucharist. Thus, for a week one remains alone with the Eucharist exposed day and night. Silence in the desert, silence in the cave, silence in the Eucharist. No prayer is so difficult as the adoration of the Eucharist. One's whole natural strength rebels against it.

One would prefer to carry stones in the sun. The senses, memory, imagination, all are repressed. Faith alone triumphs, and faith is hard, dark, stark. To place oneself before what seems to be bread and to say, "Christ is there living and true," is pure faith. But nothing is more nourishing than pure faith, and prayer in faith is real prayer.

"There's no pleasure in adoring the Eucharist," one novice used to say to me. But it is precisely this renunciation of all desire to satisfy the senses that makes prayer strong and real. One meets God beyond the senses, beyond the imagination, beyond nature.

Carlo Carretto
Letters from the Desert

I have said that this body of his is a sun. Therefore you could not be given the body without being given the blood as well; nor either the body or the blood without the soul of this Word; nor the soul or body without the divinity of me, God eternal. For the one cannot be separated from the other—just as the divine nature can nevermore be separated from the human nature, not by death or by any other being that you receive in that most gracious sacrament under that whiteness of bread.

And just as the sun cannot be divided, so neither can my wholeness as God and as human in this white host. Even if the host is divided, even if you could break it into thousands and thousands of tiny bits, in each one I would be there, wholly God and wholly human. It is just as when a mirror is broken, and yet the image one sees reflected in it remains unbroken. So when this host is divided, I am not divided but remain completely in each piece, wholly God, wholly human.

Words of God the Father
Catherine of Siena, The Dialogue

"What great care she took to accompany me to the altar this morning. It seemed to me that she had nothing else to think about except myself as she filled my whole heart with sentiments of holy love" (Letters I, 312).

Asked if the Madonna had been present at Mass, he answered: "Yes, she placed herself to the side, but I could see her, what joy! What paradise . . ."

"Has she attended only once, or is she always present?"

Padre Pio: "How can the mother of Jesus, present on Calvary at the foot of the cross, who offered her Son as victim for the salvation of souls, be absent at the mystical calvary of the altar?"

"Is our Lady present at all of the Masses that are being celebrated in the world?"

Padre Pio: "Yes."

"Do the angels also attend?"

Padre Pio: "The whole celestial court is present."

That is why Mass was both calvary and paradise for Padre Pio.

Padre Alberto D'Apolito
Padre Pio of Pietrelcina

How useful it is every so often to remain in contemplation before the tabernacle—without forcing ourselves to think of lofty things! To be able to tell Jesus simply: "You are my Master. You have given me an example. I want to do as You did."

The eucharistic visit for the apostle is like an audience, or a school, where the disciple engages in conversation with the Divine Master. Many methods are proposed for obtaining the maximum fruit from this practice. But especially suitable is the one which honors Jesus Master, Way, Truth and Life. First of all, the visit is not a complex of prayers. It is precisely a "visit," something you'd make to a dear person, your mother, for example. There is an exchange of greetings, an exchange of news, of gifts, promises, etc. The visit has the scope of establishing our lives in Jesus Christ, that is, to live in Jesus, for Jesus, with Jesus.

In making the visit, consider yourselves as representatives of humanity before the tabernacle, gathering the hearts of all men and women and children everywhere in you own, presenting all their needs to God, asking Him to give them strength in weakness, and light in obscurity. Do this so that they may be kept far from sin, so that Jesus may conquer the resistance of sinners, so that those who are consecrated to God may be granted holiness and zeal. Jesus has given us this ministry: to represent humanity before the tabernacle. This is your vocation: a ministry of love!

James Alberione, ssp
Thoughts: Fragments of Apostolic Spirituality from His Writings and Talks

March 15

Feast of St. Clement Mary Hofbauer
d. 1820

S t. Clement Mary Hofbauer was sent to Warsaw, Poland, to minister to the spiritual needs of several thousand Germans living there. This saint and his two companions lived a very simple, frugal, hand-to-mouth existence. Their food was extremely limited in quantity and variety.

A day came when there was not a penny in their pockets or a bite of food in the pantry, and there seemed little chance of immediate help. Fr. Hofbauer then went over to the church and knelt on the altar steps to tell their need to Jesus in the tabernacle. Insistent and confident as a child, Fr. Hofbauer then walked up to the tabernacle, tapped gently on the golden door, and spoke softly: "Lord, we are in great need; come quick and help us." It was not long after, when a total stranger rapped on the rectory door, leaving a sum of money generous enough to supply their needs for some time.

Child-like as it may seem, this incident emphasizes the power of petition presented to Christ in the Eucharist. . . . When we ask God for favors, we are simply accepting the invitation of Christ: "Ask, and it shall be given you; seek, and you shall find; knock, and it shall be opened to you" (Matt. 7:7).

During our visits to the Blessed Sacrament recall the picture of St. Clement Hofbauer tapping on the tabernacle door. Recall his attention, his sincerity, his humility, his confidence and his perseverance. Let us be as attentive, as sincere, as humble, as confident and as persevering in our petitions.

Rev. Armand Dasseville, OFM CAP.
Immaculata Magazine
December 1984

Father Kolbe often went to chapel to adore the most Blessed Sacrament and encouraged the friars to do likewise. He called such visits "audiences with the great King." Brother Luke Kuzba attests: Repeatedly throughout the course of the day, he visited Jesus in the tabernacle. He said that there is our strength, there the source of our sanctification . . . When he was observed there during adoration of the All-Holy, it was not possible to turn one's glance away from his figure, so fascinating it was. During adoration he was ordinarily seen kneeling without support of any kind, just before the steps of the altar.

"He kept his hands under his capuche, and his entire personal composure expressed a profound respect for and the recollected understanding" of the eucharistic mystery, another witness adds. He was so absorbed in prayer, wholly directed to the tabernacle, that he seemed not to notice anyone beside him and that "it was necessary to nudge him first, to inform him of urgent business to be attended to." Then, without protest, he would go wherever obedience or love of neighbor called him.

Jerzy Domanski, OFM CONV.
For the Life of the World,
Saint Maximilian and the Eucharist

I'd like to share a teaching that came to me one day as I sat before the Lord. I was just looking at the Blessed Sacrament and adoring Jesus and telling him I didn't have much to say except that I loved him.

I felt as though the Lord said to me, "Well, don't you know that you don't have to say anything to me? Just be with me. Come into my presence. It's not what you do for me, it's what I want to do for you."

Then I got an image of a person going out of his house and sitting in the sun. As he sat in the sun, he didn't do a thing, but he started to change color. People who saw him knew he had been in the sun because his skin showed it. The man knew it, too, because he felt the effects of the sun: the warmth and the light.

I heard the Lord saying, "So it is when you come into my presence. You will experience the effects of your time spent with me. People will see it in your actions."

It was a great teaching to me, knowing that I didn't always have to be saying things but all I had to do was be there with Jesus.

Sister Briege McKenna, OSC
Miracles Do Happen

March 18

Feast of St. Cyril of Jerusalem
c. 315

Here is how one of the Fathers of the Church, St. Cyril of Jerusalem, in the fourth century, describes the sacrifice of the Mass:

Then, having sanctified ourselves by spiritual hymns (the *trisagion*) we call upon the merciful God to send His Holy Spirit upon the gifts lying before Him (the unconsecrated species of bread and wine), that He may make the bread the Body of Christ and the wine the Blood of Christ for whatsoever the Holy Ghost has touched is sanctified and changed.

Then after the spiritual sacrifice is perfected . . . we entreat God for the peace of the Church, for the tranquility of the world . . . in a word for all who stand in need of succor we all supplicate and offer this sacrifice . . .

We commemorate also those who have fallen asleep . . . believing that it will be a very great advantage to the souls . . . When we offer to Him our supplications for those who have fallen asleep . . . we offer up Christ, sacrificed for our sins, propitiating our merciful God both for them and for ourselves (St. Cyril of Jerusalem, *Catechesis Mystagogica*, 5).

Thomas Merton
The Living Bread

March 19

Once, when I was in a difficulty and could not think what to do, or how I was going to pay some workmen, Saint Joseph, my true father and lord, appeared to me and gave me to understand that money would not be lacking and I must make all the necessary arrangements. I did so, though I had not a farthing, and the Lord, in ways which amazed people when they heard of them, provided the money. I thought the house very small, so small that it seemed impossible to turn it into a convent. I wanted to buy another, but had not the wherewithal, so there was no way of buying it, and I could not think what to do. There was a house near our own, but it was also too small to make into a church. One day after I had communicated, the Lord said to me: "I have already told you to go in as best you can," and then added a kind of exclamation: "Oh, the greed of mankind! So you really think there will not be enough ground for you! How often did I sleep all night in the open air because I had nowhere to lay my head!" This amazed me, but I saw that He was right. So I went to look at the little house, and worked things out, and found that it would just make a convent, though a very small one. I thought no more then about buying another site but arranged to have this house furnished so that we could live in it. Everything was very rough and it had only enough done to it not to make it injurious to the health. And that is the principle that should be followed everywhere.

St. Teresa of Avila
The Autobiography of St. Teresa of Avila
E. Allison Peers

Many make pilgrimages to various places to visit the relics of the Saints, wondering at the story of their lives and the splendor of their shrines; they view and venerate their bones, covered with silks and gold. But here on the Altar are You Yourself, my God, the Holy of Holies, Creator of men and Lord of Angels! When visiting such places, men are often moved by curiosity and the urge for sight-seeing, and one seldom hears that any amendment of life results, especially as their conversation is trivial and lacks true contrition. But here, in the Sacrament of the Altar, You are wholly present, my God, the Man Christ Jesus; here we freely partake the fruit of eternal salvation, as often as we receive You worthily and devoutly. No levity, curiosity, or sentimentality must draw us, but firm faith, devout hope, and sincere love.

O God, invisible Creator of the world, how wonderful are Your dealings with us! How sweetly and graciously You welcome Your chosen, to whom You give Yourself in this Sacrament! It passes all understanding, it kindles the love and draws the hearts of the faithful to Yourself. For Your faithful ones, who strive to amend their whole lives, receive in this most exalted Sacrament the grace of devotion and the love of virtue.

Words of the Disciple
The Imitation of Christ
Thomas à Kempis

Though I had believed in transubstantiation for more than a year, I had no yearning to receive. But now a hunger for the Eucharist became the last thought of the day and the first thought of the morning. I had received Jesus as Savior and Lord by faith when I was a teenager, but now I longed to receive his Body and Blood. For not only had Jesus humbled himself on our behalf in taking on human flesh to be our perfect sacrifice; he had even condescended lower—to offer us that same flesh to be the life and food of our souls! All this so that we could have him within us—not only in our hearts but in our physical bodies as well, making us living tabernacles. I felt that my heart would burst with so much joy!

Kimberly Hahn
Rome Sweet Home,
Our Journey to Catholicism

All this was once shown in a vision to Nicholas de la Flue, a holy hermit of Switzerland who was greatly enlightened by God in spiritual matters. While this good man was one day present at Mass, he saw a large tree full of the most beautiful flowers. He soon noticed that the flowers began to fall down upon those who were present. But some of the flowers, as soon as they fell, became withered and dry, while others retained their freshness and fragrance.

After Mass, he related this vision to his brother and requested him to explain its meaning. The brother replied that he too had seen the vision, and he explained it as follows: "The tree," said he, "is the Holy Mass; the beautiful flowers which it bears are the fruits of the Holy Mass; the withering of many of the flowers signifies that many of the graces which Our Lord distributes in the Mass are lost because Christians are not recollected and devout while they assist at this sacrifice, or because they afterward allow worldly thoughts to stifle all the good inspirations which they have received; the flowers which retained their odor and beauty signify the permanent fruits which those Christians derive from the Mass who assist at it with reverence and devotion and who, after having left the church, are still mindful of the great blessings which they have received from this holy sacrifice."

Fr. Michael Muller, CSSR
The Blessed Eucharist, Our Greatest Treasure

Sacrifice is necessary in our lives if we want to realize the tenderness of God's love. Sacrifice is his love in action. God sent Jesus to teach us this love. And you will find out in your own life. Have you ever experienced the joy of loving? Have you ever shared something with the sick, with the lonely, together making something beautiful for God. This is something that has to come from within us. That is why Jesus made himself the Bread of Life—to create that in our life. If it is not there it is good to examine our heart: is our heart clean? Jesus said: "Blessed are the clean of heart, for they shall see God." Now unless we see God in each other we cannot love each other. And so it is important for us to have a clean heart. With a clean heart we will be able to be only all for Jesus and to give Jesus to others. That is why Jesus made himself the Bread of Life. That is why he is there twenty-four hours. That is why he is longing for you and for me to share the joy of loving. And he says: "As I have loved you." If I can give you any advice, I beg you to get closer to the Eucharist and to Jesus . . . We must pray to Jesus to give us that tenderness of the Eucharist. Parish priest, ask your people to have adoration in your churches wherever you can. Make it even once a week, so that the tenderness of love may grow in your heart to share it with others . . . The cross is the proof that he loved us and the Tabernacle is the proof that he loves us now with tender compassion.

Mother Teresa of Calcutta
International Eucharistic Congress,
Nairobi, 1985

One day, having a little more leisure . . . I was praying before the Blessed Sacrament, when I felt myself wholly penetrated with that Divine Presence, but to such a degree that I lost all thought of myself and of the place where I was, and abandoned myself to this Divine Spirit, yielding up my heart to the power of His love. He made me repose for a long time upon His Sacred Breast, where He disclosed to me the marvels of His love and the inexplicable secrets of His Sacred Heart, which so far He had concealed from me. Then it was that, for the first time, He opened to me His Divine Heart in a manner so real and sensible as to be beyond all doubt, by reason of the effects which this favor produced in me, fearful, as I always am, of deceiving myself in anything that I say of what passes in me. It seems to me that this what took place: "My Divine Heart," He said, "is so inflamed with love for men, and for thee in particular that, being unable any longer to contain within Itself the flames of Its burning Charity, It must needs spread them abroad by thy means, and manifest Itself to them (mankind) in order to enrich them with the precious treasures which I discover to thee . . . "

St. Margaret Mary Alacoque
The Autobiography of St. Margaret Mary

O my daughter! Would that the believers in the holy Catholic faith opened their hardened and stony hearts in order to attain to a true understanding of the sacred and mysterious blessing of the holy Eucharist! If they would only detach themselves, root out and reject their earthly inclinations, and, restraining their passions, apply themselves with living faith to study by the divine light their great happiness in thus possessing their eternal God in the holy Sacrament and in being able, by its reception and constant intercourse, to participate in the full effects of this heavenly manna! If they would only worthily esteem this precious gift, begin to taste its sweetness, and share in the hidden power of their omnipotent God! Then nothing would ever be wanting to them in their exile. In this, the happy age of the law of grace, mortals have no reason to complain of their weakness and their passions; since in this bread of heaven they have at hand strength and health. It matters not that they are tempted and persecuted by the demon; for by receiving this Sacrament frequently they are enabled to overcome him gloriously. The faithful are themselves to blame for all their poverty and labors, since they pay no attention to this divine mystery, nor avail themselves of the divine powers, thus placed at their disposal by my most holy Son . . . Lucifer and his demons have such a fear of the most holy Eucharist, that to approach it, causes them more torments than to remain in hell itself. Although they do enter churches in order to tempt souls, they enter them with aversion, forcing themselves to endure cruel pains in the hope of destroying a soul and drawing it into sin, especially in the holy places and in the presence of the holy Eucharist.

Words of Our Lady spoken to
Venerable Mary of Agreda
The Mystical City of God

Father Leloir was interned at Buchenwald, where at 6 p.m. each day the prisoners and deportees were lined up for inspection by the S.S. troops. On the evening of August 23, 1944, Father Leloir had carefully concealed on his person a small white envelope containing six consecrated Hosts, which he intended to distribute secretly among his comrades. The presence of the Blessed Sacrament on the person of the priest was known to several fellow-prisoners.

Consternation filled all when the soldiers began to search the prisoners one by one. What would be the fate of the priest when the envelope containing the Hosts was found? Too well they knew what punishment would be given him. And what unspeakable irreverence would be done to the Sacred Hosts!

Down the line the S.S. troops contemptuously searched each man, and finally came Father Lelior's turn. Into his pockets one after another the Nazi soldiers pried, and found the "evidence." Father Leloir stood erect, a trifle pale, but silently praying to the Lord whose Precious Body was within the folds of the white envelope. His companions trembled and grew faint.

With an insolent air the S.S. guard tore open the envelope. Several prisoners gasped. Father Leloir stared in open amazement—as the Nazi soldiers threw the envelope scornfully to the ground saying: "Just an empty envelope."

Just an empty envelope! The Hosts had disappeared! To prevent the desecration of the Sacred Hosts and to save the priest and his fellow Catholics from certain punishment, perhaps death, Our Lord had worked this "little miracle!"

Immaculata Magazine
Eucharistic Adoration Issue

After Holy Communion, the child had a vision in which she assisted at the Sacred Mysteries in the Catacombs in company with St. Cecilia.

"I knelt," she said, "in a subterranean hall which seemed to be cut out in a mountain. Many people were kneeling around on the bare ground. Flambeaux were fastened to the wall, and there were two upon the stone altar which had a tabernacle, likewise of stone, and a door. A priest was saying Mass, all the people answering. At the end of it he took a chalice from the tabernacle. It looked like wood, and from it he distributed the Blessed Sacrament to the people, who received it on little white linen cloths spread carefully on their breast. Then they all dispersed."

This vision was a pledge that God had heard her and had accepted the sacrifice of her whole being. Her purity of heart and austerity of life rendered her worthy of figuring in the sacred cohort of early Christians who had drawn from the Most Blessed Sacrament their strength in the midst of torments. Her own life was to be a perpetual martyrdom and she, too, was to draw strength and courage from the same divine source. Like St. Cecilia she was to suffer for the Faith at a time of persecution, unbloody, it is true, but not the less dangerous to the Church. She, too, with heroism not inferior to that of the virgin-martyrs, was to confess her Redeemer denied and abandoned by the multitude.

Rev. K. E. Schmoger, CSSR
Life of Anne Catherine Emmerich

There was a worker from Belgium with a piece of bone missing in his leg, so that his ankle and foot dangled, suspended only by flesh and tendons, able to be turned a hundred and eighty degrees. When the Eucharist was raised over him in blessing, that missing bone was instantly created in his leg. The doctors had before-and-after x-rays. When the man died, an autopsy showed where the new bone had come to unite with the separated bone. The full documentation and x-rays can be seen at the office of the Medical Commission at Lourdes, together with the affirmation of many witnesses.

John M. Haffert
The World's Greatest Secret

Our Lord is in the Blessed Sacrament to receive from men the same homage he received from those who had the happiness of coming close to him during his mortal life. He is there to give everybody the opportunity of offering a personal homage to his sacred humanity. Were this the only reason for the Eucharist it should make us very happy; for the Eucharist enables us as Christians to pay our respects to our Lord in person. This presence is the justification of public worship as well as the life of it. If you take away the Real Presence, how will you be able to pay his most sacred humanity the respect and honor which are its due? . . . Without this presence, divine worship becomes an abstraction. Through this presence we go straight to God and approach him as during his mortal life. How unfortunate it would be if, in order to honor the humanity of Jesus Christ, we were obliged to go back eighteen centuries! That is all very well for the mind, but how pay an outward homage to so distant a past? We would content ourselves with giving thanks for the mysteries without actively participating in them.

But with the Eucharist we can actually come and adore him like the shepherds; we can prostrate ourselves before him like the Magi; we need no longer regret our not having been present at Bethlehem or Calvary (St. Peter Julian Eymard, *The Real Presence,* Eymard League).

Fr. Michael L. Gaudoin-Parker
The Real Presence through the Ages

I remember how, in the days of my youth, when I read and re-read the words of St. Paul, "By the grace of God, I am what I am," I thought what a gloriously bold and upright man he was, and how courageous. For I placed all of the emphasis on the words, "I am what I am,'" much in the spirit of Henley's "*I* am the captain of my soul, *I* am the master of my fate." I did not emphasize, as I should have, the words "by the grace of God." It is these words that I now emphasize. I give thanks to my wife, to the first priest I dared to talk to and who instructed me, and to God for His grace. . . .

Before I became a Catholic I used to say to myself: "Had I lived when He lived, and had I but once seen Him in the flesh, certainly had I heard His voice and looked into His eyes, never again would my life be the same. This would have been a transforming experience giving me forever life and hope." Now by the Faith He is here, present not only in the sacred tabernacle of the altar but everywhere, available for me as for you who read these lines, giving to all men who ask of Him, certainty of purpose and guidance divine.

In short, my Faith has led me to the feet of Christ who is "the way, the truth and the life." And the day on which I received Our Blessed Lord in Holy Communion has remained through all the intervening years the happiest day of my life.

Ben W. Palmer
Roads to Rome

O how unspeakable is this sacrament which sets the affections ablaze with the fire of charity and sprinkles our home's lintel, on both doorposts [lips], with the immaculate Lamb's blood! What wholesome provision for our dangerous journey we receive in this food! What strengthening manna enriches the traveller! It invigorates the weak, brings back health to the sick; it increases virtue, makes grace abound, purges away vices, refreshes the soul, renews life in the languid, binds together all the faithful in the union of charity! This Sacrament of Faith also inspires hope and increases charity. It is the central pillar of the Church, the consolation of the dead, and the fulfillment of Christ's Mystical Body.

St. Thomas Aquinas
Thomas Aquinas, Selected Writings

We must start practicing what we have said as soon as we come out from Mass. We must really make the effort, each one within his or her own limits, to offer our "bodies" to our brethren, and that is to say, our time, energy and attention— in a word, our lives. When Jesus had pronounced the words: "Take . . . this is my body; take . . . this is my blood," he didn't allow much time to pass before doing what he had promised: a few hours later he gave his life and blood on the Cross. Otherwise, it's all just empty words, lies. Therefore, after saying to our brothers and sisters: "Take, eat," we must really allow ourselves to be "eaten" and especially by those who do not act with the gentleness and kindness we expect. Jesus said: "What merit have you got if you love only those that love you, greet only those that greet you, invite only those that invite you? Everyone does this" (cf. Matt 5:46-47). On his way to Rome where he was to die a martyr, St. Ignatius of Antioch wrote: "I am the grain of Christ; that I may be ground by the teeth of wild beasts to become pure bread for the Lord." If we think about it, each one of us will realize that there are sharp teeth grinding us: criticisms, contrasts, hidden or open oppositions, different ideas in those surrounding us, differences in character. We should even be grateful to those who help us like this. They are of infinitely more benefit to us than those who approve or flatter us. In another letter, the same holy martyr wrote: "Those that praise me, scourge me."

Fr. Raniero Cantalamessa
The Eucharist, Our Sanctification

When Elizabeth Seton returned to New York she attended her own church as usual, but chose a side pew which faced the Catholic church opposite. She records that she constantly found herself speaking to the Blessed Sacrament there "instead of looking at the naked altar where I was, or minding the routine of prayers."

Later after she had become a Catholic, she burned with faith at no time more strongly than when she was about to receive Communion.

She wrote: "God is everywhere, in the very air I breathe, yes everywhere, but in His Sacrament of the Altar He is as present actually and really as my soul within my body; in His Sacrifice daily offered as really as once offered on the Cross."

On New Year's Day, 1821, Mother Seton was near death. To receive communion in those days one had to abstain from food and drink from midnight, and when a nurse requested the dying saint to take a beverage she said: "Never mind the drink. One Communion more and then eternity." Thus in the face of death she reminded us that only on this earth is Eucharistic union with Christ possible . . . an honor even the angels cannot enjoy.

John M. Haffert
The World's Greatest Secret

When Christ promised that He would give His very Flesh to eat, the Jews protested because they imagined a natural and cannibalistic eating of Christ's Body. Christ refuted this notion of the manner in which His Flesh was to be received by saying that He would ascend into Heaven, not leaving His Body in its human form upon earth. But He did not say that they were not to eat His actual body. He would thus contradict Himself, for a little earlier He had said, "My flesh is meat indeed and My Blood is drink indeed." VI., 56. He meant, therefore, "You will not be asked to eat My flesh in the horrible and natural way you think for My Body as you see it with your eyes will be gone from this earth. Yet I shall leave My Flesh and Blood in another and supernatural way which your natural and carnal minds cannot understand. The carnal or fleshy judgment profits nothing. I ask you, therefore, to have faith in Me and to trust Me. It is the spirit of faith which will enable you to believe, not your natural judgment." Then the Gospel goes on to say that many would not believe, and walked no more with Him; just as many today will not believe, and walk no more with the Catholic Church. According to the doctrine of the Catholic Church Christ's Body is ascended into Heaven. But by its substance, independently of all the laws of space which affect substance through accidental qualities, this body is present in every consecrated Host.

Fr. Charles M. Carty and Rev. Dr. L. Rumble, MSC
Q. A. Eucharist, Quizzes to a Street Preacher

Today everything which concerns the Sacred Heart of Jesus has become familiar and doubly dear to me. My life seems destined to be spent in the light irradiating from the tabernacle, and it is to the heart of Jesus that I must look for a solution of all my troubles. I feel as if I would be ready to shed my blood for the cause of the Sacred Heart. My fondest wish is to be able to do something for that precious object of my love. At times the thought of my arrogance, of my unbelievable self-love and of my great worthlessness alarms and dismays me and robs me of my courage, but I soon find reason for comfort in the words spoken by Jesus to Blessed Margaret Alacoque: "I have chosen you to reveal the marvels of my heart, because you are such an abyss of ignorance and insufficiency."

Ah! I wish to serve the Sacred Heart of Jesus, today and always. I want the devotion to his Heart, concealed within the sacrament of love, to be the measure of all my spiritual progress. The conclusion of my resolutions during the holy exercises is in my desire henceforth to do all that I have been trying to do till now in intimate union with the Sacred Heart of Jesus in the Blessed Sacrament.

Pope John XXIII
Journal of a Soul

April 5

Feast of Saint Juliana of Mount Cornillon
d. 1258

When, in the thirteenth century, the Waldenses and Albigenses . . . spread false doctrines concerning the Blessed Sacrament, divine Providence ordained that, in opposition to these errors, a public profession of faith should be made by all Christendom. The will of God was made known to an obscure and pious religious named Juliana who lived near Liege. This humble and devout person had been privileged to behold in her lifetime heavenly mysteries. . . . In a vision she saw the full moon in its splendor, one dark spot only marring the brilliance of its orb. It was revealed to her that this spot denoted the absence of a festival which should be devoted exclusively to honoring the Most Holy Sacrament. At the same time it was enjoined upon her to tell this to the bishop, and suggest that he should celebrate such a feast with the clergy of his diocese. . . . The new festival commended itself to all the faithful, and in 1264 Pope Urban IV, who had formerly been archdeacon of Liege, made it binding upon the whole Church.

The festival is called the feast of *Corpus Christi*, the body of Christ . . . It was for this day that St. Thomas of Aquinas composed the beautiful hymn *Lauda Sion*, which is recited after the epistle. At the conclusion of this sequence it is customary in some places to expose on this day the Bread of Angels in the monstrance, and give the blessing with it. After High Mass there is a solemn procession, in which the highest ecclesiastic present carries the sacred Host beneath a canopy, accompanied by the clergy.

Rev. H. Rolfus
An Explanation of the Holy Sacraments

One who thirsted eagerly for God was Charles de Foucald whose prodigal and shocking way of life provoked so much gossip in Paris that he was the butt of violent feelings and jokes among French soldiers.

Born September 15, 1858, of fabulous wealth, at one point of his shady life he stated: "I was so completely selfish, so completely vain, so completely irreligious, and utterly given over to wickedness, that I was only one step away from insanity."

God seemed to him to be infinitely remote—if He existed at all! He used to enter St. Augustine Church in Paris, repeating over and over "My God, if You exist, let me come to know You." One day, as a priest elevated the Consecrated Host, he was overheard to say: "My God, You are real!"

"In a single instant," he said, "my heart was touched and I believed." The Eucharist, until his death, dominated his whole life. To stir others to seek and find God dwelling in the tabernacle that they too may be touched to the quick, share in his discovery, and come home to the Creator, "that Power which erring men call change," he composed this prayer: *Oh Jesus present in the Blessed Sacrament in our churches, You give us solace and refuge; You give us faith, hope, love and hospitality. You build for us an inner retreat, an ardent repose. Help us to seek You and find You in the tabernacle.*

Louis Kaczmarek
Hidden Treasure, The Riches of the Eucharist

I often see the Child Jesus during Holy Mass. He is extremely beautiful. He appears to be about one year old. Once, when I saw the same Child during Mass in our chapel, I was seized with a violent desire and an irresistible longing to approach the altar and take the Child Jesus. At that moment, the Christ Child was standing by me on the side of my kneeler, and He leaned with His two little hands against my shoulder, gracious and joyful, His look deep and penetrating. But when the priest broke the Host, Jesus was once again on the altar, and was broken and consumed by the priest.

After Holy Communion, I saw Jesus in the same way in my heart and felt Him physically in my heart throughout the day. Unconsciously, a most profound recollection took possession of me, and I did not exchange a word with anyone. I avoided people as much as I could, always answering questions regarding my duties, but beyond that, not a word.

Sr. Faustina of the Blessed Sacrament
*Divine Mercy in My Soul,
the Diary of Sr. M. Faustina Kowalska*

Two sacrifices of the Old Law were, before all others, representative of the Sacrifice of the Divine Redeemer. The first is that of Abraham, who, in obedience to God's command, offers his son Isaac as a holocaust; but God accepts his good-will, and spares the life of Isaac. The second very celebrated example, also in the time of Abraham, and more nearly figurative of the Eucharist, is the sacrifice of Melchizedek, king of Salem (Jerusalem).

Abraham was returning victorious, and bearing the spoils of his victory over the five kings of Upper Asia. He meets the king of Salem, who, in thanksgiving for the victory, offers *bread and wine* as a holocaust, exclaiming: "Blessed be Abraham. . . and blessed be the Most High God, by Whose protection Thy enemies are in Thy hands." (Genesis 14: 19-20) The Prophet David, St. Paul the Apostle, the Synagogue, and all Christian tradition agree that the Messiah, the Divine Redeemer, Christ Jesus, was prefigured in Melchizedek, "a priest for ever according to the order of Melchizedek." There is then no doubt (the Fathers of the Church and Christian sentiment are in agreement) that the Holy Christian Sacrifice of our altars was foretold and represented two thousand years beforehand in the sacrifice of bread and wine offered to God by Melchizedek.

And, therefore, as the *clean oblation* foretold by Malachy foreshadows the Eucharist, so does the sacrifice of bread and wine that was offered by Melchizedek foreshadow the same Sacrament.

Cardinal Gaetano De Lai
The Real Presence of Jesus Christ in the Eucharist

"The Blessed Sacrament is the invention of Love. It is life and fortitude for souls, a remedy for every fault, and viaticum for the last passage from time to eternity. In it sinners recover life for their souls; tepid souls true warmth; fervent souls, tranquility and the satisfaction of every longing . . . saintly souls, wings to fly towards perfection . . . pure souls sweet honey and rarest sustenance. Consecrated souls find in it a dwelling, their love and their life. In it they will seek and find the perfect exemplar of those sacred and hallowed bonds that unite them inseparably to their heavenly Bridegroom.

"Indeed, O consecrated souls, you will find a perfect symbol of your vow of Poverty in the small, round, light and smooth host; for so must the soul that professes poverty be: no angles, that is to say, no petty natural affections, either for things used nor for her employments, or for family or country . . . but she must ever be ready to leave, or give up, or change . . . Her heart must be free, with no attachments whatever . . .

"This by no means signifies insensibility of heart; no, for the more it loves the more it will preserve the integrity of the vow of Poverty. What is essential for religious souls is first that they should possess nothing without the permission and approbation of Superiors, and secondly, that they should possess and love nothing that they are not ready to give up at the first sign."

Words of Our Lord to Sr. Josefa Menendez
The Way of Divine Love

The real light that led me to my Catholic home was the doctrine of transubstantiation—the change of the substance of the bread and wine into the substance of the body and blood of Our Lord at the consecration in the Mass. That is the doctrine which has proved a stumbling block and a rock of offence to so many souls. It has been mocked, derided and denounced by so many of the wise men of the world, as unreasonable, unphilosophical, a denial of the evidence of the senses and as altogether preposterous, yet it was that doctrine that landed me in the bosom of the Church. And, where, you will ask, did I, being a Protestant at the time, get that doctrine from? The answer, perhaps, will prove still more of a puzzle. My thanks for the doctrine are due to the Episcopal Book of Common Prayer, the Old and New Testaments and, it is humbly believed and trusted, to the grace of God.

One morning, after receiving Communion—it was no sacrament, but God's mercy, I solemnly believe, sent a special grace with it—a light, like a flash from Heaven, burst upon my poor soul. It was like the sun suddenly beaming through a rift in the dark storm cloud. It was no miracle, but it was a distinctive grace. It could have been nothing else. Instantly the whole doctrine of the Incarnation in all its offices and functions bearing upon man's fall and his redemption and sanctification opened to my perception. The absolute necessity, in the scheme of salvation, for the literal interpretation of our Lord's words in the sixth chapter of S. John seemed irrefutable to me, and justified beyond cavil the doctrine of the Catholic Church as to transubstantiation.

William Markoe
Roads to Rome

April 11

Feast of St. Gemma Galgani
1878-1903

We read in the lives of different Saints, that as sometimes they were unable to go to the Church for Holy Communion, God made use of an angel, who, to satisfy their hunger for the Blessed Eucharist, acted instead of the priest and took the consecrated species to them. It appears that Our Savior Himself willed to take this great gift to Gemma; and that happened quite three times. Here is how it is told us by one who was an eyewitness: "On the morning of the Friday on which dear Gemma for the first time underwent the cruel punishment of the Scourging, on seeing her horribly lacerated all over, I forbade her to get up. The poor child obeyed, and collecting her thoughts she set to prepare herself for a spiritual Communion, for which she used to make her preparation in the same way as for her sacramental Communion in the Church. She went into ecstasy, and at a given moment I saw her join her hands and return to herself, while her eyes sparkled and her face suddenly lit up as usually happened when she had some extraordinary vision. At the same moment she put out her tongue and soon withdrew it, returning into ecstasy to make her usual thanksgiving. The same thing happened at other times as well, but I was not then a witness. I learned from Gemma herself, who quite candidly told me of it, that it was Jesus and not an Angel Who came to communicate her."

Fr. Germanus, CP
The Life of Gemma Galgani

The founder of the Order of the Congregation of the Most Holy Redeemer (Redemptorists), St. Alphonsus Liguori (d. 1787), was often rapt in ecstasy before the Blessed Sacrament and was frequently heard to exclaim, "O my God, my Love, O everlasting Love, I love Thee!" It is said that no other saint visited Jesus in the Eucharist as often as did St. Alphonsus. He encouraged frequent visits to the Blessed Sacrament and even wrote a treatise called *Visits to the Most Holy Sacrament of the Altar*, which has been translated into numerous languages, to the welfare of countless souls. When he became unable to offer the Holy Sacrifice of the Mass because of his advanced years, he would ask to be carried into church, where he heard five or six Masses and spent from five to six hours in prayer before the Blessed Sacrament. The saint was often heard to remark: *One thing is certain, that next to Holy Communion no act of worship is so pleasing to God, and none is so useful, as the daily visit to our Lord Jesus Christ in the Blessed Sacrament dwelling upon our altars. Know that in one quarter of an hour which you spend before Jesus in the Blessed Sacrament you attain more than in all the good works of the rest of the day.*

Joan Carroll Cruz
Eucharistic Miracles

There is a parish in Ottawa, Canada, where a priest was appointed. He had tried everything to attract people to church.
Yet, the church was almost empty. There were only 20-30 people
at Mass on Sunday. But the priest did not get discouraged. He
invited those few people to Perpetual Adoration. He told them
that we suffer because our brothers and our children are not
here. So, let's do something! Let's have Eucharistic Adoration!
So, they started that. After three years the small community
grew with people who were attracted to the Eucharist because
it is there that the loving heart of Jesus is present, ready to in-
flame our hearts and the church was full every Sunday. Two
years ago, nine boys had gone to the seminary to become priests,
just because they had rediscovered the Eucharist. So, I think it
is important to go back to the Eucharist, and give a real place to
the Eucharist in our lives and in the lives of our families.

Cardinal Edouard Gagnon
Immaculata Magazine
Eucharistic Adoration Issue

For hundreds of years, since the Holy Thursday institution, men have chosen to become priests. Better, God has chosen them.

We are among those chosen to succeed the Apostles. Only God knows why. 365 times a year for over thirty-eight years (12,870 times) I have acted in the place of Christ and said, "This is my body. This is my blood," more that the first half of the years in Latin, the latter decade or so in the vernacular. Always for me, God's most unworthy servant, with awe and trepidation.

We hold Christ in trembling hands and we kneel before the tabernacle with head held between our hands, lest, like Judas, we betray the Lord. We must pray to be worthy of the Eucharist, which we call down on the altar and dispense to the saints, the living saints of the Church. Some priests gave the Eucharist to St. Francis of Assisi and St. Theresa of Lisieux, to St. Teresa of Avila and to all the unknown saints. Today a priest gives the Eucharist to Mother Teresa and her sisters—how unworthy we would be of that privilege! We are not the Cure who spent hours in prayer at Ars before the Eucharist, especially before the crowds started to come. But the Lord still wants us to say Mass, to call people to the Eucharist.

Priests form an innumerable family—from St. John the Apostle until now, from St. Peter to John Paul II. The priesthood must be transmitted unto the end of time. Pray before the Eucharist for priests, that they be Eucharistic priests. Pray to the Eucharistic Jesus that there will be priests.

Msgr. John F. Davis
An Audience with Jesus

The great Cardinal Mercier, a saintly and learned theologian, used to say: "Give me a priest fully appreciating the gift of his daily Mass, preparing it well, offering it devoutly, living the grace of his Mass; I tell you, this priest will be ready for canonization when he dies." I apply this statement to the faithful: Give me a Catholic fully realizing the doctrine of the Mass, really and truly living the grace of daily Mass, and I, too, will show you someone who will be a saint at the hour of death.

I am preaching the reign of the Sacred Heart. But the reign of the Sacred Heart presupposes an enlightened mind, a full appreciation of the meaning of the Holy Sacrifice of the Mass, as much as that is possible. The Mass is the only wonderful thing on earth—the rest is mere shadow. This is the obsession of my life; this is the foundation of the crusade I am preaching. In the measure we give to priests, to religious, to the faithful, the true meaning, the true sense, of this message of faith and love, the Holy Sacrifice of the Mass, we are preaching eloquently, victoriously, through His Blood and Chalice, the reign of the great King Who was crucified for us, the reign of the Eucharistic Heart of Jesus, Who wrought this miracle.

Father Mateo Crawley-Boevey, sscc
Jesus King of Love

April 16

Feast of St. Bernadette Soubirous
1844-1879

On February 11, 1858, the fourteen-year-old Bernadette and two friends went to gather firewood. They stopped near the Gave River to remove their shoes and wade across the small stream. They were near a natural grotto at a place called Massabielle. The other children waded into the icy stream and ran ahead, but Bernadette hesitated for fear that the cold water might bring on another asthma attack. Suddenly, she heard the sound of rushing wind and saw a bright light near the grotto. In this light appeared a lady whom Bernadette later described as being "so beautiful that to see her again one would be willing to die." Bernadette felt inspired to pray the Rosary, and slipped the well-worn beads out of her pocket. The lady seemed to smile, and she joined in the "Glory Be to the Father" prayers.

At a subsequent apparition, the lady asked Bernadette to return each day for fifteen days, which the young girl promised to do. During the apparitions, the lady gave Bernadette a number of messages. The main purpose of most of her requests was to ask people to do penance for their sins. The lady gave Bernadette some messages for herself which she never revealed. She also asked for a chapel to be built at the grotto, and for processions. During one of the apparitions, she asked Bernadette to drink from the spring; Bernadette, not knowing of a spring, turned and began walking toward the Gave, but the lady called her back. She indicated a spot on the ground, and Bernadette obediently dug into the earth. The people watching were astounded to see the little visionary apparently eating mud or dirt. From this spot, an underground spring welled up which today provides water for the pilgrims at Lourdes.

Ann Ball
Saints, Their Lives and Faces

During three long weeks of trial I was able to have the tremendous consolation of daily Holy Communion. How sweet it was! Jesus spoilt me for a long time, much longer than He did His more faithful brides, for, after the influenza had gone, He came to me daily for several more months and the rest of the community didn't share this joy. I had not asked for any special treatment, but I was most happy to be united each day with my Beloved. I was also allowed to handle the sacred vessels and to prepare the altar linen which was to receive Jesus. I felt that I must be very fervent and I often recalled the words addressed to a deacon: "Be holy, you who carry the vessels of the Lord."

What can I tell you, Mother, of my thanksgiving after Holy Communion—both at that time and always? I have less consolation then than I ever have! And it's very natural, for I don't want Our Lord to visit me for my own satisfaction, but only for His pleasure.

I picture my soul as a patch of bare ground and I beg the Blessed Virgin to clear it of all rubbish (my imperfections) and then build there a vast pavilion fit for heaven and adorn it with her own jewels. Then I invite all the angels and saints to come and sing hymns of love. It seems to me that Jesus is pleased to see Himself received with such magnificence. I share His delight. But it doesn't prevent me from being distracted and feeling sleepy. So I often resolve to continue my thanksgiving throughout the whole day, as I've made it so badly in choir.

St. Therese of Lisieux
The Story of a Soul

I am a twenty-four year old mother of two who God has worked a miracle with during Mass. I had been medicated for months for a debilitating depression that I had suffered with following a number of painful life experiences. My husband is a recovering alcoholic who had been both physically and emotionally abusive. In desperation I sought to receive love from an absentee parent who I had never known; I found my father after a 24 year separation. He also was unable to fill that need for a total consuming love within me. Having to say good-bye to all of my childhood dreams of "Daddy," I became so depressed and lost in hurts of the past that until I was medicated, I had sat on the couch in front of the T.V. unable to give or receive love.

During the Mass, I experienced Jesus in such a powerful way! I had known the Lord since I was a teenager, yet, I had never experienced such love and peace as in this Mass. I wept through the readings, and as the Host was consecrated, I felt all of my pain and frustration lost into my Lord before me. When I received Communion I felt healed and I knew within me that Christ, my Master, had intervened and divinely healed me. That night, I had a choice; to believe in blind faith, that I had truly experienced the Lord, or if it was just a dream. I knew what I received was real indeed.

I spoke with my psychologist and told her I had been healed by the Master and would not be returning to medication. Following our conversation, she too believed the depression was indeed gone! Praise God!

P. S., Albuquerque, New Mexico
Walking in the Light
Ann Ross Fitch and Fr. Robert DeGrandis, ssj

If there is one mystery of faith around which revolves the whole Catholic liturgy, it is the Eucharist. Christian piety has been lavish in the titles it gives to this mystery, believing it is impossible to exhaust its depth of meaning. The name "Eucharist," or thanksgiving, is to be explained either by the fact that at its institution Christ "gave thanks," or by the fact that this is the supreme act of Christian gratitude to God. Early instances of this title occur in the *Teaching of the Twelve Apostles*, in the letters of St. Ignatius of Antioch, and in the Apologies of St. Justin. Other familiar names are the Lord's Supper, the Table of the Lord, the Holy Sacrifice, the Holy of Holies, the Blessed Sacrament, or simply the Liturgy. Each of these and similar names concentrate on one or another of the three main aspects of the Eucharistic mystery, as Real Presence, as the Sacrifice of the Altar, or as the sacrament of Holy Communion.

In the New Testament there are four accounts of its institution, one by St. Paul in his letter to the Corinthians and three in the Synoptic Gospels of Matthew, Mark, and Luke. We have already seen how it was celebrated by the early Christian communities and from the beginning was a regular part of Christian worship.

While there is no institution narrative in John's Gospel, this is explainable by the fact that John wrote his Gospel to supplement what the other evangelists had already told. Moreover, his account of Christ's promise of the Eucharist is our most telling witness to the real bodily presence of Christ in the Blessed Sacrament.

Fr. John A. Hardon, SJ
The Catholic Catechism

S ister Emmerich herself speaks as follows:— "I very often saw blood flowing from the cross on the Sacred Host; I saw it distinctly. Sometimes Our Lord, in the form of an Infant, appeared like a lightning-flash in the Sacred Host. At the moment of communicating, I used to see my Saviour like a bridegroom standing by me and, when I had received He disappeared, leaving me filled with the sweet sense of His presence. He pervades the whole soul of the communicant just as sugar is dissolved in water, and the union between the soul and Jesus is always in proportion to the soul's desire to receive Him."

Very Rev. K. E. Schmoger, CSSR
Life of Anne Catherine Emmerich

I believe that the importance of this point of doctrine, its religious significance, is very significant. . . . How can man, earthbound and sinful as he is, succeed in reaching the throne of God? And then the miracle occurs, God himself takes our place and fulfills the sacrifice. Even before this happened we could offer him only what we had already received from him, somewhat in the way children can only celebrate their parents' birthdays by offering flowers gathered from their father's garden, or a present bought with money from their mother's purse. But what we are now considering is something much greater than this. Through transubstantiation, our humble offering is transformed into that of Christ, whilst still remaining our own, or rather that of the Church; this is why after the consecration, the liturgy continues to speak of the elements on the altar as *our* gifts and also as the offered body and blood of Christ. Ultimately it is always a question of that *admirabile commercium*, that wonderful exchange and intercourse, hymned in the Christmas liturgy, and of that principle in which the Fathers sum up God's whole purpose: He became man in order that we might become God! Our offering, and ourselves in and through it, can travel all the distance to God, because it has been transformed into the supremely holy and effective offering of Jesus Christ, which, in this way, retains its autonomy and yet is extended to his mystical Body (Yves Congar, OP, *The Revelation of God*).

Fr. Michael L. Gaudoin-Parker
The Real Presence through the Ages

Before the tabernacle. Lord, I want to thank you for your presence, for recognizing in this house the house of your Father, and for dwelling within it, so as not to be distant and hidden from us with the Father and the Spirit, but rather to remain among us as the way that leads to the Father, as the way by which we will also attain the possession of the Holy Spirit. I want to thank you for being here, veiled in the mystery of the host, but so fully present that you yourself teach us to pray and help us to live. You are so fully present that we come to receive from you and take with us what your presence bestows upon us: the certainty of faith, the love of your dwelling among us. Lord, you know how weak and distracted we are and how we consider everything else more important than you; but again and again you guide us back to this place where you dwell in order to change us.

Hans Urs von Balthasar
First Glance at Adrienne von Speyr

Pope John Paul II said that "Our essential commitment in life is to persevere and advance constantly in Eucharistic life and Eucharistic piety and to grow spiritually in the climate of the Holy Eucharist."

On December 1, 1981 Pope John Paul II began perpetual adoration in a chapel at St. Peter's and appealed with these encouraging words for all parishes to do the same: ". . .every member of the Church must be vigilant in seeing that this sacrament of love shall be at the center of the life of the people of God so that through all the manifestations of worship due to it, Christ shall be given back 'love for love,' and truly become the life of our souls" (*Redeemer of Man*).

This is what perpetual adoration is: centering the life of the people of God in this Sacrament of love so that Christ is given back "love for love" and truly becomes the life of our soul, our parish, and the world.

Fr. Martin Lucia, MSS
Rosary Meditations from Mother Teresa of Calcutta

"If souls but understood the Treasure they possess in the Divine Eucharist, it would be necessary to encircle the tabernacles with the strongest ramparts for, in the delirium of a devouring and holy hunger, they would press forward themselves to feed on the Bread of Angels. **The Churches would overflow with adorers consumed with love for the Divine prisoner no less by night than by day.**"

Blessed Dina Belanger

Let us gaze upon the ardent soul of the one whom the Church now venerates as Blessed Dina Belanger religious of the Congregation of Jesus and Mary. From her novitiate days she attained a high degree of intimacy with God. "My hunger for Communion," she wrote, "kept on growing. Is not a day without bread like a day without sunshine, like hours when evening is eagerly awaited?" She wanted to see Jesus alone live in her so that her whole being would be annihilated in him. Dina Belanger reflects the admirable ideal proposed by Saint Paul when he writes: "It is no longer I that live, but Christ lives in me" (Gal 2:20). In a Congregation dedicated to making Christ known through Christian education, Sister Marie de Sainte-Cecile de Rome arranges everything in her life in such a way as to allow Christ to act in her, becoming an instrument which remains entirely in his hands.

Pope John Paul II, March 20, 1993
The Link Magazine
"Eucharistic Union For The Life Of The World"
July 1994

If only we had the humility to realize that He alone is Goodness and makes us good. As soon as we come into His Presence in the Eucharist, our souls respond to the power before them like a sunflower turning toward the sun.

His silent Presence, hidden in the tabernacle, says to each one of us, "I love you. Come to me all you who labor and are burdened and I will refresh you. Come to the fountain of life and drink. Tell Me your problems. Listen to My voice. I tug at your heart, guiding your way and smoothing your path."

There is between the Eucharistic Heart of Jesus and the soul, a silent exchange of love, a sharing of pain, an inaudible dialogue between two who know each other perfectly and love each other deeply.

It is as if the soul sees itself in a perfect Mirror and knows clearly its faults and imperfections. A strange phenomenon occurs as the soul gazes at Jesus. Its own reflection becomes brighter. Its faults fade away and one day that "soul is turned—transformed into the image it reflected" (2 Cor 3:18).

This being true, why do we permit our souls to die of thirst when the Fountain of Living water is just around the corner?

Mother Angelica
To Leave and Yet to Stay

The writings of the Fathers of the Church reveal the wonder fully pluriform nature of their reflections on the Eucharist, a plurality of approaches that highlights the many aspects of the Sacrament itself. They all worked from two apparently fundamental data of faith: the Presence of Christ himself in the Sacrament and the sacrificial aspect of the Sacrament. The Presence was the Flesh born of Mary, and so the Eucharist was to be adored. With increasing perception they mentioned and reflected upon the change that takes place in the elements of bread and wine, although it is surely true that some of them realized the extent and profundity of that change and made more of it than did others. In none of them were the symbolic aspects of the Sacrament neglected. The very formation of the bread and wine mirrored the unity of the church. The Reality that the bread and wine became in the Consecration created the unity of the Church and was the motive and cause for fraternal charity. For the Fathers the Eucharist was, as well, meal and nourishment, pledge of eternal life to all who received worthily, even while it brought condemnation to the unworthy communicant, an antidote to sin, the means by which our humanity is made sharer of the divine nature, thanksgiving to the Heavenly Father for his creation and for what he had done for us in Christ, our share in Christ's heavenly offering.

St. Thomas Aquinas wrote: "The common spiritual good of the whole Church is substantially contained in the Sacrament of the Eucharist" (*S. Th.*, III, q. 65, a. 3, ad I). The teaching of Aquinas can be considered a fair summation of the writings of the Church Fathers. The Eucharist is Christ who is himself our life and all our good.

Rev. James T. O'Connor
The Hidden Manna, A Theology of the Eucharist

S he draws as close as she can to the altar. There she kneels, head erect, hands joined, body motionless, eyes riveted on the host or on the tabernacle door. She looks at Jesus, speaks to him, calls on him; she also keeps silent and listens to him. Her prayer is absorption in the divine. She tells her divine Master that she wants to be "a living victim"; she envies the candle on the altar which is consumed as it burns, shedding light and giving off the mystical perfume of wax; she would like to be like the sanctuary lamp which remains day and night in the company of the Blessed Sacrament; she presents herself to her Savior as to her all-compassionate, all-powerful Physician; then, as she beautifully says, she comes to pay her due homage to the divine king of her heart.

She tries to make up for sin; she apologizes to him; she begs graces for herself and for others. What holy familiarity with Jesus hidden in the host! In his presence she sometimes reads the letters she has received, and tells him about them, for there is no secret he does not share. In all simplicity and confidence she pours out her heart into his. She recommends to him all the intentions that have been recommended to her prayers. Eager to visit the Blessed Sacrament and to remain in its presence as long as possible, she advises others to do the same. She asks for their prayers, but hopes that they will be offered at the foot of the tabernacle. Can one find a soul more in love with the Eucharist? Margaret Mary had understood the incomparable privilege of the real presence; she was merely drawing the practical conclusions from her faith. What an eloquent lesson for us!

Joseph Dargaud
The Eucharist in the Life of St. Margaret Mary

If the Blessed Mother and St. John at the foot of the Cross had closed their eyes when Our Lord was offering Himself for the sins of the world, the spiritual effects on them would have been no different from those which we may receive as we assist at the Sacrifice of the Mass. But if their eyes were open, there would have been this difference: they would have seen the sacrifice offered in bloodshed with blood pouring from gaping holes in hands and feet and side. In the Mass, we see it performed without bloodshed.

The Mass, therefore, is not a substitute for the Cross, but the merit we gain at the Mass is the same as the merit we would have gained if we had assisted at Calvary.

Bishop Fulton Sheen
This Is the Mass

Feast of St. Catherine of Siena
1347-1380

Nor is the sacrament itself diminished by being divided, any more than is fire, to take an example. If you had a burning lamp and all the world came to you for light, the light of your lamp would not be diminished by the sharing, yet each person who shared it would have the whole light. True, each one's light would be more or less intense depending on what sort of material each brought to receive the fire. I give you this example so that you may better understand me. Imagine that many people brought candles, and one person's candle weighed one ounce, another's more than that, and they all came to your lamp to light their candles. Each candle, the smallest as well as the largest, would have the whole light with all its heat and color and brightness. Still, you would think that the person who carried the one-ounce candle would have less than the one whose candle weighed a pound. Well, this is how it goes with those who receive this sacrament. Each one of you brings your own candle, that is, the holy desire with which you receive and eat this sacrament. Your candle by itself is unlit, and it is lighted when you receive this sacrament. I say it is unlit because by yourselves you are nothing at all. It is I who have given you the candle with which you can receive this light and nourish it within you. And your candle is love, because it is for love that I created you, so without love you cannot have life.

Words of God the Father
Catherine of Siena, The Dialogue

I know a TALISMAN which never fails to open the gates of Divine Mercy. I know a RIVER which will carry us into the Promised Land. I know a PALM TREE which will overshadow and shelter us from the burning heat of our earthly exile. I know a SPRING whose refreshing waters slake our thirst in the desert of this life. I know a STAR which will guide us as the pillar of cloud guided Israel, across the sandy ocean of our existence to the end of the journey. I know a DEW which God sheds from Heaven and which must sustain us for the long remainder of the road we have to travel. I know a TREE whose Wood can sweeten the bitter waters which are our portion to drink here below, and make them give us a foretaste of the Heavenly Canaan. I know a VICTIM Whose Sacrifice ascends in an odor of sweetness to the God of Abraham. And this Talisman, this River, this Palm Tree, this Star, this Dew, this Victim is the DIVINE EUCHARIST!

Father Augustine-Marie
Perpetual Eucharistic Adoration Newsletter
October 1988

A nd what do we ourselves offer when we offer our bodies and blood with Jesus at Mass? We offer what Jesus offered: life and death. By "body" we offer all that actually constitutes our physical life: time, health, energy, ability, sentiments, perhaps just a smile, that only a spirit living in a body can give and which is so precious at times. By "blood," we express the offering of our death; not necessarily our final death, or martyrdom for Christ or our brethren. Death means also all that right now prepares and anticipates our death: humiliations, failures, sickness that cripples us, limits due to age or health, everything that "mortifies" us. When St. Paul exhorts us by the mercy of God to present "our bodies," he didn't mean just our senses and carnal appetites, but all of ourselves, body and soul; especially our minds and our wills. In fact he goes on to say: "Do not be conformed to this world but be transformed by the renewal of your mind, that you may prove what is the will of God, what is good and acceptable and perfect" (Rom 12:2).

Fr. Raniero Cantalamessa
The Eucharist, Our Sanctification

Twelve frightened men who feel that death is hovering near crowd around the Son of Man whose hand is lifted over a piece of bread and over a cup. Of what value is this gesture, of what use can it be? How futile it seems when already a mob is arming itself with clubs, when in a few hours Jesus will be delivered to the courts, ranked among scoundrels, tortured, disfigured, laughed at by His enemies, pitiable to those who love Him, and shown to be powerless before all. However, this Man condemned to death does not offer any defense; He does nothing but bless the bread and the wine and, with eyes raised, pronounce a few words.

It seems that, after nineteen centuries of extraordinary glorification, the small Host for which so many cathedrals have sprung up, the small Host that has rested in millions of breasts and that has found a tabernacle and worshippers even in the desert—it seems that the triumphant Host of Lourdes and of the Eucharistic Congresses of Chicago and Carthage remains as unknown, as secret as when it appeared for the first time in a room in Jerusalem. Light is in the world as in the days of St. John the Baptist, and the world does not know it.

Francois Mauriac
Holy Thursday, An Intimate Remembrance

It made him happy to see a group of his friars around the altar in adoration. When he showed guests about Niepokalanow, at times Germans from the highest ranks of society, he either began or ended the visit in the chapel to greet, as he explained, the Master of the house. Indicating the religious adoring the most Blessed Sacrament, he would say: "There is the most important work department in the friary."

This adoration was carried out simply before the tabernacle, except on first Fridays of the month when the Blessed Sacrament was exposed in a monstrance, and only during the day, not at night. Notwithstanding the ardent desire of the saint to have perpetual adoration, he took account of the exhaustion of the friars after a hard day's work. At times, however, he would give an individual permission for nocturnal adoration.

Jerzy Domanski, OFM CONV.
For the Life of the World,
Saint Maximilian and the Eucharist

The patient in the first case was a man in Lisbon, Portugal, who suffered from Parkinson's disease. As the creeping paralysis rose from his lower limbs, advancing closer and closer to the heart, the patient was plunged into deep melancholy. His wife pleaded with him repeatedly to go to another Marian Shrine like Lourdes which was only ninety miles away. One day, in mockery, because he knew that, like himself, his attending physician did not believe in miracles, he said to his wife in the doctor's presence: "I'll go if he does."

It occurred to the doctor that a trip to the church at Fatima might cheer his patient, or at least it would be a temporary distraction, so he surprised the ill man by saying: "All right, let's go."

The day they arrived at the shrine was the 13th of the month so there was a large crowd of pilgrims. The non-believing doctor and his non-believing patient were among the first in the rows of invalids. I (the writer of this book) was just about as close to them as possible, carrying the canopy over the Holy Eucharist as It was raised by the priest to bless the patient.

The man suddenly pushed himself up in his wheel chair. Tremblingly he began to move and feel his legs. Then, over and over he pleaded to those around him: "I am not dreaming, am I? I am not dreaming?"

The doctor's mouth fell open in amazement and he slowly sank to his knees. Tears began to roll down his cheeks. "This was not for you," he exclaimed through his sobs. "This was for me."

John M. Haffert
The World's Greatest Secret

When I grant you the grace of devotion, give thanks to God, not because you deserve to enjoy it, but because I have had mercy on you. And if you feel no devotion, but suffer dryness of soul, persevere in prayer, sigh, and knock (Matt. 7: 7; Luke 11: 9); persist until you merit to receive some crumb or drop of saving grace. You have need of Me; I have no need of you (2 Macc 14: 35). You do not come to sanctify Me, but I come to sanctify and raise you. You come in order to be hallowed and united to Me; that you may receive fresh grace, and be inspired anew to amendment of life. Do not neglect this grace (I Tim 4: 14), but prepare yourself with all care, and invite your Beloved into your heart.

Not only must you make a devout preparation before Holy Communion, but also carefully foster your devotion after receiving the Sacrament. No less vigilance is required after Communion than devout preparation beforehand. For a constant vigilance after Communion is the best preparation for receiving richer graces; and a man will be entirely undisposed to do this if he straightway turns to outward pleasures. Beware of much talk (Prov 10: 19): remain in some quiet place, and savour the presence of God; for you possess Him whom the whole world cannot take away from you. I am He to whom you should offer your whole self, that, set free from care, you may no longer live in yourself, but in Me (John15: 4, Gal 2:20).

Words of Christ
The Imitation of Christ
Thomas à Kempis

Feast of St. Dominic Savio
1842–1857

Before his First Communion, Dominic made four promises: 1. I will go often to confession and I will go to Holy Communion as often as I am allowed. 2. I will try to give Sundays and holy days completely to God. 3. My best friends will be Jesus and Mary. 4. Death but not sin . . .

Don Bosco and the boys at the Oratory had been anxiously awaiting word of Dominic. His father's letter arrived; it began, "With my heart full of grief I send you this sad news. Dominic, my dear son and your child in God gave his soul to God on March 9th after having received with the greatest devotion the Last Sacraments and the papal blessing."

Dominic's friends were the first to realize his sanctity. They began praying to him, and soon reports of a cured toothache or a passing mark on an exam were brought to Don Bosco. In 1876, Dominic appeared to Don Bosco in one of the saint's vivid dreams. At this time he made several predictions, and when asked, told Don Bosco that he was in Heaven. Dominic himself was beautiful and glorious, and he appeared in the company of many other blessed souls. He gave Don Bosco three slips of paper; in one the priest saw the faces of Oratory boys who were living in their baptismal innocence. In the second he saw those who had fallen but were trying to rise from their sin. When he opened the third paper (boys living in mortal sin), it gave off such a disgusting and nauseating stench that Don Bosco abruptly awoke; he found that the disgusting odor still clung to his clothes.

Ann Ball
Modern Saints, Their Lives and Faces

The early Christians took the greatest care to conceal the doctrine as well as the celebration of the holy mysteries from pagans and even from catechumens. This was done out of reverence and awe; also as a precaution, to prevent the uninitiated and uninstructed from being present at divine worship, which could have given rise to misconceptions and brought down on them persecution. They were well aware that the teaching of the cross was unto the Jews a stumbling-block, unto the Gentiles foolishness. Accordingly it was never mentioned in the presence of Jews or Gentiles, and even the catechumens who were desirous of being baptized, and who were admitted to Christian instructions, were obliged to leave the church after the first part of the Mass was ended, before the offertory. The doctrine of the Adorable Sacrament of the Altar and of the holy sacrifice of the Mass was not expounded to them until after their Baptism. On this subject St. Cyril of Jerusalem says: "When catechumens are present we do not speak of the holy mysteries in a manner that they can understand; we are often compelled to make use of enigmatical language, which the faithful who are duly instructed will comprehend, but which awaken no suspicions in the mind of the uninstructed." It certainly would not have been necessary to use these precautions had the matter in question been merely a commemorative feast, at which common bread and wine were partaken of.

Rev. H. Rolfus
An Explanation of the Holy Sacraments

Perhaps the most amazing phenomenon in the modern world is the existence of the perfectly incorrupt and life-like body of the holy Maronite monk, St. Charbel Makhlouf, who was born on May 8, 1828, in the village of Biqa-Kafra in the high mountains of Northern Lebanon. . . . Having received a thorough theological education at seminaries conducted by his order, he was ordained a priest on July 23, 1859 and was assigned to the Monastery of St. Maroun, where he spent sixteen years in the practice of monastic virtues. In 1875 he received the permission of his superiors to retire to the Hermitage of Saints Peter and Paul, which was a little distance from the monastery and which was used by the priests during days of quiet retreat. It was in this secluded sanctuary that he spent the remaining twenty-three years of his life in the practice of severe mortification. It is recorded by his companions that he wore a hair shirt, practiced corporal discipline, slept on the hard ground, and ate only one meal a day, that being the remains of the meals of his companions.

Nothing outstanding is recorded of him except his remarkable devotion to the Holy Eucharist and his preference for saying daily Mass at 11:00 a.m., so he could spend almost all the morning in preparation and the rest of the day in thanksgiving.

In 1898 he suffered a seizure while saying Mass, and a priest assisting at the Holy Sacrifice was forced to pry the Holy Eucharist from his grasp. The holy monk died eight days later on Christmas Eve at the age of seventy.

Joan Carroll Cruz
The Incorruptibles

Some narrators say it happened in 1246 and others that it took place in 1226. There lived in the village of Santarem (Portugal) a poor woman whose life was made miserable by her unfaithful husband. Weary of so much unhappiness, she decided to consult a sorceress who promised the woman that all her difficulties would disappear if she would bring her a consecrated Host. After great hesitation, the poor woman decided to commit the sacrilege. After being heard in confession at the Church of St. Stephen, she proceeded to the altar and upon receiving the Blessed Sacrament, removed It from her mouth and carefully wrapped It up in her veil. Hurrying to the sorceress' cave, she didn't notice the drops of Blood that fell from her veil. . . . Confused, she ran home and hid the Holy Sacrament in a wooden chest.

Her husband returned and in the middle of the night, they awoke to see the house lit up by mysterious rays of light which penetrated through the chest. The woman confessed her sin to her husband and both of them spent the rest of the night in adoration. At daybreak, the parish priest was informed and people from far and near rushed to the woman's house to contemplate the Holy Miracle.

The Blessed Sacrament was then taken in procession to the Church of St. Stephen where it was placed in a small case of wax. . . .When the Tabernacle was opened for adoration of the Blessed Sacrament, the wax case was found broken in pieces and the Holy Sacrament encased in a beautiful crystal pyx. This pyx was placed in a gold-plated silver monstrance and can be seen today.

Fr. Sam Tiesi, TOR
Remain with Me

The Blessed Sacrament attracts the saints in certain wonderful ways: while on the other hand the saints have sometimes the power to attract the Blessed Sacrament. . . . It is because of this that we read so often in the lives of the saints that our Lord has appeared to them in such or such a form, and most often in the guise of an infant. . . .Our Lord appeared as a child to St. Ida three times successively, and each time greater than before, and she was deluged with joy for forty days. St. Veronica of Binasco, saw Him with her bodily eyes, all environed with angels. . . Vaulem, the Cistercian, saw in the Host the Infant Jesus, holding in His hand a crown of gold adorned with precious stones. He was whiter than snow, His countenance serene, and His eyes sparkling. When Peter of Toulouse was holding the Host over the chalice at Mass, the Infant Jesus appeared to him in marvelous beauty. Frightened at the brightness, he shut his eyes; but the vision still continued. He turned his head aside; but still he saw our Lord, sometimes on his hand, sometimes on his arm, whichever way he turned. The same thing happened to him almost every day for three or four months. A parish priest at Moncada, in the kingdom of Valentia, was tormented by doubts about the validity of his ordination. One Christmas day, while he was saying Mass, a little girl four years and a half old saw a Babe in his hands, instead of the Host, at the elevation. He bade her watch the next day, and the same thing occurred. Not content with that, he took with him to the altar three altar breads, consecrated two of them, communicated with one of them, and then showed the other two to the child. She at once perceived the same vision in the consecrated Host, but not in the other.

Fr. Frederick William Faber
The Blessed Sacrament

Then one day, I made a "fatal blunder"—I decided that it was time for me to go to Mass on my own. . . I slipped quietly into the basement chapel for daily Mass. I wasn't sure what to expect . . . I took a seat as an observer in the back pew.

All of a sudden lots of ordinary people began coming in off the streets—rank-and-file type folks. They came in, genuflected, knelt and prayed. . . .Their simple but sincere devotion was impressive.

Then a bell rang and a priest walked out toward the altar. . . As an evangelical Calvinist, I had been taught that the Catholic Mass was the greatest sacrilege that a man could commit—to resacrifice Christ—so I wasn't sure what to do.

I watched and listened as the readings, prayers and responses—so steeped in Scripture—made the Bible come alive. I almost wanted to stop the Mass and say, "Wait. That line is from Isaiah; the song is from the Psalms. Whoa, you've got another prophet in that prayer." I found numerous elements from the ancient Jewish liturgy that I had studied so intensely.

All of a sudden I realized, this is where the Bible belongs. . . Then we moved into the Liturgy of the Eucharist, where all my covenant conclusions converged.

I wanted to stop everything and shout, "Hey, can I explain what's happening from Scripture? This is great. Instead I just sat there, famished with a supernatural hunger for the Bread of Life."

After pronouncing the words of consecration, the priest held up the Host. I felt as if the last drop of doubt had drained from me. With all of my heart, I whispered "My Lord and my God. That's really you! And if that's you, then I want full communion with you. I don't want to hold anything back."

Scott Hahn
Rome Sweet Home, Our Journey to Catholicism

Active participation in the Mass, intelligent and humble reception of the Blessed Sacrament with a pure heart and the desire of perfect charity—these are the great remedies for the resentment and disunity that are spread by materialism. Here in this greatest of sacraments we can find the medicine that will purify our hearts from the contagion which they inevitably contract in a world that does not know God.

But in order to protect ourselves still more, to strengthen our position and to sink our roots deeper into the charity of Christ, it is necessary that we seek opportunities to adore Christ in this Blessed Sacrament and to give testimony to our faith outside the time of Mass. Therefore we visit our churches in order to pray to Him in silence and alone. We go to benediction of the Blessed Sacrament. We make Holy Hours, or we spend time in adoration, by day or by night, before the Sacramental Christ enthroned upon the altar. All these contacts deepen our awareness of the great mystery that is the very heart of the Church and open our souls to the influence of the Son of God "Who gives life to whom He wills" (John 5:21).

Thomas Merton
The Living Bread

On arriving at the Cova da Iria, near the holm oak, moved by some interior impulse, I asked the people to shut their umbrellas. We began to say the Rosary and shortly after we saw the reflection of the light and after that Our Lady on the holm oak.

What do you want from me?

I want to tell you to have a chapel built here in my honour. I am the Queen of the Holy Rosary. Continue praying the Rosary daily. The war is coming to an end and the soldiers will come back to their homes soon.

I had many things to ask you, to cure sick people, to convert sinners etc.

I will cure or convert some of them. Others I will not. They must repent and beg pardon for their sins. Do not offend God any more. You have offended Him so much.

. . . The miracle of the sun, promised in July, occurred as a proof of the truth of the apparitions in Fatima. The rain stops and the sun revolves three times round itself, sending in all directions luminous rays of different colours, yellow, lilac, orange and red. At a certain moment it seemed to be detached from the sky and to fall on the crowd. After ten minutes of this wonderful sight, the sun returned to its normal state . . .

After Our Lady had disappeared in the immense distance of the sky, we saw at the side of the sun St. Joseph with the Child Jesus and Our Lady dressed in white with a blue mantle. It seemed that St. Joseph and the Child Jesus were blessing the world with gestures of their hands in the form of a cross.

Lucia dos Santos
The Apparitions of Fatima

One day as St. Bernard was about to say Mass in the church of St. Ambrose at Milan, the people brought to the church a lady of high rank who had been sick for many years. She had lost her sight, her hearing and her speech, and her tongue had become so long that it protruded out of her mouth. St. Bernard, having exhorted the people to join him in praying for her, began to celebrate Mass, and as often as he made the Sign of the Cross over the Host, he made it over the sick woman also. As soon as he had broken the Host and said, *"Pax Domini sit semper vobiscum,"* she was instantly cured. The people, filled with joy and astonishment, began to ring the bells, and soon the whole city hastened to the church to witness the miracle and to give thanks to God (Life of St. Bernard).

Fr. Michael Muller, CSSR
The Blessed Eucharist, Our Greatest Treasure

Since ordination in 1956, I have spent one-third of my priesthood in administration on the national or diocesan level and two-thirds of it in parish ministry. Just as the Eucharist and eucharistic people were so influential in leading me to the altar, I credit those same factors for the fact that I am still an active priest today.

Extended prayer before the reserved Presence on a regular basis, ideally each day, but actually about 90% of the time, has been an essential lifeline. While I have been blessed with enormous successes, accomplishments, and recognition, there have been a balancing amount of weaknesses and wounds, poor choices and burdensome crosses. I don't think I would have survived spiritually without that kind of ongoing, extensive prayerful reflection.

The development of a Perpetual Adoration Chapel in our parish with 400 lay people spending an hour each week before the exposed sacrament fits nicely into that pattern. When you enter the chapel for a period of prayer at least one parishioner will always be there. That encourages me; I presume my presence heartens them.

Monsignor Joseph M. Champlin
Emmanuel Magazine
January/February 1994

There are so many advantages in making a holy hour in the presence of Our Lord. As He was about to suffer, Jesus Himself asked His apostles to watch one hour with Him (Matthew 26:40).

We all need direction, focus, and a good sense of our priorities. The holy hour gives us ample opportunity to listen to God. The voice of the Spirit is a gentle one. It is not easily heard amid the clamor of daily routine. An hour spent in the presence of the Blessed Sacrament enables us to keep a balance between the spiritual and the practical in our lives.

Loving reparation to Jesus in the Blessed Sacrament is one of the principal purposes of spending an hour with Him. Pope John Paul II strongly maintains that reparation is an integral part of the renewal of the Church and the world envisioned by the Council. The Fathers of the Council frequently spoke of our duty to offer ourselves and our entire lives in union with the sacrifice of Christ. In his Apostolic Letter, "On the Mystery and Worship of the Holy Eucharist," the Holy Father returns to this theme. In speaking of the worship proper to the Eucharistic mystery which is directed to God the Father through Jesus, he writes: "And this adoration of ours contains yet another special characteristic. . . it is also a response that tries to repay that love immolated even to the death on the Cross; it is our 'Eucharist,' that is to say our giving Him thanks, our praise of Him for having redeemed us by His death and having made us shares in immortal life through His resurrection."

Most Reverend Thomas V. Daily
Bishop of Brooklyn
Pastoral Letter on the Holy Eucharist

May 17

Feast of St. Pascal Baylon
1540-1592

St. Pascal Baylon experienced many unusual receptions of the Eucharist. As a Franciscan lay brother, Pascal served his community in a number of lowly positions. He performed many miracles—so many, in fact, that during the consistory that heard the case for his canonization, the number of miracles recounted prompted a cardinal to cry out, "The like has never been seen!"

As an adolescent, Pascal was entrusted with the care of his father's sheep. While on the mountainside, he would often fall on his knees in adoration on hearing the bell that signaled the consecration of the Mass. During these times when his occupation prevented his attendance at services in the church, an angel often appeared before him bearing the Host for his reception.

The saint was distinguished by his ardent love of the Eucharist. When he was able, he would spend hours on his knees before the tabernacle. Often the fervor of his prayers raised him from the ground. During his lifetime he was known by all as the saint of the Blessed Sacrament—thus it was with good reason that Pope Leo XIII proclaimed St. Pascal Baylon the patron of all Eucharistic societies and congresses.

Joan Carroll Cruz
Eucharistic Miracles

Although Charles de Foucauld wrote rules for "Little Brothers" and "Little Sisters," these religious communities did not come into existence until Father Rene Voillaume and four other French priests began to live at El Abiodh Sidi Cheikh, on the fringes of the Sahara. They adopted a life of adoration and prayer inspired by de Foucauld's original rule. Scattered by the Second World War, the communities or "fraternities" regrouped after 1945 and live a simple lifestyle, supporting themselves in the midst of working class situations. But, at the heart of their lives they are sustained by adoration of the presence of Jesus in the Holy Eucharist. Father Voillaume, the first Superior of this Congregation of "Little Brothers," has written much on the need for prayerful response to Christ's presence as the unique "Bread of Life," which is uniquely capable of satisfying the hungers of the human family.

"You will always be right in imitating the attitude of soul—which is so simple, so logical, so full of love—of Frere Charles of Jesus towards the Blessed Sacrament. Our devotion to the Eucharist must be profound, honest, totally embraced as essential. When one has acquired the disposition of receiving this gift of God with the soul of a child, one is upset by the reasoning of certain people, especially priests and religious, who dispute the devotion towards the Eucharist and sometimes question its legitimacy on liturgical or historical grounds . . . Why not, in the simple logic of faith, love the Eucharist with all the love with which we love Jesus himself? This is what filled Father de Foucauld with the spontaneity of a child" (Rene Voillaume, *Lettres aux Fraternites*, Paris).

Fr. Michael L. Gaudoin-Parker
The Real Presence through the Ages

L et no one, therefore, approach this wondrous Table without reverent devotion and fervent love, without true penitence or without remembering his redemption. For it is the pure Lamb that is eaten in the unleavened bread . . . Approach the Lord's Supper, the table of wholeness and holiness, child of faith, in such a way that at the end you may enter into the wedding feast of the Lamb . . .There we shall be filled with the abundance of God's house; then we shall behold the King of Glory and the Lord of Hosts in his beauty, and shall taste the bread of our Father's kingdom; our host shall be our Lord Jesus Christ, whose power and reign are without end. Amen.

St. Thomas Aquinas
Thomas Aquinas, Selected Writings

Feast of St. Bernardine of Siena
1380-1444

St. Bernardine of Siena remarks that men remember more continually and love more tenderly the signs of love which are shown to them in the hour of death. Hence it is the custom that friends, when about to die, leave to those persons whom they have loved some gift, such as a garment or a ring, as a memorial of their affection. But what hast Thou, O my Jesus, left us, when quitting this world, in memory of Thy love? Not, indeed, a garment or a ring, but Thine own body, Thy blood, Thy soul, Thy divinity, Thy whole self, without reserve. "He gave thee all," says St. John Chrysostom; "he left nothing for himself . . . " St. Bernardine of Siena says that Jesus Christ, burning with love for us, and not content with being prepared to give his life for us, was constrained by the excess of his love to work a greater work before he died; and this was to give his own body for our food. This Sacrament, therefore, was rightly named by St. Thomas, "*the* Sacrament of love, the pledge of love . . ." St. Bernard calls this sacrament "the love of loves;" because this gift comprehends all the other gifts bestowed upon us by our Lord . . . The Eucharist is not only a pledge of the love of Jesus Christ, but of paradise, which he desires also to give us. "In which," says the Church, "a pledge of future glory is given us." Hence St. Philip Neri could find no other name for Jesus Christ in the Sacrament save that of "love;" and so, when the holy Viaticum was brought to him, he was heard to exclaim, "Behold my love; give me my love."

St. Alphonsus de Liguori
The Holy Eucharist

A very beautiful experience in Hawaii shows the great and indiscriminate love of Jesus. In one of our healing services, Father Kevin walked down the aisle processing with the Blessed Sacrament. I stood at the microphone praying for healing as they focused on Jesus. A young Catholic woman had brought a Mormon friend with her. The Mormon girl had deformed hands. They had hoped we would pray with the girl. To their great surprise we were not praying individually with people, but we brought Jesus among them and told them to focus on him.

Just as in Lourdes, Father held up the monstrance and blessed the people. The young Mormon girl explained later that she did not really understand our teaching on the Eucharist, but realized that we Catholics thought this Host was the real presence of Jesus.

Looking at the sacred Host as Father Kevin blessed the people, she asked Jesus to ease the pain of her deformed hands. As she looked at the Host, she felt something come from it and go through her body. As she walked out of the church, she nudged her Catholic friend and said, "Look." She held out her hands and they were healed.

Miracles do happen! We believe that the Lord, as much as he was doing for the Mormon girl, was also saying to us Catholics, "Do you see and believe in my power?"

Sister Briege McKenna, osc
Miracles Do Happen

Feast of St. Rita of Cascia
1381-1457

S t. Rita of Cascia is known to have observed every year not just one Lent, but the equivalent of two others. During these fasts she took only a little coarse food whose flavor was altered with the roots of a bitter plant. So extreme were these fasts that the sisters marveled that her health was sustained on so little. To this she replied that the food which nourished her they could not see, this food being the sacred wounds of Jesus Christ and, of course, the Holy Eucharist.

Joan Carroll Cruz
Eucharistic Miracles

Weekly reception of the Eucharist was customary already in apostolic times. In the *Didache*, the faithful are admonished that, "having come together on the Lord's Day, you are to break bread and give thanks, after you have confessed your sins, so that your sacrifice might be undefiled. But anyone who is estranged from his friend should not join us, until both have become reconciled, lest your sacrifice be polluted." Equally clear is the description of the Sunday morning service given by St. Justin during the middle of the second century: "On the day which is called Sunday, we have a common assembly . . . The Eucharistic elements are distributed and consumed . . . "

From the end of the second century there are numerous indications that priests and laity received Holy Communion everyday. Tertullian mentions that Christians daily extend their hands, according to the prevalent custom, to receive the body of Christ. St. Cyprian states that in Africa "we who are in Christ, daily receive the Eucharist as the food of salvation." From Egypt we have the witness of Clement of Alexandria, and also of Origen, who says that "the Lord hates those who think that only one day is a festival of the Lord. Christians partake of the Lamb every day, that is, they daily receive the flesh of the Word of God." St. Basil in Asia Minor writes that "it is commendable and most beneficial to communicate and partake of the body and blood of Christ every single day."

Regarding the European practice, St. Ambrose wrote of northern Italy that Mass was celebrated every day, at which priest and people received of the "food of saints." Jerome says the same for Spain. The custom in France, at least among the hermits, was "to feed daily on the most pure flesh of the Lamb."

Fr. John A. Hardon, SJ
The Catholic Catechism

I have a friend who is impressed by what the world calls "power ful" and "successful" people. Imagine, if he had the gift of faith, how he would be attracted to the chapel to be in the presence of and be influenced by the One from Whom all power flows, the very Source of Life. In the Powerful Presence, I am made aware of my own utter powerlessness: I did not choose to live; I did not choose my parents or the Age in which I live; I cannot prolong my life here indefinitely, and I do not control the lives of those with whom I share my life.

The world sets me in a struggle against my true nature as it fosters the illusion that I am self-sufficient.

In those quiet moments before Our Lord in the Blessed Sacrament, I am freed from that illusion . . . The sand of self-confidence on which the world would have me build my life is replaced by the rock of God-confidence . . . Conflict and anxiety and fear give way to peace beyond expression. The world inflicts wounds upon us which God alone can heal. In those quiet moments before Our Lord in the Blessed Sacrament, I experience that Healing Power and catch a glimpse of that Divine Compassion we are called to share.

In the presence of the Source of life, I am made aware that all of life is a gift to be humbly accepted and appreciated. It's not so much that I choose to go to the chapel as it is that I am drawn there. "Come to me all you who are weary and find life burdensome, and I will refresh you. Take my yoke upon your shoulders and learn from me, for I am gentle and humble of heart. Your souls will find rest, for my yoke is easy and my burden light."

John Gile
Immaculata Magazine
December 1984/January 1985

Feast of St. Madeleine Sophie Barat
1779-1865

In beginning his account of the Passion of Our Lord, St. John says: "Jesus, having loved His own who were in the world, loved them to the end," which means, not that He loved them only up to death but as much as He could love them. And how did He love them? By leaving them this divine gift through which He gives Himself to us and so begins on earth the blessed union that will continue in Heaven. If you could only understand the value of one Holy Communion! A single Communion should make us other Christs! And yet, after all these years during which we have had the happiness of uniting ourselves to Our Lord, of receiving Him in Holy Communion many times each week . . . how cold we still are. We go before Our Lord in His Tabernacle and we do not know what to say to Him, though we have received Him this morning and we shall receive Him again tomorrow! A God has come down to us and we do not love Him. Faith and love are wanting to us. But it takes only a moment for that love to flame up in our hearts. We must love Jesus Christ; we must imitate Him!

Saint Madeleine Sophie talks to the community
Saint Madeleine Sophie Barat
Foundress of the Religious of the Sacred Heart

Not only has Our Lord seen fit to speak to some of His saints from the Eucharist, but it has also pleased Him to favor certain of His saints by appearing to them within the consecrated Host. In this way He has rewarded their devotion, strengthened them in trials and crowned their virtue.

One recipient of such favors was St. Philip Neri, who is the founder of the Congregation of the Oratory. St. Philip often employed a gentle jest to veil the miracles that constantly surrounded him.

There were times, however, when his spiritual experiences could not be dismissed or disguised. One such instance occurred as he celebrated Mass on Christmas Eve.

After the Consecration, St. Philip saw the Host transform itself into the Child Jesus. The saint's rapture was noticed by others in the church; to those who questioned him about this, he confided that the beauty of the vision surpassed earthly description. On other occasions, St. Philip was privileged to behold within the Sacred Host a multitude of angels and the glory of Paradise.

Joan Carroll Cruz
Eucharistic Miracles

All of these questions are very real to me; they constantly beg for an answer. Oh, yes, I have had answers, but it seems that they don't last very long in my quickly changing world. The Eucharist gives meaning to my being in the world, but as the world changes, does the Eucharist continue to give it meaning? I have read many books about the Eucharist. They were written ten, twenty, thirty, even forty years ago. Although they contain many deep insights, they no longer help me to experience the Eucharist as the center of my life. Today, the old questions are there again: How can all of my life be Eucharistic, and how can the daily celebration of the Eucharist make it that way? I have to come up with my own response. Without such a response, the Eucharist may become little more than a beautiful tradition.

Henri Nouwen
With Burning Hearts,
A Meditation on the Eucharistic Life

To a spiritual daughter, who marvelled at seeing him standing for over two hours at the altar, with his wounded and swollen feet, Padre Pio said: "I cannot get tired, because when I celebrate holy Mass I am not standing, but hanging on the cross together with Jesus, and I suffer inadequately all that Jesus suffered on the cross, as much as is possible for a human creature. The Lord has deigned to associate me with the great work of human redemption, and this despite my every demerit, and only because of His supreme goodness."

Holy Mass was Calvary for Padre Pio, but it was also his Paradise. He saw the heavens open, the splendour of God, and the glory of the angels and the saints.

Padre Alberto D'Apolito
Padre Pio of Pietrelcina

The Eucharist has an extraordinary potential for bringing about personal and global transformation. If ever it is vitalized into being a sacrament of communion through effective personal sharing, it can successfully challenge the comfortable cultural values most people blindly accept. If Christians ever begin to practice what Jesus has taught and exemplified when he took, blessed, broke and gave bread to be distributed, many of the world's problems would be solved at both personal and institutional levels.

A true Eucharist is never a passive, comforting moment alone with God, something which allows us to escape the cares and concerns of our everyday life. Eucharist is where all these cares and concerns come to a focus, and where we are asked to measure them against the standard lived by Jesus when he proclaimed for all to hear that the bread that he would give would provide life for the entire world. But it will do so only if, finding ourselves with a basket of bread, we have peered deeply enough into the heart of Christ to know what to do with it.

Paul Bernier, sss
Bread Broken and Shared

It is not medieval, but biblical for a Christian to realize when considering the sacrament, that we are given the bodily Self of the Lord . . . that we are given the possibility of addressing ourselves in faith and love, in adoration and acceptance, to that Lord bodily present to us . . . It is actually plain heresy to say (in theory and hence in practice) that Jesus Christ in the Sacrament of the altar is not to be honored with an external cult of adoration . . . that exposition is to be rejected.

Karl Rahner, SJ
The Christian Commitment

"What made me happiest when I left the world was the thought that I would be able to go to communion often, because I had been permitted to go only rarely up to then. I would have been the happiest person in the world if I had been able to receive more often, and spend the night alone before the Blessed Sacrament. I was so unafraid that even though in most things I was very timid, I would not even think of my fears as soon as I was in this place of my delight. The eve of communion days I felt myself buried in such deep silence that I could bring myself to speak only by doing myself violence, on account of the greatness of the action I would accomplish the next day. When I had received communion I would have wished not to have to drink, eat, see, or speak, so great were the consolation and peace I felt. I kept myself hidden as much as possible, to learn in silence how to love my Sovereign Good, who was urging me so powerfully to return him love for love."

"Once, when I yearned to receive communion, my divine Master appeared to me as I was carrying out the sweepings, and said, 'My daughter, I have heard your sighs, and the desires of your heart are so agreeable to me that if I had not already instituted the sacrament of my love, I would do so now for love of you, to have the joy of coming to dwell in your soul and to rest there like a lover in your heart.' This filled me with such great love that I felt my soul completely unnerved, and unable to express itself."

Joseph Dargaud
The Eucharist in the Life of St. Margaret Mary

Feast of St. Justin Martyr
110-165

S t. Justin was born about 110 A.D. in Palestine. He was converted to Christianity around 135 and turned his skills as a philosopher to a defense of the Faith. In the year 150 he wrote his great *Apology*. Although he was not an outstanding writer (his periodic Greek style tends to use what we would call "run-on" sentences), the work is of great interest because we find in it our first extant description of the Mass as it was celebrated in Rome in the second century.

(65) And when the one who is presiding has given thanks, and all the people have cried out, those whom we call deacons give the bread and wine and water over which the thanksgiving was made [lit., "the eucharistized bread and wine and water"] to be received by each of those present, and then they carry it to those who are absent.

(66) This food we call Eucharist, which no one is allowed to share except the one who believes that our teaching is true, and who has been washed with the washing that is for the remission of sins, and unto regeneration, and so lives as Christ has handed down. For we do not receive these as common bread and common drink; but just as Jesus Christ our Savior, having been made flesh by the word of God, had both flesh and blood for our salvation, so likewise have we learned that the food over which thanks has been given by the prayer of the word which comes from him, and by which our blood and flesh are nourished through a change [Gk. *kata metabolen*], is the Flesh and Blood of the same incarnate Jesus (*The First Apology*).

Rev. James T. O'Connor
The Hidden Manna, A Theology of the Eucharist

Cardinal Edouard Gagnon, former president of the Pontifi-cal Council for the Family and presently president of the Pontifical Committee for International Eucharistic Congresses, spoke at a Catholics United for Faith conference in the fall of 1993, in which he made an appeal for greater devotion to the Real Presence as a means of keeping the family together. He pointed out that Pope John Paul II is fostering belief in the Real Presence of Christ in the Eucharist to "save the family." The Cardinal asked the rhetorical question, "Where is Christ?"

In reply: "He is in the Eucharist . . . in the Mass, in our churches and we have to put the Eucharistic Christ back in our lives . . . It is the first thing parents should tell their children. It is never too soon to teach your children about the Eucharist . . . I say it is a duty to tell your child. Their whole life and their eternal life depends on Christ."

We have forgotten that the Catholic Church was recognized everywhere for the presence of God in the Person of Christ in the tabernacle . . . We should all work to reopen our churches. . . If the churches are open, the people will come."

Cardinal Edouard Gagnon
Immaculata Magazine
Special Eucharistic Adoration Issue

The Miracle of Lanciano, Italy

In about the 700th year of Our Lord, in a monastery then named for St. Longinus, the Roman centurion who pierced the side of Christ with a lance, a priest monk of the Order of St. Basil was celebrating the Holy Mass according to the Latin Rite. Although his name is unknown, it is reported in ancient documents that he had recurrent doubts regarding transubstantiation (the change of bread and wine into the body and blood of Christ). He had just spoken the solemn words of Consecration when the Host was suddenly changed into a circle of flesh, and the wine was transformed into visible blood. The priest praised God for blessing him in such a way and invited all present to view the miracle. Word spread and people came from far and wide to view the miracle.

The Flesh remained intact and the Blood congealed into five pellets which exhibited peculiar physical characteristics. The Host and the five pellets were placed in an ivory reliquary.

Many verifications of the miracles have been done throughout the centuries, the last in 1970. The following conclusions were ascertained: the flesh was striated muscular tissue of the myocardium having no trace of preservative agents. The flesh and the blood were of human origin, belonging to the same blood type, AB. Their findings conclusively excluded the possibility of fraud.

The ostensorium containing this miracle is now kept in a tabernacle over the high altar in the Church of St. Francis.

Fr. Sam Tiesi, TOR
Remain with Me

Though all the children of the Church largely incur this fault, yet more to be blamed are the unworthy and wicked priests; for by the irreverence with which they treat the blessed Sacrament the other Catholics have been drawn to undervalue it. If the people see that their priests approach the divine mysteries with holy fear and trembling, they learn to treat and receive their God in like manner. Those that so honor Him shall shine in heaven like the sun among the stars; for the glory of my divine Son's humanity will redound in a special measure in those who have behaved well toward Him in the blessed Sacrament and have received Him with all reverence; whereas this will not happen to those who have not frequented this holy table with devotion. Moreover the devout will bear on their breast, where they have so often harbored the holy eucharist, most beautiful and resplendent inscriptions, showing that they were most worthy tabernacles of the holy Sacrament. This will be a great accidental reward for them and a source of jubilation and admiration for the holy angels and all the rest of the blessed. They will also enjoy the special favor of being able to penetrate deeper into the mystery of the presence of the Lord in the sacrament and to understand all the rest of the wonders hidden therein. This will be such a privilege, that it alone would suffice for their eternal happiness, even if there were no other enjoyment in heaven. Moreover the essential glory of those, who have worthily and devoutly received the holy Eucharist, will in several respects exceed the glory of many martyrs who have not received the body and blood of the Lord.

Words of Our Lady spoken to
Venerable Mary of Agreda
The Mystical City of God

During this retreat I have been reading St. Gregory and St. Bernard, both of them concerned with the *interior life* of the pastor, which must not be affected by external material cares. My day must be one long prayer: prayer is the breath of my life. I propose to recite all fifteen decades of the rosary every day, if possible in the chapel before the Blessed Sacrament, with the intention of recommending to Our Lord and to Our Lady the more urgent needs of my children in Venice and in the diocese: the clergy, young seminarists, consecrated virgins, public authorities and poor sinners.

Angelo Roncalli, Cardinal Patriarch of Venice

(Pope John XXIII)

Journal of a Soul

Give me Yourself, and it is enough; nothing but You can satisfy me. Without You I cannot exist; without Your visits I cannot live. Therefore I must often approach You, and receive You as the medicine of salvation, lest if I be deprived of this heavenly food, I faint by the way. For, O most merciful Jesus, it was Yourself who, when You had been preaching to the people and healing their many diseases, said, 'I will not send them away to their homes hungry, lest they faint on the way' (Matt 15:32). Deal in like manner with me now, since You remain in this Sacrament for the comfort of the faithful. You are the sweet refreshment of the soul, and whoever receives You worthily will be a partaker and heir of eternal glory. It is essential to me, who am so prone to frequent falls, and who so quickly grow lukewarm and careless, that I renew, cleanse, and enkindle myself by frequent prayer and confession, and by the holy reception of Your Body; if I neglect these for long, I may fall away from my holy purpose.

Words of the Disciple
The Imitation of Christ
Thomas à Kempis

Anyone who has offered his heart to God belongs to God, and God is the Lord of his life! This is particularly clear in the giving of offerings. We offer to God, in acknowledgment and gratitude, the bread and the wine which are in fact the symbol of our suffering and efforts, our hope and our love, and of our working together with Him. These gifts are representative of us because, like all gifts, they are the symbol of those who offer them. They express our willingness to please and our friendliness and readiness to offer what we have to Him who has showered us with all good things. We do not offer gifts because they are necessary, but because they are an acknowledgment of the other and express our gratitude.

And God rewards us in His divine way! Our gifts, which are simple but true expressions of our lives, become for us divine marvels. By the strength of God's Word, they are transformed from bread and wine into the Body and Blood of Christ. What a miraculous transformation! God is unequaled in His gifts. We bring a little bread and wine, the fruits of our labors and of our working together with God, and He, in these very offerings, offers Himself and becomes our food!

It is, therefore, important to note this transformation and to take part in it with our hearts and our love. This tribute, in the form of gifts offered, is complete when we put into the bread and wine our own lives, our suffering, sickness, hardships, our families and the world itself. This is also the moment of our sacrifice, and of our understanding with Christ who offers His life for us in every Mass.

Fr. Slavko Barbaric, OFM
Celebrate Mass with Your Heart

Christ's words were too literal, and He cleared up too many false interpretations, for any of His hearers to claim that the Eucharist (or Body and Blood He would give) was a mere type or symbol, or that its effects depended upon the subjective dispositions of the receiver. It was Our Lord's method whenever anyone *misunderstood* what He said to correct the misunderstanding, as He did when Nicodemus thought "born again" meant re-entering his mother's womb. But, whenever anyone correctly understood what He said, but found fault with it, He *repeated* what He said. And in this discourse, Our Lord repeated five times what He had said about His Body and Blood. The full meaning of these words did not become evident until the night before He died. In His last will and testament, He left that which on dying no other man has ever been able to leave, namely, His Body, Blood, Soul, and Divinity, for the life of the world.

Fulton J. Sheen
Life of Christ

An accident in the middle of the desert paralyzed one of my legs. When the doctor arrived—eight days later—it was too late; I shall be lame for the rest of my life.

Stretched out on a mat in the cell of an old Saharan fort, I looked at the marks made by time on the mud wall, whitewashed in lime by the soldiers of the Foreign Legion. The heat made it difficult to think . . . I remained silent, trying mentally to take my soul beyond the compounds of my room into the little Arab-style chapel where I knew the Eucharist was . . . My leg was hurting terribly, and I had to work up the force to stop my mind wandering. I remembered Pius XII once asking in one of his audiences, "What does Jesus do in the Eucharist?" Even today, after so many years, I do not know how to reply.

In the Eucharist Jesus is immobilized not in one leg only, but both, and in his hands as well. He is reduced to a little piece of white bread. The world needs him so much and yet he doesn't speak. Men need him so much and he doesn't move!

The Eucharist is the silence of God, the weakness of God.

It is as though the world and the Eucharist were walking in opposite directions.

One has to be courageous not to let oneself be carried along by the world's march; one needs faith and will-power to go cross-current towards the Eucharist, to stop, to be silent, to worship. And one needs really strong faith to understand the impotence and defeat which the Eucharist represents and which is today what the impotence and defeat of Calvary was yesterday.

And yet this powerless Jesus, nailed down and annihilated, is the God of the Impossible, Alpha and Omega, the beginning and the end.

Carlo Carretto
Letters from the Desert

A doration of Christ in this sacrament of love must also find expression *in various forms of eucharistic devotion*: personal prayer before the Blessed Sacrament, Hours of Adoration, periods of exposition—short, prolonged and annual (Forty Hours)—Eucharistic benediction, Eucharistic processions, Eucharistic congresses (John Paul II). A particular mention should be made at this point of the Solemnity of the Body and Blood of Christ as an act of public worship rendered to Christ present in the Eucharist, a feast instituted by my predecessor Urban IV in memory of the institution of this great Mystery. (Bull *Transiturus*) All this therefore corresponds to the general principles and particular norms already long in existence but newly formulated during or after the Second Vatican Council (Paul VI, *Mysterium Fidei*).

The encouragement and the deepening of Eucharistic worship are *proofs of that authentic renewal* which the council set itself as an aim and of which they are *the central point*. And this, venerable and dear brothers, deserves separate reflection. The church and the world have a great need of Eucharistic worship. Jesus waits for us in this sacrament of love. Let us be generous with our time in going to meet Him in adoration and in contemplation that is full of faith and ready to make reparation for the great faults and crimes of the world. May our adoration never cease.

Pope John Paul II
On the Mystery and Worship of the Eucharist

After Holy Communion one day He made me understand the significance of these words in the Canticle of Canticles: "Draw me: we will run after Thee to the odour of Thy ointments." So, Jesus, there is no need to say: In drawing me, draw also the souls I love. The simple words "Draw me" are enough! When a soul has been captivated by the intoxicating odour of Your ointments, she cannot run alone. Every soul she loves is drawn after her—a natural consequence of her being drawn to You.

As a river sweeps along it carries with it all it meets down to the depths of the sea, and so, my Jesus, the soul which plunges into the boundless ocean of Your love carries with it all its treasures. You know that my treasures are those souls which You have linked with mine. You have entrusted these treasures to me and so I dare borrow Your own words, those You used on the last evening You spent as a mortal traveller on earth.

St. Therese of Lisieux
The Story of a Soul

I f we love the Blessed Sacrament, and if we delight to spend our time in adoration of this tremendous mystery of love, we cannot help finding out more and more about the charity of Christ. We cannot help gaining an intimate and personal knowledge of Jesus Who is hidden under the sacramental veils. But in proportion as we grow in our knowledge and love for Him, we will necessarily grow in the knowledge of His will for us. We will come to understand more and more how seriously He means us to take His "new commandment" that we love one another as He has loved us.

Indeed, if we fail to take this commandment seriously and if we find our devotional life concentrated upon a selfish desire for pious feelings that enclose us within ourselves and narrow our hearts, making us insensible to others or even contemptuous of them, we can be sure that our devotion is an illusion. We do not know Christ because we do not keep His word. For he only manifests Himself to those who do His will. And He wills to come to us in this Sacrament of His love not only in order to console us as individuals, but in order that we may give Him our hearts and let Him dwell in them, that through us He may love our brothers with our own love.

Thomas Merton
The Living Bread

Feast of St. Anthony of Padua
1195-1231

The miracle of St. Anthony of Padua is well known. He was preaching on the truths of the faith to a large crowd in Rimini, when he was challenged by a Jew, who denied the truth of the Eucharist, saying: "You confound me by your words, because you are more learned than I am, but let us come to deeds; prove it to me by them." St. Anthony accepted the challenge, and permitted the Jew to name the proof he required. A mule was kept without food for three days, and at the end of the time the Jew, accompanied by a great crowd, led it out to the place in which he was to meet the Saint. The latter was celebrating Mass, and when he reached the Communion he went forth with the Sacred Host, and turning to the mule said: "In the name of Jesus Christ, Whom I, though unworthy, hold in my hands, I command you to come forth and do reverence to your Creator, that you may confound these heretics." The Jew now threw a handful of hay and oats to the hungry animal, but at a sign from the Saint it left them untouched, although famishing with hunger, and approaching the Saint bent its knees before him, and bowed its head as a mark of veneration. The miracle was plain for all: the Jew, as well as others, was converted. A chapel was erected on the spot in memory of the event, and is preserved to the present day.

Cardinal Gaetano De Lai
The Real Presence of Jesus Christ in the Eucharist

Divine Savior, while I meditate on the proofs of Your Presence under the Eucharistic veils, enlighten my mind, enkindle my heart, and inspire me with that keen and living faith which is already a vision of Your Eternal Beauty.

Jesus Christ is present in the Eucharist with His Body, His Blood, His Soul, and His Divinity. Do you want clear and convincing proof of it?

Let us cite only one example: A priest was saying Mass in a church of the town of Bolsena and, after pronouncing the words of consecration, doubted the reality of the Body of Jesus Christ in the Sacred Host. At that same instant the Sacred Host was all covered with blood. It seemed as though Jesus Christ would reproach his minister for his infidelity, and make him sorry for it and, at the same time, show us by this great miracle how firmly convinced we ought to be of His Holy Presence in the Eucharist. The Sacred Host shed blood with such abundance that the corporal, the cloth, and the altar, itself, were covered with it.

The Pope, who was informed of this miracle, ordered that this corporal, all blood-stained, should be brought to him; and, being sent to the town of Orvieto it was received there with great pomp and exposed in the church. Every year this precious relic is still carried in procession on the Feast of Corpus Christi. Ought not that to confirm our faith? But, my God, what need of proofs have we after the very words of Jesus Christ?

St. John Vianney
Perpetual Eucharistic Adoration Newsletter
October 1988

One evening, we had an opportunity to be at a Mass where there was a eucharistic procession at the end. I had never seen this before. As I watched row after row of grown men and women kneel and bow when the monstrance passed by, I thought, these people believe that that is the Lord, and not just bread and wine. If this is Jesus, that is the only appropriate response. If one should kneel before a king today, how much more before the King of Kings? The Lord of Lords? Is it safe not to kneel?

But, I continued to ruminate, what if it's not? If that is not Jesus in the monstrance, then what they are doing is gross idolatry. So, is it safe to kneel? This situation highlighted what Scott had said all along: The Catholic Church is not just another denomination—it is either true or diabolical.

Kimberly Hahn
Rome Sweet Home,
Our Journey to Catholicism

It was over 50 years since Jesus took his place at table with the apostles for the Last Supper. At the time, Tiberius was emperor at Rome, Pontius Pilate the governor of Judea and Herod the tetrarch of Galilee (Luke 3:1). Annas and Caiaphas were the high priests (3:2). Later that night, in the courtyard of their house, Peter denied so much as knowing Jesus (22:54-62). The following morning, the opportunity to hear Jesus brought Pilate and Herod together. Weakness and contempt became friends that day (23:12).

The world had changed since then. Tiberius, Pilate, Herod, Annas, Caiaphas, the apostles and even Peter, were long gone. Jerusalem lay in ruins, smashed to the ground (see 19:41-44) and trampled underfoot (see 21:20-24). Even the temple was destroyed—with not one stone left upon another (see 21:5-6)—as was the house of the high priest along with the dwellings of the very rich overlooking the temple area from the western hill.

But throughout the world of Paul, in what are now Syria, Turkey, Greece and Cyprus, Christians (Acts 11:26) assembled to do what Jesus did the night of his Last Supper. They took bread, gave thanks, broke it and gave it to one another, saying, "This is my body, which will be given for you." They also took the cup after eating, pronouncing it the "cup of the new covenant in my blood, which will be shed for you." They did this in memory of Jesus the Christ, who died and rose that all might live (22:19-20; see also 9:16; 24:30).

Eugene LaVerdiere, sss
Dining in the Kingdom of God

In the great, triumphal apparition of June 16, 1675, our Lord had told her, "I ask you that the first Friday after the octave of Corpus Christi be consecrated to a special feast in honor of my heart. Receive communion on that day, and offer it in reparation to my divine heart; make amends to me for all the indignities which I suffered while I was exposed on the altar. . . . I promise you that my heart will pour itself out in abundant graces of divine love on those who thus celebrate this feast, and who by their words and example will cause it to be celebrated by others."

Margaret Mary was in adoration before the Blessed Sacrament at the time. It was during the octave of Corpus Christi. Jesus complained of the ingratitude shown him in the sacrament of his love. He insistently asked for a feast on which homage and reparation would be offered him for the outrages he endured during the exposition of the Blessed Sacrament. It is no exaggeration to say that the feast of the Sacred Heart is obviously a Eucharistic feast of reparation. Consequently, working for the institution, the celebration of this feast, is working for the glorification of Christ in the Host. In this way again, Margaret Mary lived for the Eucharist. We all know the long-drawn-out procedure required; the difficulties, the opposition, even the hostility that she met with; and when the matter finally got to Rome, long and prudent delays intervened before the feast of the Sacred Heart was finally approved and definitely established in the Universal Church.

Joseph Dargaud
The Eucharist in the Life of St. Margaret Mary

One must spend some time in a desert like Sinai, surrounded by the barrenness of rocks and sand, in order to appreciate more fully God's loving and providential care of his Chosen People. In the desert there was no source of food or drink. Humanly speaking, survival was impossible. The Israelites had to depend totally on God's providential love. God did not abandon them. He fed them miraculously with manna and quail. Likewise by his divine power he supplied them with water when there was no natural source of water.

The history of God's providential care and the miraculous means he used to supply all the needs of his people were an ideal preparation for the gift of the Holy Eucharist to come centuries later. Just as the Israelites had to have faith and trust in God, so Jesus asked for faith in himself when he was about to give us the gift of himself hidden under the species of bread and wine.

Like the Israelites, we are wandering through the desert of life in this land of exile. We are on our pilgrimage to the Promised Land—our union with our loving Father for all eternity.

David E. Rosage
The Bread of Life

Feast of St. Juliana Falconieri
1270-1341

A similar difficulty prevented St. Juliana Falconieri from receiving Our Lord when her last hour had come. After having thought of every possible means of satisfying her desire for Communion, she at last entreated her confessor to bring the Sacred Host near her, that she might at least humbly kiss It. This being refused her, she begged that It might be laid upon her breast, in order that her heart might feel some refreshment from being near to Jesus; and when the priest, in compliance with her request, spread the corporal on her breast and laid Our Lord upon it, she exclaimed with the greatest delight: "O my sweet Jesus!" As she drew her last breath, the Sacred Host disappeared, and as it was not to be found, the bystanders were sure that our Saviour, in the Blessed Sacrament, had united Himself to her heart, to strengthen her in her passage and accompany her to Heaven.

Fr. Michael Muller, CSSR
The Blessed Eucharist, Our Greatest Treasure

Jesus in the **promise** of the Eucharist points out the superiority of the bread which He is about to give them over the manna rained down from Heaven, saying, "And the bread that I will give, is My Flesh, for the life of the world." John 6:52. The Jews understood Christ to be speaking **literally** and not **figuratively**, for they say among themselves, "How can this man give us His Flesh to eat?" John 6:53. If Christ were talking in a figure of speech, in a metaphor, it would have been His duty not only as the Son of God, but as a teacher, to correct the Jews and say to them, "You take a wrong meaning to My words. You think that I am referring to My flesh—I know you are a civilized people and that you are not cannibals—I am only speaking of a souvenir, a symbol, a token. See that multitude going away from Me? They are leaving Me because they think I meant it. I came to save them, to win them. I want them. Do you think I would let them go like that if I did not mean it? If I could unsay it, do you not realize that I would call them back and explain? Ah, no. I meant it so much that you, too, must go, or accept it." The Jews would have remained had they believed that He meant no more than a symbol or token. Christ knew that they would revolt at the **thought of eating His very flesh**, but He let them go with the idea which would become a fundamental doctrine of His Church. Why did He not correct these first **Protestors** of the Christian World?

Fr. Charles M. Carty and Rev. Dr. L. Rumble, MSC
Q. A. Eucharist, Quizzes to a Street Preacher

Feast of St. Aloysius Gonzaga
1568-1591

I t is said of St. Aloysius Gonzaga that he used to receive Communion once a week and that he was accustomed to spend three days in preparation before it and three days in thanksgiving after it. How did he manage to do this? Was he all the time prostrated before the Altar or reading a spiritual book? Not at all; he went wherever obedience called him, quietly performing his duties and keeping his heart lifted up to God. He offered up all his actions to Jesus Christ by way of thanksgiving, and he made now and then some short acts of faith, hope and charity, some acts of self-oblation or admiration or supplication. By this means, the angelic youth was enabled to walk continually with God; one Communion was the preparation for another; thus, he constantly advanced in purity of heart and in love for Jesus Christ.

Fr. Michael Muller, CSSR
The Blessed Eucharist, Our Greatest Treasure

Feast of St. Thomas More
1478-1535

When Thomas More was Chancellor of England some of his friends reproached him for going to Communion so often. With all his duties and responsibilities they thought that this piety took up too much of his time. He answered their objections with these words: "Your reasons for wanting me to stay away from Holy Communion are exactly the ones which cause me to go so often. My distractions are great, but it is in Communion that I recollect myself. I have temptations many times a day; by daily Communion I get the strength to overcome them. I have much very important business to handle and I need light and wisdom; it is for this very reason that I go to Holy Communion every day to consult Jesus about them."

John M. Haffert
The World's Greatest Secret

The Apostle, St. Paul, wrote, "Glorify and bear God in your body" (I Cor 6: 20). There is no time in which these words, taken literally, apply so well, as during the time immediately after receiving Holy Communion. How unfeeling it is, then, for someone to receive Communion and leave the church at once as soon as Mass is over, or as soon as he has received Our Lord! We may remember the example of St. Philip Neri, who had two altar boys with lighted candles go to accompany a man who had left the church right after his Communion. What a beautiful lesson! For the sake of good manners, if for no other reason, when a person receives a guest he pauses to give his attention to him and takes interest in him. If this guest is Jesus, then we will only have reason to be sorry that His bodily presence within us scarcely lasts fifteen minutes or a little more. In view of this, St. Joseph Cottolengo used to personally oversee the baking of hosts for Mass and Communion. To the sister assigned to this he gave the following instruction: "Make the hosts thick so that I can linger a long time with Jesus. I do not want the Sacred Species to quickly dissolve."

Father Stefano Manelli, OFM CONV.
Jesus Our Eucharistic Love

(Recorded on June 24, 1973, Feast of the Sacred Heart, Sister
  Agnes was in chapel. She describes in her journal):

Suddenly I saw a blinding light shining from the tabernacle. I immediately prostrated myself in adoration and when I lifted my eyes, I saw a soft light which enveloped the altar like a mist or a dense smoke in which appeared a cohort of angels turned towards the Blessed Sacrament whose pure and clear voices proclaimed "Holy, Holy, Holy." When they finished I heard a voice on my right praying:

"Most Sacred Heart of Jesus, truly present in the Holy Eucharist, I consecrate my body and soul to be entirely one with Your Heart, being sacrificed at every instant on all the altars of the world and giving praise to the Father, pleading for the coming of His Kingdom.

"Please receive this humble offering of myself. Use me as you will for the glory of the Father and the salvation of souls.

"Most Holy Mother of God, never let me be separated from Your Divine Son. Please defend and protect me as Your special child. Amen."

This was the prayer of the Handmaids of the Eucharist which I knew well and which I recited aloud. During this prayer, I heard the voice of the same heavenly person (guardian angel) who had come to my side in the hospital in Myoko. It seemed even more beautiful and pure when she recited these prayers than when she had told me in the hospital, "Add these words after each decade." The sound of her voice resounded in my ears like a true echo of Heaven.

John M. Haffert
The Meaning of Akita

(Our Lady later added the word "truly" present in the Holy Eucharist to the first sentence of the prayer. Ed.)

When, at the consecration, I hold the delicate host in my hands and repeat the words "He broke the bread. . . ," I can sense something of the sentiments that filled the heart of Jesus at that moment: how he completely gave his human will to the Father, overcoming every resistance and repeating to himself these well-known words from Scripture: "Sacrifices and offerings thou hast not desired, but a body hast thou prepared for me; Lo, I have come to do thy will, O God" (cf. Heb 10:5-9). What Jesus gives his disciples to eat is the bread of his obedience and his love for the Father.

Then I understand that to "do" what Jesus did that night, I must, first of all, "break" myself and that is, lay before God all hardness, all rebellion towards him or towards others, crush my pride, submit and say "yes," fully, to all that God asks of me. I too must repeat the words: Lo, I have come to do thy will, O God! You don't want many things from me; you want me and I say "yes." To be Eucharist like Jesus signifies being totally abandoned to the Father's will.

Fr. Raniero Cantalamessa
The Eucharist, Our Sanctification

Father Fahsel describes Therese's ecstatic Communion succinctly: "Her arms are raised and she gazes in the direction in which the Sacred Host is being held in the hands of the priest. While he says the remaining prayers she looks up with a blessed smile as if transfigured, and then down. I asked her afterwards why she did this and she answered: 'I see the Saviour as a radiant figure. Then the radiance becomes a flame which comes upon me and enters my mouth. I know nothing more, am wholly absorbed in the Saviour.' It is striking that she looks down with particular attention. She explains that she sees the wound marks of the Redeemer's feet in a special effulgence."

Still another wonder-awakening phenomenon is Therese Neumann's reception of the Holy Eucharist without the ministration of a priest. Gorres tells us of a Communion of this kind by St. Catherine of Siena. Angels brought Communion to the Jesuit boy-saint, Stanislaus Kostka, and nearer our time is the case of Blessed Imelda. This little girl yearned to receive her Eucharistic Lord and when this desire was denied because of her tender age, heaven itself intervened.

Albert Paul Schimberg
The Story of Therese Neumann

Feast of St. Cyril of Alexandria
c. 376

As for blessings for the soul, St. Cyril of Alexandria, Father and Doctor of the Church, wrote: "If the poison of pride is swelling up in you, turn to the Eucharist; and that Bread, which is your God humbling and disguising Himself, will teach you humility. If the fever of selfish greed rages in you, feed on this Bread; and you will learn generosity. If the cold wind of coveting withers you, hasten to the Bread of Angels; and charity will come to blossom in your heart. If you feel the itch of intemperance, nourish yourself with the Flesh and Blood of Christ, Who practiced heroic self-control during His earthly life; and you will become temperate. If you are lazy and sluggish about spiritual things, strengthen yourself with this heavenly Food; and you will grow fervent. Lastly, if you feel scorched by the fever of impurity, go to the banquet of the Angels; and the spotless Flesh of Christ will make you pure and chaste."

Father Stefano Manelli, OFM CONV.
Jesus Our Eucharistic Love

Feast of St. Irenaeus of Lyons
c. 125

He is thought to hail from the East (Smyrna) since he heard St. Polycarp as a boy. After studies in Rome, he became a presbyter of the church of Lyons. After fulfilling his commission of taking letters to Pope Eleutherius regarding toleration for the Montanist sect of Asia Minor, he was made bishop on his return to Lyons (c.178) to succeed the martyred Pothinus.

Iraneus' achievement in his great work *Adversus Haereses* —against all kinds of false teachings pervading the Church through Gnosticism—rightly earns him the title of being the first great Catholic theologian. He develops the Pauline notion of "recapitulation" (cf. Eph 1:10) in showing not only how God's revelations to previous ages are summed up in the Incarnation, but also that, through his filial obedience of love, Christ reconciles and restores all humanity and creation into communion with God. His Christ-centered approach brings out the wholesomeness of creation, especially in the Eucharist, in which the new creation comes about. The presence of Christ is real, though spiritual, for Christ guarantees the continuity of revelation while uniting and integrating our material world into the communion of God's design, which consists in bringing all things under the Lordship of Christ, the Head. For in him is manifest the glory of God: man fully alive.

Fr. Michael L. Gaudoin-Parker
The Real Presence through the Ages

Animated by this heavenly food, St. Lawrence braved the flames, St. Vincent the rack, St. Sebastian the shower of arrows, St. Ignatius of Antioch the fury of lions, and many other martyrs every kind of torture which the malice of the devil could invent, content if they could but return their Saviour love for love, life for life, death for death.

They embraced the very instruments of their tortures; yea, they even exulted and gloried in them. Now this was the effect of the Holy Eucharist; this life-giving Bread imparted to them courage and joy in every pain and trial. For this very reason, in the early times of the persecutions, all Christians, in order to be prepared for martyrdom, received the Blessed Sacrament every day, and when the danger was too pressing for them to assemble together, they even carried the Sacred Host to their own homes, that they might communicate themselves early in the morning. The same was done by Mary, Queen of Scots, during her captivity in England when she was deprived of the ministry of a priest.

Fr. Michael Muller, CSSR
The Blessed Eucharist, Our Greatest Treasure

June 30

Feast of the First Roman Martyrs

S t. Cyprian was martyred in the fierce persecution of Valerian, on 14th September, 258. Pope St. Stephen suffered his martyrdom in Rome in the same persecution, on 2nd August. Having been conducted, by order of Valerian, to the Temple of Mars, that he might offer sacrifice to that idol; at the prayer of the holy Pontiff, the edifice tottered, as if shaken with an earthquake, and was partly ruined; the soldiers and the guards fled in terror: and St. Stephen, finding himself free, escaped with his people to the catacombs. Pursued shortly afterwards by the soldiers, it was found that "he was offering the Sacrifice of the Most High," and while so engaged was slain on the episcopal chair on which he was seated. His body was buried, together with the episcopal chair stained with his blood, on the spot. Such is the account in the *Acts of the Martyrs*, 2nd August, and in Baronius *ad annum* 252-259.

Here we find that the Roman Pontiff "offers sacrifice to the Most High," no other certainly than that of which St. Justin, Origen, St. Irenaeus and St. Cyprian speak; namely, the Sacrifice of the Mass.

Cardinal Gaetano De Lai
The Real Presence of Jesus Christ in the Eucharist

The prophecy of John the Baptist, considered the last of the Old Testament prophecies, is found at the beginning of the New Testament. It is an important prophecy. John the Baptist's life and words were a direct preparation for Christ's coming . . . John lived in the desert, prayed, fasted and announced the arrival of the Kingdom of God. People came to him from Jerusalem and its surroundings, listened to him and were converted. He baptized them in water and at the same time told them that one would come after him who would baptize with water and the Holy Spirit. One day Jesus Himself went to John and asked to be baptized. In St. John's Gospel we read: *The next day John saw Jesus coming to him, and said, "Behold the Lamb of God, who takes away the sins of the world! This is He of whom I said, 'After me comes a man who is preferred before me.' And I knew Him not: but that He might be manifest to Israel, I am come baptizing with water"* (John 1:29-31).

The words, *Behold the Lamb of God*, are repeated during Holy Mass just before Communion. That is an important moment when the blessed Bread is acknowledged as the Lamb mentioned in the Scriptures, identified by John and shown to the world. The event in Egypt concerning the unblemished lamb reminds us of John's prophecy concerning the wonder of the divine work, and allows us to understand the role of the Messianic Lamb, who came to reunite the people. After His departure, He miraculously remains with His people in the Eucharist. This is why the lamb is the symbol, the sign, of Jesus. This is, nevertheless, only a continuation of His mission.

Fr. Slavko Barbaric, OFM
Celebrate Mass with Your Heart

We would see, moreover, how true it is what Our Lord once said to St. Matilda (Lib. 3, Revel., C. 28), "At the moment of Consecration," said He, "I come down first in such deep humility that there is no one at Mass, no matter how despicable and vile he may be, towards whom I do not humbly incline and approach, if he desires Me to do so and prays for it; secondly, I come down with such great patience that I suffer even My greatest enemies to be present and grant them the full pardon of all their sins, if they wish to be reconciled with Me; thirdly, I come with such immense love that no one of those present can be so hardened that I do not soften his heart and enkindle it with My love, if he wishes Me to do so; fourthly, I come with such inconceivable liberality that none of those present can be so poor that I would not enrich him abundantly; fifthly, I come with such sweet food that no one ever so hungry should not be refreshed and fully satiated by Me. Sixthly, I come with such great light and splendor that no heart, how blinded soever it may be, will not be enlightened and purified by My presence. Seventhly, I come with such great sanctity and treasures of grace that no one, however inert and indevout he may be, should not be roused from this state."

Fr. Michael Muller, CSSR
The Blessed Eucharist, Our Greatest Treasure

Mother Teresa comments on Eucharistic Adoration/Exposition: "I will tell you a beautiful thing. Up until 1973, we did not have adoration in our houses for one hour daily for each Sister as we do now. But in 1973 there was a unanimous request, 'Mother, please let us have adoration every day.'

"We have much work to do, much. So I said, 'How can we do it, we have so much work to do?' But the Sisters insisted, so we started. And to tell the truth, I have not had to change anything in the timetable regarding work. We still do the same amount of work each day, plus that daily hour of adoration.

"I advise you also to start having that adoration. Our love for Jesus is more intimate, our love for each other more understanding, our love for the poor more compassionate, and we have twice as many vocations—thanks to the gift that God has given us, the Eucharist!"

Perpetual Eucharistic Adoration Newsletter
March 1989

In this sense I say the Eucharist makes the Church through contemplation. It is by staying still, in silence, and possibly for long periods, before Jesus in the Blessed Sacrament, that we perceive what he wants from us, put aside our own plans to make way for his, and let God's light gradually penetrate the heart and heal it. It's something like what happens to the trees in spring with the chlorophyll process. Green leaves sprout from the branches; these absorb certain elements from the air which, in the light of the sun, are "fixed" and become nourishment for the plant. Without these little green leaves the plant couldn't grow and bear fruit and would not contribute to regenerating the oxygen we ourselves breathe. We must be like those green leaves! They are a symbol of those Eucharistic souls who, contemplating the "Sun of Justice," Christ, "fix" the nourishment which is the Holy Spirit himself, to the benefit of the great tree, the Church. It is what St. Paul says in other words: "And we all, with unveiled face, beholding the glory of the Lord, are being changed into his likeness, from one degree of glory to another; for this comes from the Lord who is the Spirit" (2 Cor 3:18).

Fr. Raniero Cantalamessa
The Eucharist, Our Sanctification

My mother's commitment to the first Friday devotions and to the first Saturday devotions in hail, rain, and snow were a concrete, visible sign of her commitment, reverence, and fidelity to the great gift of the Eucharist. Her tender and consistent devotion to the nightly family rosary and our annual visits to Our Lady's Shrine of Monk always left me with a sense of wonder about life and what was beyond this life.

The beautiful and attractively framed picture of a priest celebrating the Eucharist, that hung on our kitchen wall, was eye-catching for me. It vividly portrayed a priest raising the host at the consecration of the Mass, with angels descending from heaven and two altar boys kneeling on either side of the priest, reverently holding the end of his chasuble.

I was always attracted to that picture. That scene encased in a large gold frame often haunted me and hunted me. As a little boy, I often fantasized about becoming an altar server some day . . . That picture, more than anything else I can remember, placed the idea of priesthood in my mind. . . . I felt drawn to the Eucharist and drawn to the priesthood, although I was never really certain that this is what I wanted to do with my life . . . These childhood and adolescent experiences influenced the way I choose to live out my specific calling in life. A priest is called to promote unity and reconciliation within himself, with others, and with God.

In effect, I am a priest today because of God's graced invitation to consecrate my energies to a life of feeding people with the bread of life and the word of life.

Fr. Thomas J. Morgan
Emmanuel Magazine
September 1994

I still remember an evening meditation on Dutch television during which the speaker poured water on hard, dried-out soil, saying, "Look, the soil cannot receive the water and no seed can grow." Then, after crumbling the soil with his hands and pouring water on it again, he said, "It is only the broken soil that can receive the water and make the seed grow and bear fruit."

After seeing this I understood what it meant to begin the Eucharist with a contrite heart, a heart broken open, to receive the water of God's grace.

Henri Nouwen
With Burning Hearts,
A Meditation on the Eucharistic Life

Why did Our Blessed Lord use bread and wine as the elements of this Memorial? First of all, because no two substances in nature better symbolize unity than bread and wine. As bread is made from a multiplicity of grains of wheat, and wine is made from a multiplicity of grapes, so the many who believe are one in Christ. Second, no two substances in nature have to suffer more to become what they are than bread and wine. Wheat has to pass through the rigors of winter, be ground beneath the Calvary of a mill, and then subjected to purging fire before it can become bread. Grapes in their turn must be subjected to the Gethsemane of a wine press and have their life crushed from them to become wine. Thus do they symbolize the Passion and Sufferings of Christ, and the condition of Salvation, for Our Lord said unless we die to ourselves we cannot live in Him. A third reason is that there are no two substances in nature which have more traditionally nourished man than bread and wine. In bringing these elements to the altar, men are equivalently bringing themselves. When bread and wine are taken or consumed, they are changed into man's body and blood. But when He took bread and wine, He changed them into Himself.

Bishop Fulton J. Sheen
Life of Christ

Once when my confessor [Father Sopocko] was saying Mass, I saw, as usual, the Child Jesus on the altar, from the time of the Offertory. However, a moment before the Elevation, the priest vanished from my sight, and Jesus alone remained. **When the moment of the Elevation approached, Jesus took the Host and the chalice in His little hands and raised them together, looking up to heaven,** and a moment later I again saw my confessor. I asked the Child Jesus where the priest had been during the time I had not seen him. Jesus answered, "In My Heart." But I could not understand anything more of these words of Jesus. (Diary 442)

That same day, when I was in church waiting for confession, I saw **the same rays issuing from the monstrance and spreading throughout the church. This lasted all through the service. After the Benediction, [the rays shone out] on both sides and returned again to the monstrance.** Their appearance was bright and transparent like crystal. (Diary 370)

Rev. George W. Kosicki, CSB
Tell My Priests, The Words of Our Lord to Priests About His Mercy as Revealed to Sr. Faustina Kowalska

On February 26, 1930, Saint Maximilian celebrated Mass in the "old chapel" of Niepokalanow "according to the intentions of the Immaculate", i.e., to conquer the world through her for the Sacred Heart of Jesus; it was his last homage to the Blessed Sacrament before leaving for the Far East. During the sea voyage, at the hour of adoration in common in Niepokalanow, he united himself spiritually to Jesus in the Blessed Sacrament with his heart, adoring Him from afar. He celebrated Mass on board ship or in churches of port cities. At Nagasaki, Father Kolbe, as Father Mieczislaus Mirochna, his disciple from 1930, attests, "very often visited the Blessed Sacrament. In any difficulty, he ran to Jesus in the Blessed Sacrament to seek the necessary strength. He desired to work by means of perpetual adoration of the Blessed Sacrament. He explained that veneration of the Blessed Virgin Mary was necessary to bring us to the worship of the Savior Jesus Christ. In the celebration of Mass, his devotion was evident to all who attended: his eyes were fixed on the Host. Each day he visited the Blessed Sacrament more than ten times with great devotion."

Jerzy Domanski, OFM CONV.
For the Life of the World,
Saint Maximilian and the Eucharist

What reasons have Catholics for believing that Our Saviour gave the Apostles His real body and blood? . . . His words, both on the occasion of the promise and at the Last Supper, if taken literally, denote a true, and not a merely symbolic presence of Himself in the Holy Eucharist. He could not have expressed this more clearly or more forcibly than He did: "He that eateth My flesh and drinketh My blood hath everlasting life . . . For My flesh is meat (food) indeed, and My blood is drink indeed . . . This *is* My body . . . This *is* My blood." . . . Those who deny the doctrine of the Real Presence do indeed adduce numerous arguments, but an honest examination of these arguments will show that they all have one common basis—the difficulty of understanding *how* Our Lord's real body and blood can be simultaneously present in thousands of places in a manner imperceptible to human senses. Now, this is only a repetition of the argument brought up by those who listened to Christ Himself at Capharnaum: "How can this man give us His flesh to eat? . . . This saying is hard, and who can hear it?" The weakness of this argument is that it measures divine power by human standards. He who has assured us that the Holy Eucharist contains His body and blood is the all-powerful, all-truthful God. Shall we twist His assertions to suit our ideas just because our puny intellects cannot understand *how* the miracle of the Real Presence takes place? Should we not rather exclaim with St. Peter: "Thou hast the words of eternal life," and humbly acknowledge as divine truth the sublime doctrine which the Son of God has made known to us with His own lips?

Rev. Francis J. Connell, CSSR

The Seven Sacraments

It is with this love that you come to receive my gracious glorious light, the light I have given you as food, to be administered to you by my ministers. But even though all of you receive the light, each of you receives it in proportion to the love and burning desire you bring with you. It is just like the example I gave you of the people whose candles received the flame according to their weight. Each of you carries the light whole and undivided, for it cannot be divided by any imperfection in you who receive it or in those who administer it. You share as much of the light (that is, the grace you receive in this sacrament) as your holy desire disposes you to receive.

Words of God the Father
Catherine of Siena, The Dialogue

Jesus Christ, Who wishes to lead a soul to the Eucharist as to her sovereign grace, prepares her by a certain grace of sentiment which at first may be little appreciated. On First-Communion Day the feeling of happiness caused by the presence of Jesus is the first call; without the soul's knowing it, this initial grace grows imperceptibly, very much like the germination of a seed in the earth. Well cared for, it later develops into a need, a disposition, a habit of thought, an instinct. Everything then points to the Eucharist; if the Eucharist is missing, everything is missing with it. A soul under the influence of this grace directs her piety, her virtues to the Blessed Sacrament. She experiences the need of Holy Mass and Communion. She feels drawn to enter churches to see the tabernacle. Something continually impels her in that direction. What is that power? The sovereign grace which, after having educated her, has become the mother of all her other graces, the moving principle of all her actions. She says: "I feel drawn to the Blessed Sacrament. It is not a sacrifice for me to be in Its presence. In fact, I am happy only there." It could not be otherwise, for she is living according to her special grace . . .

The sap of a tree lies in the heart of it; it is protected by the wood and the bark. Everything in the tree tends to preserve it during the winter frosts, because it is the life of the tree.

Well, your sovereign grace is the sap of your spiritual life. It will make all the branches of your life fruitful. Preserve it and defend it as the heart, the soul of your supernatural life.

Saint Peter Julian Eymard
In the Light of the Monstrance

On one occasion, when I was reciting the Hours with the community, my soul suddenly became recollected and seemed to me to become bright all over like a mirror: no part of it—back, sides, top or bottom—but was completely bright, and in the center of it was a picture of Christ Our Lord as I generally see Him. I seemed to see Him in every part of my soul as clearly as in a mirror, and this mirror—I cannot explain how— was wholly sculptured in the same Lord by a most loving communication which I shall never be able to describe. This, I know, was a vision which, whenever I recall it, and especially after Communion, is always of great profit to me. It was explained to me that, when a soul is in mortal sin, this mirror is covered with a thick mist and remains darkened so that the Lord cannot be pictured or seen in it, though He is always present with us and gives us our being; with heretics it is as if the mirror were broken, which is much worse than being dimmed. Seeing this is very different from describing it, for it cannot be properly explained. But it has helped me a great deal and has also caused me deep regrets at the many occasions when, through my faults, my soul has become darkened and so I have been unable to see the Lord.

St. Teresa of Avila
The Autobiography of St. Teresa of Avila
E. Allison Peers

Feast of Kateri Tekakwitha
1656-1680

Kateri Tekakwitha, the "Lily of the Mohawks," was born the daughter of a Mohawk chief and a Christian mother at Ossernenon, New York in 1656. She was baptized by a Jesuit in 1676 and moved to a Christian village. She cared for the sick and aged and took a vow of perpetual virginity. Her name, which translates, "she-who-feels-her-way-along," was so named because of her weakness of vision due to a smallpox disease. She made her first Holy Communion on Christmas day, 1677, and from that time on advanced rapidly on the road to holiness.

At 4:00 a.m. she could be seen kneeling outside the chapel in the snow waiting for it to open. She attended three Masses daily, and always managed two hours in preparation for Holy Communion and two hours in thanksgiving; and she made frequent visits to the Blessed Sacrament. Her motto was: "Who will teach me what is most agreeable to God so that I may do it?"

Louis Kaczmarek
Hidden Treasure, The Riches of the Eucharist

Feast of St. Bonaventure
1221-1274

During a brief period in the life of St. Bonaventure, the saint's humility sometimes prevented him from receiving the Holy Eucharist—this despite his great desire to communicate. But his fears were completely overcome one day, as is recorded in the acts of his canonization:

"Several days had passed, nor durst he yet presume to present himself at the heavenly banquet. But whilst he was hearing Mass and meditating on the Passion of Jesus Christ, Our Saviour, to crown his humility and love, put into his mouth by the ministry of an angel part of the consecrated Host, taken from the hand of the priest. "

Joan Carroll Cruz
Eucharistic Miracles

How great a difference there is between the Ark of the Covenant and its relics, and Your most holy Body with its ineffable powers: between those sacrifices of the old Law which foreshadowed the Sacrifice to come, and the true Victim of Your Body, which fulfills all the ancient rites!

Alas, why does not my heart burn within me at Your adorable presence? Why do I not prepare myself to receive Holy Communion, when the Patriarchs and Prophets of old, Kings and Princes with all their people, showed so great a devotion in Your holy worship?

The holy King David danced before the Ark with all his might (2 Sam 6: 14.), recalling Your blessings to his fathers; he wrote psalms, and taught his people to sing with joy; inspired by the grace of the Holy Spirit, he often sang and played on the harp; he taught the people of Israel to praise God with the whole heart, and to bless Him every day. If all these performed such acts of praise and devotion before the Ark of the Covenant, how much greater devotion and reverence should I and all Christian people have in the presence of this Sacrament, and in receiving the most adorable Body of Christ?

Words of the Disciple
The Imitation of Christ
Thomas à Kempis

"She assisted at Mass with intense devotion. When the celebrant began: 'In nomine Patris,' etc., she contemplated Jesus on the Mount of Olives, and begged for the Faithful the grace of assisting devoutly at the Holy Sacrifice and for priests that of offering It in a manner pleasing to God; lastly, she implored Our Lord to cast upon all as gracious a look as He once cast on St. Peter.

"At the Consecration, she offered the Saviour to His Father for the whole world, chiefly for the conversion of sinners, for the relief of the souls in purgatory, for the dying, and for her Sisters in religion. She imagined the altar surrounded at this moment by crowds of adoring angels who dared not raise their eyes to the Sacred Host. She said to herself that, although it might be very bold in her, yet she could not deprive herself of the consolation of gazing upon her Lord.

"She often saw a brilliant light surrounding the Sacred Host and in the Host a cross of dark color, never white. Had it been white, she would not have distinguished it. It did not seem to be larger than the Host, but the latter was Itself often larger than usual."

Rev. K. E. Schmoger, CSSR
Life of Anne Catherine Emmerich

It is sad to realize that so many believe Jesus is Present in the Blessed Sacrament and seldom visit Him. Men travel across the oceans to see ancient ruins, paintings, landscapes and celebrities, but they do not think of going into a simple church around the corner to visit the Creator of all beauty.

Man complains of his tensions, hang-ups and frustrations and for these human weaknesses he consumes bottles of pills and other remedies. He spends time and money trying to ascertain who he is and how he came to be. He is tormented by his past and entertains visions of grandeur or despair for the future.

We have a need to empty ourselves, know ourselves, accept ourselves and rise above ourselves.

Our need is not so much in changing what we are as in knowing how best to change who we are. How does darkness turn into light? How does ice turn into fire? How does a limited intelligence comprehend the mystery of life, death and what is to come?

"Whoever remains in Me, with Me in him, bears fruit in plenty." These words of Jesus at the Last Supper give us a way of holiness that is both simple and easy. The Holy Eucharist is God within us and with us—it is God in us and we in God.

To maintain a close relationship with the God of Love, we must remain in that Holy Presence often. As the rays of the sun change and alter whatever they touch, so the Eternal Son, ever present in the Blessed Sacrament, changes whoever places himself in His Presence.

Mother Angelica
To Leave and Yet to Stay

St. Peter of Alcantara experienced visions of the Blessed Mother during his childhood and was known for his devotion to the cross of Christ. After his ordination as a Franciscan priest he served for a time as a confessor of St. Teresa of Avila. From the time of his first Holy Mass, he was often found in ecstasy before the tabernacle. When approaching the divine mysteries, the saint lost all consciousness of things about him and prayed as though only he and Jesus existed. On account of his frequent ecstasies, wherever he traveled he was given a cell next to the chapel so that he might be near the high altar and pray there whenever he pleased. . . .

The holiness of St. Peter of Alcantara is well illustrated in Chapter 38 of the *Autobiography of St. Teresa of Avila*, in which St. Teresa relates that:

. . . from none of the visions that I have seen have I ever gathered that any soul has escaped Purgatory save the souls of this Father [she does not identify this friar of her order], of the Dominican Father [P. Ibanez] and the saintly Fray Peter of Alcantara.

After his death St. Peter of Alcantara appeared to St. Teresa of Avila a number of times. Referring to the great austerities he had practiced, he exclaimed, "O blessed penance, which has secured for me so glorious a reward!"

Joan Carroll Cruz
Eucharistic Miracles

On the evening of Holy Thursday the beloved Apostle John rested his head on the breast of Christ. Now Christ rests His head on the breasts of His friends, and that every day of our lives, if we so wish. On Holy Thursday we recognize the blessing of this Presence, an impression of security, as if we actually heard the Lord say: "It is I, do not be afraid."

I can still picture myself when I was a child remembering that moment of Christian history and reliving it. I can still remember kneeling there as a young man before the repository, and the longer I would kneel, the more difficult it would become to tear myself away. The contrast between the darkness of the church lighted only by candles and the glitter of the outside world struck me even then. Then I could hear: "And if I be lifted up, I will draw all things to myself " (Jn. 12:32). The words pierced the silence. Yet they brought a tenderness to the day.

On Holy Thursday many lives are decided, many vocations take shape, I am sure. Many are called to the priesthood on that day. On Holy Thursday the plan of God for mankind in the Eucharist is revealed and fulfilled. The plan of God for many other individuals who kneel before the Real Presence becomes known. On one Holy Thursday I came to realize that you never walk alone. *O Jesus, present in the Blessed Sacrament, Holy Thursday is a gift of Yourself to the Church. May the Heart of Jesus in the most Blessed Sacrament be praised, adored, and loved at every moment in all the tabernacles of the world even to the end of time.*

Msgr. John F. Davis
An Audience with Jesus

July 21

Feast of St. Laurence of Brindisi
1559-1619

The privilege of receiving the Holy Eucharist from the hands of Jesus Himself was experienced by a number of saints, including St. Laurence of Brindisi, a Capuchin, whose unusual talents and rare virtue were called upon by Pope Clement VIII for several unusual missions. One of these was his chaplaincy to the Imperial army of Prague.

With the Turks still menacing nearby Christian countries, the Imperial army of 18,000 men assembled to do battle with the Turks, who numbered 80,000. Vastly outnumbered, the Christians appealed to St. Laurence for advice and encouragement. After delivering a rousing discourse, the saint, despite his mature years, mounted a horse and with the cross held high in his hands led the troops against the infidels. The crushing defeat of the Turks was attributed by all to the prayers and inspiration of the saint. It is told that on his return from the campaign he joined his brethren at Gorizia, where Our Lord appeared to them and gave them all Holy Communion with His own hand.

St. Laurence of Brindisi had the grace never to allow his secular activities to influence his advancement in virtue, and his sanctity was such that he often fell into ecstasy while offering Holy Mass.

Joan Carroll Cruz
Eucharistic Miracles

When Elias was fleeing from Jezabel, he lay down under a tree in the wilderness and longed for death.

And he cast himself down and slept in the shadow of the juniper and behold an angel of the Lord touched him, and said: arise and eat! He looked, and behold there was at his hand a hearth cake and a vessel of water; and he ate and drank and fell asleep again. And the angel of the Lord came a second time, and touched him and said to him, "arise and eat," for thou hast yet a great way to go. And he arose and ate, and walked in the strength of that food forty days and forty nights unto the mount of God, Horeb (III Kings 19: 5-8).

So God intervened in the life of Elias at this crisis in his career, sent him miraculous food and drink, and then led him a forty days' journey through the desert to the mountain where the prophet heard the divine voice, and received his definitive mission. So too, in the Blessed Eucharist, the Logos intervenes in our lives, gives them a new meaning, a direction we could never have chosen or imagined, and leads us to the fulfillment of our vocation.

Every Communion therefore is a "viaticum"—it is food and drink to sustain us in our journey toward God. But while ordinary food and drink only supports our bodily life, this food is also our guide on our journey. For Jesus Who gives Himself to us in the Eucharist is "the way, the truth and the life" (John 14: 6). As St. Bernard says: "He is the way that leads to truth; He is the Truth who promises life, and He is the Life which He Himself gives."

Thomas Merton
The Living Bread

That night I couldn't sleep. I was very disturbed. I felt as though God were trying to tell me something. About four o'clock in the morning, I was still awake. I was turning and twisting. So, I got up and knelt at the side of the bed and said, "Jesus, what is it that you want to say to me?"

I felt the Lord saying to me, "You must make me known in the Eucharist. People are coming to you. People will come from all over looking for healing. They will say, 'Oh, if only we could get Sister Briege to touch us' or 'If Sister Briege could only lay hands on us, then we'd be healed.'

"Many are making false gods out of people in healing ministries. They are seeking after people and not me. I come every day in the Eucharist. I promised to give you life and to give it to you more abundantly, to fill you with strength for your pilgrimage.

"I want you to go out now into the world and point to me in the Eucharist. I want you to tell people to take their eyes off Briege McKenna and fix their gaze on the Eucharistic Lord, to put their faith in me. You can disappoint them, and you will disappoint them, as will any person who attracts people to themselves. But if you point them to me, then they will never be disappointed."

Again, this showed me that I had to be a signpost, pointing to Jesus. From this experience in prayer, I began centering my teaching on the Eucharist.

Sister Briege McKenna, OSC
Miracles Do Happen

"I live in the midst of sinners that I may be their life, their physician, and the remedy of the diseases bred by corrupt nature. And in return they forsake, insult and despise Me! . . .

"Poor pitiable sinners, do not turn away from Me . . . Day and night I am on the watch for you in the tabernacle. I will not reproach you . . . I will not cast your sins in your face . . . But I will wash them in My Blood and in My Wounds. No need to be afraid . . . come to Me . . . If you but knew how dearly I love you.

"And you, dear souls, why this coldness and indifference on your part? . . . Do I not know that family cares . . . household concerns . . . and the requirements of your position in life . . . make continual calls upon you? . . .But cannot you spare a few minutes in which to come and prove your affection and gratitude? Do not allow yourselves to be involved in useless and incessant cares, but spare a few moments to visit and receive this Prisoner of Love!

"Were you weak or ill in body surely you would find time to see a doctor who would cure you?. . . Come, then, to One who is able to give both strength and health to your soul, and bestow the alms of love on this Divine Prisoner who watches for you, calls for you and longs to see you at His side.

"When about to institute the Blessed Sacrament, Josefa, these were My feelings, but I have not yet told you what My Heart felt at the thought of My chosen souls; My religious, My priests . . . but I will tell you all this later on. Go, now, and do not forget that My Heart loves you . . . and, Josefa, do you love Me? "

Our Lord to Sr. Josefa Menendez
The Way of Divine Love

July 25

On the Feast of St. James the Greater, this Apostle appeared to Gertrude, adorned with the merits of those pilgrims who had visited his shrine. . . . she asked our Lord why this Apostle was so honored by pilgrimages, that his relics appeared even more revered than those of the holy Apostles Peter and Paul. Our Lord replied: "The fervor of his zeal for the salvation of souls has obtained this special privilege for him. As I took him away from the world so soon according to the decrees of My providence, that he was unable to convert many persons, which he most ardently desired to do, his desire still remains before Me fresh and flourishing. What he was unable to do during his life I permit him to accomplish after his death, by bringing an immense number of pilgrims to his shrine, absolving them from their sins and strengthening them in the Catholic faith."

Then, as she desired to obtain the remission of her sins through the merits of this Apostle and as she could not undertake the pilgrimage, she approached Holy Communion. . . . she beheld herself seated at a table with our Divine Lord, which was laden with various delicious viands. As she offered our Lord His precious Body, which she had received, for the increase of the beatitude and glory of this Apostle, St. James presented himself before God as a prince, to thank Him for the favors which he had received through this Adorable Sacrament. He then asked that God would work in the soul of Gertrude all the good which He had ever deigned to work in any soul through his merits, because she had offered this Adorable Sacrament in his honor.

Monsignor William J. Doheny, csc
The Revelations of Saint Gertrude

Because of this, if we truly understood the wonder of the Eucharist, we would never miss Mass on those days when the Church asks us to be present. We go so many miles at so much inconvenience to attend a concert or a meeting or a theater presentation. And yet, the greatest of actors and singers and musicians who have ever lived are insignificant when we compare them to the living God. The moments of drama which can be portrayed on a stage are elements of lives which do not touch us directly. The drama of the cross which is re-presented and re-enacted in the drama of the Mass touches us to the core of our being because it is through this awesome sacrifice of Jesus that we are saved, that we have a chance at heaven and happiness, that we are given grace to live our lives in light. As we pray in the Mass of the Second Sunday of Ordinary time: "Father may we celebrate the Eucharist with reverence and love, for when we proclaim the death of the Lord you continue the work of His redemption who is Lord forever and ever."

The Most Reverend Theodore E. McCarrick
Archbishop of Newark
All Praise and All Thanksgiving,
A Pastoral Letter on the Eucharist

Q. How does Jesus, received in Communion, become a source of healing for living and dead members of the family tree?

A. In two ways: among the living, and between the dead and living.

First, by the *unifying* (corporate healing) effects of his Eucharistic physical body among *living* members of his mystical body: "Is not the bread we break a participation in the Body of Christ? Because there is one loaf, we [the living] who are many, are one body, for we all partake of the one loaf" (I Cor 10:16-17). In early Church assemblies, one loaf was broken and shared, symbolizing the unity of the Body of Christ, the Church, nourished by himself, the one Bread of life (cf. John 6:33-58).

Second, by his *living* body *dying* symbolically and "proclaimed" as such by our Communion (I Cor 11:26), he becomes the link between ourselves and our deceased relatives. "Christ died and returned to life so that he might be the *Lord of both the dead and the living*" (Rom. 14:9).

We "see the goodness of the Lord in the land of the living" (Ps 27:13), that is, among our *living* relatives, by his releasing us from the bondages derived from our dead relatives, as Aaron stopped the transmission of the plague (that had killed 14,700 people), by standing between the contaminated dead and the living. The trans-generational bondage transmitted from the dead ancestors to us, the living, is broken by Jesus' stance, as the plague was broken by Aaron's stance between the two (Num 16:48).

John H. Hampsch, CMF
Healing Your Family Tree

A most remarkable miracle happened at Walduren in the year 1330: A priest named Otto, during the celebration of his Mass, accidentally upset the chalice after the Consecration, and the Sacred Blood was spilt upon the corporal. All at once there appeared upon the corporal the figure of Jesus Christ hanging on the cross, and around it twelve figures of the sacred head crowned with thorns and disfigured with blood. The priest was frightened almost to death and endeavored to conceal the accident by hiding the corporal in the altar. When the priest was lying on his deathbed, his agony was unusually great and horrifying. Thinking that his great sufferings were caused on account of his having so concealed the corporal, he called for a priest, to whom he made his confession, asking him to look for the corporal, and giving him permission to reveal the miraculous fact. The corporal was found and forwarded to Pope Urban V, who confirmed the miracle as being authentic. This event is well known throughout Germany.

Fr. Michael Muller, CSSR
The Blessed Eucharist, Our Greatest Treasure

"Above all I exhort thee to call upon me and ask me to help thee; for thou must know, that I am the special Advocate and Protectress of those who desire to arrive at great purity for receiving holy Communion. Whenever they invoke me for this purpose, I present myself before the throne of the Most High, and, as one well knowing the disposition required for harboring God Himself, I ask His favor and grace for those who are about to receive Him in the holy Sacrament. I have not lost in heaven the solicitude and zeal, which I exhibited upon earth. Having asked me, proceed to ask also the intercession of the angels, for they also are very anxious to see souls approach the holy Eucharist with great devotion and purity."

Words of Our Lady spoken to
Venerable Mary of Agreda
The Mystical City of God

In 1916 at Fatima an angel of peace came to Francesco, Jacinta, and Lucia. He prepared the way for the later apparitions of Mary. When he appeared the third time in dazzling beauty before the three seers, he held in his left hand a chalice, and in his right over the chalice, a host from which drops of blood could be seen falling into the chalice. Leaving the host and the chalice suspended in mid-air, he prostrated himself touching the ground with his forehead.

Then he said the following prayer three times: *Most Holy Trinity, Father, Son, and Holy Spirit, I adore you profoundly. I offer you the most precious Body, Blood, Soul, and Divinity of our Lord Jesus Christ, present in all the tabernacles of the world, in reparation for all the outrages, sacrileges, and indifferences by which He is offended. By the infinite merits of His most Sacred Heart and through the intercession of the Immaculate Heart of Mary, I pray for the conversion of poor sinners.*

The angel then rose and took the chalice and host into his hands. He communicated the host to Lucy, the contents of the chalice he gave to Jacinta and Francisco, saying, "Take and drink the Body and Blood of Jesus Christ, horribly outraged by ungrateful men. Make reparation for their sins and console your God."

P. Fernando Leite
The Apparitions of Fatima

Feast of St. Ignatius of Loyola
1491-1556

He also had many visions when he said Mass, and when he was drawing up the constitutions he had them with great frequency. He could now affirm this more easily because every day he wrote down what passed through his soul and he had it now in writing. He then showed me a fairly large bundle of writings and allowed me to read a good part of them. Most were visions that he saw in confirmation of parts of the constitutions, at times seeing God the Father, at other times all three Persons of the Trinity, at other times Our Lady who interceded and at other times confirmed.

In particular he spoke to me about certain decisions over which he had said Mass each day for forty days, each day with many tears. The question was whether the churches would have any income and whether the Society could make use of that.

(The question concerned the degree of poverty the Society of Jesus would embrace, specifically whether the houses and churches of the Society should be permitted to have any fixed income. Ignatius decided not to allow a fixed income.)

The habit which he observed while he was drafting the Constitutions was to say Mass each day and to present the point that he was treating to God and to pray about it; he always said the prayer and the Mass with tears.

John C. Olin
The Autobiography of St. Ignatius Loyola

Feast of St. Alphonsus DeLiguori
1696-1787

No consideration of the Eucharist of this type could omit St. Alphonsus de Liguori, the founder of the Redemptorist congregation. He wrote his well-known *Visits to the Most Blessed Sacrament* in 1745. They immediately inflamed the hearts of men with a love of the Eucharist. No finer work is there to prepare us for the reception of Communion, to help us in the thanksgiving, and to provide prayerful helps for those who visit the Eucharistic God each day.

St. Alphonsus tells of a Spanish Poor Clare who loved to make long visits to the Blessed Sacrament. The other nuns asked what she did during those long silent hours. "I could kneel there forever," she answered. "And why not? God is there. You wonder what I do in the Presence of God. I marvel. I love. I thank. I beg."

Here is the essence of Eucharistic prayer. Here are the four ends of Eucharistic prayer. Under the guidance of St. Alphonsus all of our time spent before the Eucharist can fall into the four categories, 1. adoration 2. thanksgiving 3. reparation and 4. petition. Every time I receive the Eucharist at Mass, this is my thanksgiving—perhaps just a few minutes at the altar adoring the Eucharistic Presence, thanking God for all His graces, telling the Lord of my sorrow for the sins of a lifetime, and begging Him for the graces and favors I need. We can also do this in the Holy Hour with a prolonged period for each segment. I know of no better informal structure or heart-to-heart arrangement for a visit to the Eucharist.

Msgr. John F. Davis
An Audience with Jesus

A priest who was in the German prison camp Dachau describes the Mass after all the German guards were in bed. He said, "Our lives were in danger if we were ever discovered. A young priest had to memorize the names of all of those who had received communion, but it was forbidden for us to gather in groups for prayer. After night call and bed check, we would set our guards, darken the windows, and the lucky one to be chosen to celebrate for this momentous occasion would carefully brush his pathetic prison garb, put the stole over his shoulders and by the small light of his smuggled candle begin the commemoration of that other great passion of which our own was the physical continuation. We could understand the Mass.

"All that could crowd into the room were there, tears of joy running down our cheeks. Christ the Lord, who knew what suffering was, was coming to suffer with us, to bring us strength and consolation. The small hosts were broken into as many particles as possible so the greatest number could communicate. We had to keep a secret roster of those who received. We missed some of the liturgy perhaps, but I think that God looked down into that prison room and found a particularly refreshing response to his cry of love from the cross, 'I thirst.' There was nothing that could keep us from doing all in our power to be closer to God."

Mother Teresa
Jesus through Mary Foundation Address

Feast of St. Peter Julian Eymard
1811-1868

At the age of twelve St. Peter Julian Eymard was already making night adoration in his home from eleven to midnight on Thursday, thus fulfilling the Sacred Heart's request to St. Margaret Mary and exemplifying the truth that night adoration in the home leads to Holy Hours in church. Peter Julian's mother, we are told, was so edified when she thus discovered her boy in adoration that she did not have the heart to scold or disturb him.

"It was devotion to the Sacred Heart that saved me," Father Eymard could say in later years. Oh, how much youngsters and grown-ups nowadays need devotion to the Sacred Heart of Jesus to be saved from the contagion of sin, to be rescued from the indifference and mediocrity of our times, and to be set on fire with love of God and of souls!

Like St. Pius X after him, Father Eymard regretted the practice of those who upon entering a church, go and kneel in front of a statue of the Sacred Heart, instead of concentrating their prayerful attention on the Tabernacle where He is present in person. And he would exhort in letters and sermons: "Find the Sacred Heart where it is, living, all-good, and all-merciful, in the Eucharist. Unfortunately that divine and loving Heart is not known and loved, even by many devout people, who play at any number of little devotions, good in themselves, but neglect the one devotion which ought to be the life and the end of all the others: the Heart of Jesus that gave us Calvary and the Eucharist."

Jules V. Simoneau, sss
Immaculata Magazine
December 1984/January 1985

August 4

Feast of St. John Vianney
(1786-1859)

When St. John Mary Vianney arrived at the obscure little village of Ars, someone said to him with bitterness, "Here there is nothing to do." "Therefore, there is everything to do," replied the Saint.

And he began immediately to act. What did he do? He arose at 2:00 A.M. in the morning and went to pray near the altar in the dark church. He recited the Divine Office, he made his meditation and he prepared himself for Holy Mass. After the Holy Sacrifice, he made his thanksgiving; then he remained at prayer until noon. He would be always kneeling on the floor without any support, with a Rosary in his hand and his eyes fixed on the Tabernacle.

Things continued this way for a short time.

But then . . . he had to start changing his timetable; and things reached a point requiring radical changes in his program. The Eucharistic Jesus and the Blessed Virgin Mary, little by little, drew souls to that poor parish, until the Church did not seem big enough to contain the crowds, and the confessional of the holy Curate became swamped with endless lines of penitents. The holy Curate was obliged to hear confessions for ten, fifteen and eighteen hours a day! How did such a transformation ever come about? There had been a poor Church, an altar long unused, an abandoned tabernacle, an ancient confessional and a priest of little talent with no means to do anything. How could these things achieve such a remarkable change in that obscure village?

Father Stefano Manelli, OFM CONV.
Jesus Our Eucharistic Love

The lay faithful "consecrate the world to the Father!" The people of God really are a priestly people. The ordained, ministerial priest consecrates the bread and wine to be the Body and Blood of Christ and the lay faithful, by means of the presence of the Eucharistic body and Blood of Christ, now consecrate the world—and their lives, their families, their works and possessions. The lay faithful transform the world, that all may be divinized in Christ.

The lay faithful are charged with "living" the Eucharistic sacrifice so that Christ may be all in all. The Council Fathers conclude Section #48 of *Sacrosanctum Concilium . . .* with this sweeping picture of the daily transformation of the world:

"Through Christ the Mediator, [the Christian laity] should be drawn day by day into even closer union with God and with each other, so that finally God may be all in all."

This means in practice that every one of our actions and desires, pains and joys, disappointments and hopes, loves and frustrations—all that we are, all that we do and think, all that we have—everything can be offered in—"spiritual sacrifice" in union with the Eucharist sacrifice for the sake of others.

Your pain and joy is precious, don't waste it! Offer it! Offer it for the members of your family, for families of the whole church and world in order that in Christ we may be one family, one Body of Christ to the glory of God the Father.

Rev. George W. Kosicki, csb
Living Eucharist,
Counter Sign to Our Age and Answer to Crisis

Charles de Foucauld (1858-1916) was born into a French aristocratic family and after a rather dissipated life as a cavalry officer with the rank of lieutenant was filled with a sense of spiritual unrest. This led him back to the faith after his conversion by the Abbe Huvelin, an experienced spiritual director, at the church of St. Augustin in Paris. His attempts to follow a religious vocation with the Trappists proved futile. He left the order in 1897 because he sought a life of greater solitude and went to the Holy Land where, at Nazareth, he served as a gardener and general factotum at the Poor Clare Monastery until 1900. He returned to France and was ordained a priest the following year. A few months later he left for Algeria in North Africa, where a holy restlessness for God had originally stirred his heart. Here he lived as a hermit in the desert, first at the oasis of Beni Abbes, and then later in the remote Hoggar Mountains and at the oasis of Tamanrasset among the Tuaregs. Apart from applying himself to learn the difficult Tuareg language, which he mastered enough to compile dictionaries and translations, his life was mainly absorbed in simple prayer before the Blessed Sacrament, penance, and works of charity. Though greatly admired, he never made a single convert. He died most tragically, being assassinated by one of the people he befriended. The reason for this may have been because of confusion and suspicions regarding his complicity with the French army. But, the real reason must be one of the secrets which the desert keeps close to its heart.

Fr. Michael L. Gaudoin-Parker
The Real Presence through the Ages

The center of the spiritual life of Padre Pio was the Eucharistic Jesus. His devotion polarized around the tabernacle. Jesus, the Word Incarnate, was not distant in time and space to Padre Pio, but very close to him, living with him under the same roof, hidden under the eucharistic Species.

Hour by hour, day and night, he would linger in conversation with the Divine Inhabitant of the tabernacle. When asked where he could be found if he was not in his cell or in the confessional, he answered: "Come and look for me in the choir, in the presence of Jesus in the Blessed Sacrament."

The sleepless nights, spent in prayer, were a preparation for Mass and union with Christ in Holy Communion. The days, lived in prayer, in the confessional, in his priestly ministry, were a hymn of thanksgiving. His thoughts, his looks, his sighs, were always for Jesus in the Blessed Sacrament, from whom he could not separate himself without suffering, as if attracted by a powerful magnet.

Padre Alberto D'Apolito
Padre Pio of Pietrelcina

Feast of St. Dominic
1170-1221

St. Dominic was once saying Mass in London, England, in the presence of the King and Queen and 300 other persons. As he was making the Memento for the living, he suddenly became enraptured, remaining motionless for the space of a whole hour. All present were greatly astonished, and did not know what to think or to make of it. The King ordered the server to pull the priest's robe, that he might go on with his Mass. But on attempting to do so, the server became so terribly frightened that he was unable to comply with the King's order.

After an hour's time, St. Dominic was able to continue the Mass, when, behold! At the Elevation of the Sacred Host, the King and all who were present saw, instead of the Host in the hands of the priest, the Holy Infant Jesus, at the sight of which all experienced great interior joy. At the same time they beheld the Mother of God in great brilliancy and splendor and surrounded by twelve bright stars. She took the hand of her Divine Infant to bless with it all those who were present at the Mass. At this blessing many experienced an ineffable joy and shed tears of tenderness. At the Elevation of the chalice, everyone saw a cross uprising from it, with Jesus Christ hanging upon it in a most pitiable condition and shedding all His blood. The Blessed Virgin was also seen sprinkling, as it were, the Sacred Blood over the people, upon which everyone received a clear knowledge of his sins and a deep sorrow for the same, so much so that everyone who saw them could not help weeping with them.

Fr. Michael Muller, CSSR
The Blessed Eucharist, Our Greatest Treasure

Had you the purity of the Angels and the holiness of Saint John the Baptist, you would still be unworthy to receive or touch this Sacrament. For it is not due to any merit of his own that a man is allowed to consecrate and handle the Sacrament of Christ, and receive the Bread of Angels (Ps 78:26) as his food. High the office, and great the dignity of a priest, to whom is granted what is not granted to Angels; for only a rightly ordained priest has power to celebrate the Eucharist and to hallow the Body of Christ. The priest is the minister of God, using the words of God by His own command and appointment: but God Himself is the principal agent and unseen worker, to whose will all things are subject (Wis 12:18), and whose command all creatures obey.

In all that relates to this sublime Sacrament, you should have regard to God's word, rather than your own senses or any visible sign. Therefore, when you approach the Altar, let it be with awe and reverence. Consider from whom this ministry proceeds, that has been delivered to you by the imposition of the Bishop's hands (I Tim 4:14.). You have been made a priest and ordained to celebrate the Sacrament: see, then that you offer this sacrifice to God faithfully, regularly, and devoutly, and that your life is blameless (I Tim 3: 2; 2 Pet 3:14). Your obligations are now greater; you are bound to exercise stricter self-discipline and to aim at a higher degree of holiness. A priest should be adorned with all virtues, and show an example of holy life to others (Titus 2:7). His life should not be like that of worldly men, but like that of the Angels (Phil 3:20), or of perfect men on earth.

Words of Christ
The Imitation of Christ
Thomas à Kempis

Father Hunolt, of the Society of Jesus, relates that two students were once discoursing together about the hour of their death. They agreed that if God would allow it, he who should die first should appear to the other to tell him how he fared in the other world. Shortly afterwards, one of them died and appeared soon after his death to his fellow-student, all shining with heavenly brightness and glory, and in answer to his inquiries, told him that by the mercy of God he was saved and was in possession of the bliss of Heaven. The other congratulated him on his felicity and asked him how he merited such unspeakable glory and bliss. "Chiefly," said the happy soul, "by the care with which I endeavored to receive Holy Communion with a pure heart." At these words the spirit disappeared, leaving in his surviving friend feelings of great consolation and an ardent zeal to imitate his devotion. "You have heard these things; blessed shall you be if you do them."

Fr. Michael Muller, CSSR
The Blessed Eucharist, Our Greatest Treasure

Feast of St. Clare
1194-1253

The infamous tribe of Saracens, thirsting for Christian blood, was ready to commit any crime or act of audacity and had already penetrated the outer wall of San Damiano and had entered the cloister. The poor ladies were overcome with anguish and, their voices trembling with fright, they ran to take refuge around their mother. Clare, however, was not afraid; although ill herself, she asked to be taken to the cloister door and to have placed there as her only protection against the Saracens the ivory-covered silver pyx wherein was kept the Body of Christ.

She knelt in prayer before the Lord and with many tears prayed to Him, "Could it be your will, Lord, to deliver your servants whom you have nourished in your love into the hands of pagans? Guard them, Lord, for in this hour I am unable to take care of them." From the ciborium . . . the voice of a child was heard, "I will care for you always." Clare continued, "Lord, if it is your will, please protect this city, which continues to live in your love." And Christ replied, "It will suffer much, but I will come to its aid and protection."

At that very moment the frenzy of those dogs was changed into fear and they climbed down the walls faster than they had scaled them; the power of that prayer had cast fear into their ranks. But Clare firmly enjoined the Sisters who had heard the voice, "My dearest daughters, as long as I am alive, make certain that you will tell no one of this voice."

P. Theophile Desbonnets
Assisi, In the Footsteps of Saint Francis

If My dear people truly recognized Me in the host, they would not be so quick to leave, and wander in their thoughts after receiving My Precious Body and Blood. It is only confirmation on how many of My people go through habitual motions and routine actions, instead of true devotion and dedication! Where is their commitment? I am committed to them. I respect them. Cannot they be loyal to true friendship? I wish to assist them and help them in their times of need. They must allow Me, and listen to Me. How, child, do you listen?

Another question many of My people ask: "How can I listen? What are the signs? How do I know I am being obedient and listening?"

My response is: "How can I tell them, if when they come to receive Me, they do not take the time to allow Me to instruct, counsel, guide or fill them with My love? To listen, is to firstly absorb Me, and to allow Me to fill you with My love. That is the first step. SPEAK TO ME OPENLY, SINCERELY, TRUTH-FULLY AND INTIMATELY. STOP BEING OBSESSED WITH SELF-IMAGE, PROBLEMS AND DAILY OCCURRENCES. Come openly to Me, and talk to Me! Then My peace will slowly be absorbed into you, and you will know that your hearts are primed for counsel!"

It begins with Eucharist for all those who desire reception of Me, and it continues with respectful mannerisms and devoted faithfulness!

Words of Our Lord
I Am Your Jesus of Mercy
The Riehle Foundation

On 16th September, 1903, the Bishop, Monsignor Dubillard, was carrying the ostensorium. Amongst the last stretchers of the sick was one on which lay the daughter of General Clement. For seventeen years she had suffered most severe pains, and her leg, reduced to a state of inflexibility, had lesions even to the bone. Her doctor and friends said it was folly to expect a cure. Yet she would go to Lourdes. The journey was a real martyrdom. She fainted three times while being conveyed from the station to the Sanctuary. Still she had faith. On the morning of the 16th she received Holy Communion at the Grotto, and in the afternoon wished to be present for the procession. Jesus passed by; she heard a sound, but could not move, and fell back on her couch as if bitterly disillusioned. The Bishop, who had passed by slowly, perceived her. He turned back, and blessing her anew, placed the ostensorium on her head. This was the moment of grace. The general's daughter felt that she was cured, she uttered a cry and, although for many years she had not touched the ground, she leaped down and, dressed as she was, proceeded to follow the procession. The miracle was evident, the enthusiasm of the crowd was beyond bounds.

How often have not similar miracles been repeated! Suggestion, not knowing how to harmonize the facts with their blind mentality, say the incredulous. Miracle, whereby God intervenes to prove that He Who can do all things is present in the adorable Eucharist, say we.

Cardinal Gaetano De Lai
The Real Presence of Jesus Christ in the Eucharist

August 14

S aint Maximilian desired to write a book on the teaching of the Church with a chapter entitled "Dogma: The Most Blessed Sacrament," perhaps eventually to be published as a booklet. He wished to write of dogma "in a popular, lively style, illustrating the doctrine with miracles attested by competent witnesses (for example, bearing on the Eucharist)." The constant demands of the apostolate did not permit him to write such a work. But in the material for a book on the Immaculate, we find the description of the apparition of our Lady to Alphonse Ratisbonne in the Church of Sant'Andrea delle Fratte, Rome, together with an account of a moral miracle bearing on the Eucharist. In an instant, this unbelieving Jew, without hearing so much as a word from the all holy Virgin, understood the entire Catholic Faith, including the truth about the Eucharist.

Jerzy Domanski, OFM CONV.
*For the Life of the World,
Saint Maximilian and the Eucharist*

Assumption of the Blessed Virgin Mary
Feast of St. Tarsicius
Third Century

S aint Tarcisius, the boy martyr of the Holy Eucharist, is called the Patron Saint of First Communicants.

It was to young Tarsicius that the Blessed Sacrament was entrusted to be carried, as inconspicuously as possible, as Holy Viaticum to imprisoned Christians who had been condemned to death.

One day when Tarsicius refused to show them what he was carrying, a band of pagan Roman ruffians attacked him and beat him with sticks before stoning him to death.

When his assailants turned over Tarsicius' body and searched him, they could find no trace of the Most Blessed Sacrament either in his hands or on his clothing—Christ had miraculously disappeared. Christians took up the body of the young martyr and buried it with great respect in the cemetery of Callistus.

In the fourth century, Pope St. Damasus composed an epitaph for the young martyr's tomb which he had carefully restored and beautified.

The epitaph leaves no doubt that belief in the Real Presence of Our Lord's Body and Blood in the Blessed Sacrament was the same then as it is now. **"Christ's secret gifts by good Tarsicius borne, the mob profanely bade him to display; He rather gave his own limbs to be torn than Christ's celestial to mad dogs betray."**

Perpetual Eucharistic Adoration Newsletter
March 1989

"I do not know," the pastor had said, "whether she will see the Saviour today." This occurs only when she has passed the night in expiatory suffering. Then she can receive an entire host, although ordinarily she swallows a small part with difficulty. The parish Mass was over now and the pastor took his time, even though his little lamb was almost passing away with longing for the sacred food. I almost felt like begging him in sympathy to hurry. First the children were dismissed in order, and I do not know what else was done in the church. Only then did he put on a surplice and stole and finally appear at the corner of the altar, holding the white host above the ciborium. Although she was tiredly leaning over the kneeling-bench before, now she sat upright with her hands respectfully folded, waiting. "He nodded to me to come close to Therese's chair for the most sacred moment. This I could easily do without being noticed by her. I knelt alongside her, about a step from her, so that I could see and observe everything. The priest came a step nearer. Therese in a rapture opened both arms wide and stretched them toward the Sacred Host. Her eyes were not directed to the host but to a Figure which I could not see. She can see the Saviour Himself, the Risen One, whom I see only under the veil of bread. Fully a minute, if not longer, the priest stood still and I used the time to calmly and carefully see and observe all as well as to impress it on my mind."

Albert Paul Schimberg
The Story of Therese Neumann

In the desert of Sinai, God's caring love supplied the only means of survival for the Chosen People; likewise, through the Holy Eucharist, Jesus has supplied us with all our needs for our journey. Like the Israelites, we need food for our journey. Each day Jesus invites us to the inexhaustible fount of nourishment in the eucharistic banquet.

Each day as we come to join our eternal High priest in celebrating the Eucharist, we are assured that we are not journeying alone, but that Jesus is with us and within us every step of the way. As the lyrics of one modern song proclaims: "Lord Jesus, you shall be our song as we journey . . . "

The Mass is the very source in which we find hope and encouragement when the road seems rough and the traveling quite difficult if not seemingly impossible. Our courage and strength are renewed as we meet Jesus in his eucharistic celebration.

When life's deserts are hot, the mountains high and the valleys deep, we find great comfort and joy in the awareness that Jesus loves us. His presence in the Eucharist speaks to our heart of his overwhelming love, a love which wants to be with us at all times.

When we contemplate God's loving presence among us, our hearts can certainly exclaim with the Israelites: "Manna—what is this?"

David E. Rosage
The Bread of Life

The Blessed Sacrament is God. Devotion to the Blessed Sacrament is simply divine worship. Turn it which way we will, throw the light of love and knowledge now on one side of it, now on another, still the result is the same, the one inexhaustible sweet fact of the Real Presence. In the hands of the priest, behind the crystal of the monstrance, on the tongue of the communicant, now, and for a thousand times, and almost at our will and pleasure, there are the Hands and Feet, the Eyes and Mouth, the swift Blood and living Heart of Him whom Thomas touched and Magdalen was fain to touch, the Soul that delighted Limbus with its amazing beauty and set the prisoners free, nay the Eternal, Incomprehensible, Almighty Word who is everywhere and yet fixed there, the flashing fires of whose dear glory we could not bear to see, and so for love of us He stills them and He sheathes them in the quiet modesty of the Blessed Sacrament.

Fr. Frederick William Faber
The Blessed Sacrament

Feast of St. John Eudes
1601-1680

You should adore our Lord Jesus Christ, who makes himself present to us on the altar, so that we might offer him the homage and adoration we owe. Pray that just as he changes the lower earthly nature of bread and wine into his body and blood he might change and transform also the sluggishness, coldness and dryness of our earthly and arid heat into the fire, tenderness and agility of the holy divine affections and dispositions of his divine and heavenly heart. Then you should remember that Christians are one with Jesus Christ, as members with their head. . . . They should also be there as hosts and victims who are but one host just as they are one priest with Jesus Christ. They need to be immolated and sacrificed with the same Jesus Christ for the glory of God.

John Eudes
What We Must Do to Assist Worthily at the
Holy Sacrifice of the Mass

November 19 [1936]. During Mass today, I saw the Lord Jesus, who said to me, "Be at peace, My daughter; I see your efforts, which are very pleasing to Me." And the Lord disappeared, and it was time for Holy Communion. After I received Holy Communion, I suddenly saw the Cenacle and in it Jesus and the Apostles. **I saw the institution of the Most Blessed Sacrament.** Jesus allowed me to penetrate His interior, and I came to know the greatness of His majesty and, at the same time, His great humbling of Himself. The extraordinary light that allowed me to see His majesty revealed to me, at the same time, what was in my own soul. (Diary 757)

Rev. George W. Kosicki, csb
Tell My Priests, The Words of Our Lord to Priests About His Mercy as Revealed to Sr. Faustina Kowalska

Feast of St. Pius X
1835-1914

Pope St. Pius X had extensive pastoral experience before being elevated to the papacy. The most glorious actions were his decrees urging the frequent reception of Holy Communion and lowering the age for First Holy Communion.

O Most sweet Jesus, who came into this world to give to all souls the life of Your grace, and who, to preserve and increase it in them, willed to be the daily Remedy of their weakness and Food for each day, we humbly beseech You, by Your Heart so burning with love for us, to pour Your divine Spirit upon all souls in order that those who have the misfortune to be in the state of mortal sin may, returning to You, find the life of grace which they have lost.

Through this same Holy Spirit, may those who are already living by this divine life devoutly approach Your divine Table every day when it is possible, so that, receiving each day in Holy Communion the antidote of their daily venial sins and each day sustaining in themselves the life of Your grace and thus ever purifying themselves the more, they may finally come to a happy life with You. Amen.

Rev. Charles Dollen
Prayer Book of the Saints

One of the great apparitions of Our Lady was in the Irish village of Knock. On August 21, 1879, surrounded by light, wearing a brilliant golden crown, and a long white gown covered by a dazzling white cloak, she appeared. On her right appeared St. Joseph inclining reverently towards her; on her left St. John the Evangelist, attired as a bishop and holding a book, his hand raised as if preaching. To St. John's left was an altar on which stood a lamb, surrounded by angels' wings, a symbol of the Holy Sacrifice of the Mass. This wondrous spectacle lasted two hours in the rain. No word was spoken to the fifteen persons of different ages, occupations and intelligence who knelt while witnessing the apparition. Since nothing was spoken, it was to become known as "The Silent Apparition," to bring to our attention the importance of the Holy Sacrifice of the Mass, and that Christ is truly present in the Blessed Sacrament which we should venerate in silence, awe and reverence.

Wherever approved apparitions of our Blessed Lady have taken place, churches or chapels have been erected in order that the Holy Sacrifice of the Mass may be offered for the greater honor and glory of God, and as places to keep the Blessed Sacrament.

Louis Kaczmarek
Hidden Treasure, The Riches of the Eucharist

St. Bonaventure tells how Francis of Assisi "burned with love for the Sacrament of our Lord's Body with all his heart, and was lost in wonder at the thought of such condescending love, such loving condescension. He received Holy Communion often and so devoutly that he roused others to devotion too. The presence of the Immaculate Lamb used to take him out of himself, so that he was often lost in ecstasy."

Of this continuing condescension Francis says, "Every day he humbles himself just as he did when he came from his heavenly throne into the Virgin's womb; every day he comes to us and lets us see his abjection, when he descends from the bosom of the Father into the hands of the priest at the altar. He shows himself to us in this sacred bread just as he once appeared to his apostles in real flesh. With their own eyes they saw only flesh, but they believed that he was God, because they contemplated him with the eyes of the spirit. We, too, with our own eyes, see only bread and wine, but we must see further and firmly believe that this is his most holy Body and Blood, living and true."

For Francis his love for the Eucharist was intimately connected to his love for the incarnation of God through Jesus Christ. To believe in one led ultimately to the belief in the other. This belief was centered on the assurance that God loves us so much that He comes into the world He created to save it. He took on flesh to save all flesh. This belief was not mere speculation for Francis. It was a mystical fire that burned within his whole soul, and this fire did not destroy, it saved.

John Michael Talbot
The Fire of God

But anyone who would approach this gracious sacrament while guilty of deadly sin would receive no grace from it, even though such a person would really be receiving me as I am, wholly God, wholly human. But do you know the situation of the soul who receives the sacrament unworthily? She is like a candle that has been doused with water and only hisses when it is brought near the fire. The flame no more than touches it but it goes out and nothing remains but smoke. Just so, this soul brings the candle she received in holy baptism and throws the water of sin over it, a water that drenches the wick of baptismal grace that is meant to bear the light. And unless she dries the wick out with the fire of true contrition by confessing her sin, she will physically receive the light when she approaches the table of the altar, but she will not receive it into her spirit.

If the soul is not disposed as she should be for so great a mystery, this true light will not graciously remain in her but will depart, leaving her more confounded, more darksome, and more deeply in sin. She will have gained nothing from this sacrament but the hissing of remorse, not because of any defect in the light (for nothing can impair it) but because of the water it encountered in the soul, the water that so drenched her love that she could not receive this light.

Words of God the Father
Catherine of Siena, The Dialogue

Feast of Saint Louis IX
1214-1270

In the person of St. Louis IX were the qualities which form a great king, a hero of romance, and a saint! With his death, the century of knights ended. One day a messenger, breathless with haste, burst in upon the king with surprising and exciting news. "Your majesty," he cried, "hasten to the Church! A great miracle is occurring there. A priest is saying holy Mass, and after the consecration, instead of the host there is visible on the altar Jesus Himself in His human figure. Everybody is marveling at it. Hurry before it disappears."

To the astonishment of the messenger, the saintly monarch calmly replied:

" Let them go to see the miracle who have any doubt regarding the Real Presence of our Lord in the Holy Sacrament. As for me, even if I saw Jesus on the altar in His visible form, and touched Him with my hand, and heard His voice, I should not be more convinced than I now am, that He is present in the consecrated Host. The word of Christ is sufficient for me. I need no miracle."

Louis Kaczmarek
Hidden Treasure, The Riches of the Eucharist

On the First Friday of each month, the above-mentioned grace connected with the pain in my side was renewed in the following manner: The Sacred Heart was represented to me as a resplendent sun, the burning rays of which fell vertically upon my heart, which was inflamed with a fire so fervid that it seemed as if it would reduce me to ashes. It was at these times especially that my Divine Master taught me what He required of me and disclosed to me the secrets of His loving Heart. On one occasion, whilst the Blessed Sacrament was exposed, feeling wholly withdrawn within myself by an extraordinary recollection of all my senses and powers, Jesus Christ, my sweet Master, presented Himself to me.

St. Margaret Mary Alacoque
The Autobiography of St. Margaret Mary

❝ . . . [The] cult of adoration has a valid and solid motive. The Eucharist, in fact . . . differs from the other Sacraments in that it not only produces grace, but permanently contains the very author of grace. When therefore the Church commands us to worship Christ hidden beneath the Eucharistic veils, and to ask him for supernatural and earthly gifts, which we always need, she manifests the living faith wherewith she believes in the presence of her Divine Spouse beneath those veils, shows forth her gratitude and enjoys close familiarity with him.❞

Pope Pius XII
Mediator Dei

Feast of St. Augustine
354-430

Your light shone upon me in its brilliance, and I thrilled with love and dread alike. I realized that I was far away from you. It was as though I were in a land where all is different from your own and I heard your voice calling from on high saying, "I am the food of full-grown men. Grow and you shall feed on me. But you shall not change me into your own substance, as you do with the food of your body. Instead, you shall be changed into me" (*St. Augustine, Confessions*).

Fr. Michael L. Gaudoin-Parker
The Real Presence through the Ages

Private time spent in the presence of the Blessed Sacrament is one of the most effective ways of drawing closer to Jesus. The world is filled with noise. We all need quiet time to gather our thoughts, to speak to God and to listen to Him. If we can do this in the presence of the Blessed Sacrament, we are very fortunate. Our visits should include acts of adoration, thanksgiving, reparation and petition. These can also be times for devotion to the Sacred Heart of Jesus. The Sacred Heart symbolizes the human manifestation of God's infinite love for us. It is here, in love poured out, that Eucharistic devotion and devotion to the Sacred Heart find their meeting place.

Jesus is present in the Most Blessed Sacrament to complete the work which His Father entrusts to Him. He is there to fill our soul with the love which led Him to die on the Cross for us. He is there to take over our hearts and to lead us to the love of God and neighbor. He is there to make us stronger and more resolute in loving Him.

Parishes should consider the formation of a Society of the Blessed Sacrament. Members would commit themselves to prayerful adoration in certain shifts. Jesus gave His all for us. We should be giving more of ourselves to Him. These extended times in His presence would afford a marvelous opportunity to pray for the needs of the universal Church and for the needs of our own Parishes and our families. They would be times for quiet listening, times to give thanks and make reparation. What graces might be ours if, as a united people, we fostered such devotion! I ask Mary, the Mother of Jesus, the Mother of the Church and our Mother, to help us in these efforts.

Most Reverend Thomas V. Daily
Bishop of Brooklyn
Pastoral Letter on the Holy Eucharist

At Lourdes, even Mary has stepped aside to make way for Christ. There is no place in the world where Christ in the Eucharist is more glorified. The procession of the Eucharist by candlelight is the high point of each day. Here the pilgrims are joined in faith, and all the countries of the world are united as the procession winds from the grotto to show that Jesus is the Gift of the Virgin Mary. Now she stands at the side of her Son so that He may console.

The Eucharist in our churches and in our shrines creates a world of its own. It breathes an atmosphere of faith, love, hope and hospitality. Most of us who do not live sheltered lives find ourselves between the noisy, worldly, excited environment in which we are forced to live and the peaceful presence of the Eucharist. The Eucharist obliges us worldlings to build for ourselves an inner retreat, an underground refuge. We have lost much ground. As the poet says, "the world is too much with us." We have forgotten the necessity for the delicate balance, and the noise has consumed us. We can retrace our steps, I suppose, if we get rid of all that distracts us from Christ. There are too many plans and programs and directives I would think. When Pius X was asked his program, he pointed to the cross and said, "That is my program." So the Eucharist is our program, our directive. We must tear down the walls that have estranged us from the prayer of the Eucharist in our churches to bring Christ near to us.

Msgr. John F. Davis
An Audience with Jesus

During a prayer time the week before Easter, I was amazed by how much the monstrance seemed to symbolize the Catholic Church. Like many Protestants, I had been concerned that Mary, the saints and the sacraments were roadblocks between believers and God so that to get to God, one would have to go around them. They seemed to complicate life with God unnecessarily like accretions on the sides of sunken treasures; they had to be discarded to get to what was important.

But now I could see that the opposite was true. Catholicism was not a distant religion, but a presence oriented one. Catholics were the ones who had Jesus physically present in churches and saw themselves as being tabernacles after receiving the Eucharist. And because Jesus is the Eucharist, keeping him in the center allows all of the rich doctrines of the Church to emanate from him just as the beautiful gold rays stream forth from the Host in the monstrance.

Kimberly Hahn
Rome Sweet Home,
Our Journey to Catholicism

The center of activity and attention in most parishes is not focused on our Eucharistic Lord, but rather on social activities. "Unless the Lord built the house, they labor in vain who built it." Spiritual priorities are replaced by financial concerns. "My house is meant for a house of prayer, but you have made it a den of thieves." In most tabernacles, Jesus is left unloved and unwanted as the world ignores the only One who can solve its problems. "Take care of Me and My concerns and I will take care of you and your concerns." "If you find your delight in the Lord, He will grant you your heart's desire."

The Eucharistic Heart of Jesus is infinitely appreciative of the love you have for Him in the Blessed Sacrament. "The Lord takes delight in His people." This is why every holy hour you make changes the thorns in His Heart into many flowers of indescribable consolation. With Mary we offer to Him any suffering in our own life caused by the feeling of not being appreciated, in order that all humanity may come to truly appreciate Jesus in this most Blessed Sacrament.

"They are happy who dwell in Your House . . . they are happy whose strength is in You."

Fr. Martin Lucia, MSS
Rosary Meditations from Mother Teresa of Calcutta

I was celebrating Holy Mass in a private chapel in Europe. I don't know why, but a man who was scandalizing the people . . . was present. It was really shocking the way he acted . . . It was truly satanic. But the people were struck, you may be sure, when at the consecration this man fell on his knees, trembling and staring at the altar, wide-eyed, apparently seeing something astounding. . .

When the Mass was over, this person rushed into the sacristy . . . "Please, tell me, what have you been doing at the altar?" "Why, I have been celebrating Holy Mass." He demanded to know what Mass is. I explained to him how the same Jesus, who was nailed to the Cross on Calvary, and who shed the last drop of His Blood for us sinners, does the same thing now on the altar but in an unbloody way. "That is what we call the Mass." Imagine my surprise when this man claimed to have seen what I had just described. When I asked him to tell me just what he had seen, he told me he saw me come from the sacristy to the altar and reading from a big book and going back and forth. "Then you bowed; you said something; and then you lifted up a round white object, when suddenly you disappeared and in your place, I saw a wonderful personage with arms outstretched; what beauty, what majesty! I can still see that face, those features, those eyes, the blood gushing from those wounds. His lips were moving as though he were talking to someone. And His body was shining like the sun. Then, after some time, this wonderful personage disappeared and you returned."

Father Mateo Crawley-Boevey, sscc
Jesus, King of Love

September 3

Feast of St. Gregory the Great
d. 604

From the day he became Pope, Saint Gregory applied himself vigorously to the duties of the Church, appointing overseers to look after its secular affairs so he could devote himself to the celebration of Holy Mass where his homilies on the Gospel and the Eucharist became the talk of Rome.

He dealt with codifying rules for selecting deacons and priests to make these offices more spiritual. Until Saint Gregory's time, for example, deacons were elected not because of their spirituality but because they had good voices to help sing the liturgy.

Because he so loved the solemn celebration of the Eucharist, Saint Gregory devoted himself to compiling the Antiphonary—containing the chants of the Church used during the liturgy (which is called today by his name, Gregorian Chant)—and setting up the foundation for the Schola Cantorum, Rome's famous training school for choristers.

Saint Gregory never rested and wore himself down almost to a skeleton. Even as he lay dying, he directed the affairs of the Church and continued his spiritual writing. He died in 604 and was buried in St. Peter's Church. Saint Gregory is venerated as the fourth Doctor of the Latin Church and his influence on the daily life of the Church is evident even in our own time.

Perpetual Eucharistic Adoration Newsletter
April 1990

Is there any real difference between Jesus in heaven and Jesus in the Eucharist? No, it is the same Jesus. The only difference is in us. We now on earth cannot see or touch him with our senses. But that is not a limitation in him; it is a limitation in us.

We speak correctly of believing in the Real Presence. But we should grow in our understanding of what this implies.

The living, breathing Jesus Christ is in the Blessed Sacrament. This is the reality. When we speak of presence, however, we are saying something more.

Two people may be really near each other physically, but not present to each other spiritually. To be present to someone means to have another person in mind by being mentally aware of their existence, and to have them in one's heart by loving that other person . . .

Jesus is on earth in the Blessed Sacrament. Why? In order that we might come to him now no less than his contemporaries did in first century Palestine. If we thus approach him in loving faith, there is no limit to the astounding things he will do. Why not? In the Eucharist he has the same human lips that told the raging storm, "Be still!" and commanded the dead man, "Lazarus, come forth!"

There are no limitations to Christ's power, as God, which he exercises through his humanity in the Eucharist. The only limitation is our own weakness of faith or lack of confidence in his almighty love.

Rev. John A. Hardon, SJ
Soul Magazine

In 1926 the terrible Masonic persecution of the Church in Mexico erupted. Fr. Maldonado continued his priestly work during the ups and downs of these tragic times, all through the intense persecution under the Mexican President Calles, and into the presidency of Cardenas.

Fr. Maldonado spent many hours prostrate before the Blessed Sacrament, praying with his arms extended in the form of a cross. Because of the persecution, there were times when he could not go out but had to stay hidden indoors. At such times he had the opportunity to spend long hours in prayer and adoration before the Blessed Sacrament.

After many close calls, he was discovered. He hid the Blessed Sacrament in a pyx pressed against his chest. The soldiers beat him with the butts of their rifles and screamed at him to loosen his hands and give them "that thing in his chest." They yelled horrible blasphemies referring to the Eucharist. Fr. Maldonado grabbed the pyx very tightly in his hands, but his persecutors continued to blaspheme and yelled again and again, "Open the hand." By this time they had tortured him so badly that all of his teeth were broken, his left eye destroyed, his right arm fractured and a leg dislocated from the beatings with the rifle butts. Yet, in his agony, he held on tightly to the pyx to protect the Blessed Sacrament.

When the tormentors cut the cords of his hand with a knife, he no longer could protect the Blessed Sacrament and it fell to the floor. It is not clear what happened after that but sources have said there was a man in the room, still somewhat Catholic. He was frightened at what was going to happen to the Hosts, and picked them up and consumed them rather than see them desecrated.

Louis Kaczmarek
Hidden Treasure, The Riches of the Eucharist

Please come before the Blessed Sacrament . . . I will speak to you there.

Here, I am present in My Tabernacle, waiting for My people so that I can fill them with My peace. Pay homage to Me, your Lord . . . I, Who am your source of life!

Do you know what it means to be in front of the Blessed Sacrament?

It is I, Who am here. It is I, Who stands before you! It is I, Who shall grant your heart's desire. It is I, Who awaits, My dear one.

I have been waiting for so long for all to come to Me, so that I can give them true happiness!

Words of Our Lord
I Am Your Jesus of Mercy (Vol. 1)
The Riehle Foundation

I said before that the Blessed Sacrament was the triumph of the Church over the world, of spirit over matter, of grace over nature, of faith over sight . . . The Blessed Sacrament is everything to us. If we wish to be all for Jesus, there is our way, there is Himself. If we desire to see how Jesus is all for us, or which is another thing, how He is all in all to us, the Blessed Sacrament is at once that double revelation. All the doctrines of the Church, creation, incarnation, grace, sacraments, run up into the doctrine of the Blessed Sacrament, and are magnificently developed there. All the art and ceremonial, the liturgical wisdom and the rubrical majesty of the Church are grouped around the Blessed Sacrament. All devotions are united and satisfied in this one. All mysteries gravitate to this, touch upon it and are crowned by it. Nowhere are the marvelous perfections of the invisible God so copied to the life and displayed to His creatures. All the mysteries of the Incarnation are gathered into one in the Blessed Sacrament. All the lives and actions of Jesus are found therein. All the other sacraments subserviently minister to this, and it is the one and only Sacrament which Jesus Himself received. It does His work better than anything else does, and answers as nothing else does all the ends He had in view. With the Body and the Blood and the Soul of Jesus it brings with it His Divine Person, and the Persons of the Father and of the Holy Ghost, in a way so real and sublime as to be beyond expression, but which we signify by the theological word "concomitance," as if the Holy Trinity came in the train of our Saviour's Body, as its equipage and company. It is the greatest work of God, and the sabbath of all His works; for therein the Creator's love and power and wisdom find their rest.

Frederick William Faber
The Blessed Sacrament

September 8

The Birthday of the Blessed Virgin Mary

We cannot forget that the mystery of the Eucharist is inseparable from another reality: the role of the Blessed Virgin Mary in the life of Christ and in the life of the Church. In the Mass, Jesus entrusted to us his redeeming sacrifice. It is Mary who prepared the way for this sacrifice. Through her act of obedience, she allowed God to use her so that Christ the Redeemer might take on a human nature. Indeed the body and blood shed for us on the cross and offered on the altar were fashioned miraculously by God within her. The Christ we receive in Communion is the Christ who was born of the Virgin Mary. The Christ we adore in the tabernacle is the Christ who became man through her. Thus every time the Mass is celebrated, Mary is present in a very special way, just as she was present at the sacrifice of Calvary. When we receive him, we are united in an effable way to his Mother and to all the saints and angels, and every time we honor Jesus in his Eucharistic presence, we are made aware of her whose faith helped make him present to us.

As your Bishop, I wish to assure you of my prayers. At Mass every day, I pray that we may be united by the offering we make of ourselves, joined to the sacrifice of our Redeemer. Every day, too, as I pray before the Blessed Sacrament, you are present in my thoughts. Brothers and sisters, please remember to pray for me. I very much depend on your prayers.

Bishop John J. Myers
Immaculata Magazine
Special Adoration Issue

All these thoughts on the Eucharist make it clear to us that in this Sacrament, in which He not only gives grace to us but also gives Himself, we are led to a supreme peak of spiritual fulfillment. This Sacrament is not given to us merely in order that we do something, but that we may *be* someone: that we may be Christ. That we may be perfectly identified with Him. Comparing the Eucharist with confirmation, St. Thomas says that confirmation brings us an increase of grace in order to resist temptation, but the Eucharist does even more: it increases and perfects our spiritual life itself, in order that we may be perfected in our own being, our own personality, by *our union with God* . . . In other words, by our union with Christ in the Eucharist we find our true selves. The false self, the "old man" is burned away by the fervor of charity generated by His intimate presence within our soul. And the "new man" comes into full possession of Himself as we "live, now not we, but Christ liveth in us."

Thomas Merton
The Living Bread

"I will tell you My reasons for washing the feet of My apostles before the Last Supper. "In the first place I would teach souls how pure they must be to receive Me in Holy Communion. "I also wished to remind those who would have the misfortune to sin that they can always recover their innocence through the Sacrament of Penance. "And I washed the feet of My apostles with My own hands, so that those who have consecrated themselves to apostolic work may follow My example, and treat sinners with humility and gentleness, as also all others that are entrusted to their care.

"I girded Myself with a white linen cloth to remind them that apostles need to be girded with abnegation and mortification, if they hope to exert any real influence on souls. . . . "I wished also to teach them that mutual charity which is ever ready to excuse the faults of others, to conceal them and extenuate them, and never to reveal them.

"The hour of Redemption was at hand. My Heart could no longer restrain its love for mankind nor bear the thought of leaving them orphans.

"So, to prove My tender love for them and in order to remain always with them till time has ceased to be, I resolved to become their food, their support, their life, their all. Could I but make known to all souls the loving sentiments with which My Heart overflowed at My Last Supper, when I instituted the Sacrament of the Holy Eucharist!

"My glance ranged across the ages, and I saw the multitudes who would receive My Body and Blood, and all the good It would effect . . . How many souls who had been enfeebled by sin and the violence of passion would come back to their allegiance and recover their spiritual energy by partaking of this Bread of the strong!

Words of Our Lord to Sr. Josefa Menendez
The Way of Divine Love

Beloved sons, in these present times the darkness has alas obscured even the tabernacle; around it there is so much emptiness, so much indifference, so much negligence. Each day, doubts, denials and sacrileges increase. The Eucharistic Heart of Jesus is wounded anew by his own, in his own house, in the very place where He has taken up his divine dwelling in your midst.

Become again perfect adorers and fervent ministers of Jesus in the Eucharist who, through you, makes himself again present, immolates himself anew and gives himself to souls. Bring everyone to Jesus in the Eucharist: by adoration, by communion and by a greater love.

Help everyone to approach the Eucharistic Jesus in a worthy manner, by cultivating in the faithful an awareness of sin, by inviting them to present themselves for the sacrament of Holy Communion in the state of grace, by educating them in the practice of frequent confession, which becomes necessary before receiving the Eucharist for those who are in mortal sin.

Beloved sons, build a dam to hold back the flood of sacrileges. Never before as in these present times have so many communions been made in such an unworthy manner.

The church is deeply wounded by the multiplication of sacrilegious communions! The time has come when your heavenly Mother says: enough!

I myself will fill up the great void about my Son Jesus, present in the Eucharist. I will form a barrier of love about his divine presence. I myself will do this through you, beloved sons, whom I wish to set up as a guard of love round about all the tabernacles of the earth."

Words of Our Lady to Father Gobbi
Our Lady Speaks to Her Beloved Priests
Fr. Don Stefano Gobbi

I celebrated a healing Mass for the people of Naga in the chapel of the Carmelite Monastery on a Saturday morning. I did not know the condition of any of the people at the Mass as no one had asked me to pray for any special intention. I stressed the importance of forgiveness, led them in *The Forgiveness Prayer*, and gave everyone general absolution. During the homily I was led to tell the people to look up during the elevation of the Body and Blood of Christ. "As you are looking at the Lord Jesus and adoring Him in faith," I said, "pray for healing. Especially if you pray for others," I added, "you will be healed."

One woman, Nena Bichara, took my words as gospel truth. She had been suffering from a goiter for three years. The doctors could do nothing about it except to recommend surgery that, of course, she did not want to undergo. During the elevation of the Body of Christ she prayed for different people. Then she added, "and also, Lord, do not forget my goiter." At once she felt a power hit her. She knew instantly that she was healed. She nudged her son next to her and said, "I am healed." He answered, "Be quiet, mommy. People will think you are crazy." After the Mass she called her doctor and insisted on an examination. He told her to come next week as it was already Saturday afternoon, but, like the persistent widow in the gospel, she got her way. The doctor could find no trace of the goiter! Three months later in Manila she went to another doctor who did not know her case. She asked for a complete examination and asked the doctor to be sure to check for goiters. The doctor told her, "You do not have any sign of a goiter. You have never had one." Praise God!

Fr. Robert DeGrandis, SSJ
Healing through the Mass

Feast of St. John Chrysostom
c. 347-407

Born around 350 and dying in exile from his See, Constantinople, in 407, John Chrysostom, contemporary of Ambrose and Augustine, is the great figure of the Eastern Church in the fourth century. His doctrine on the Eucharist was marked by its very realistic references to the Presence of Christ in the Sacrament and to his many references to the sacrificial nature of the Lord's Supper. His words on the theme are abundant. Typical of them are the following from his *Homily 82 on the Gospel of Matthew*, where he comments on the institution of the Eucharist as found in Matthew 26.

Let us therefore everywhere be attentive to God. Let us not contradict him although what he says appears to be contrary to our reasoning and understanding. Thus we carry out in the Mysteries not only what appears to our senses but what his words tell us. For his word is not able to deceive; our senses are easily deceived. Because the Word says, "This is my Body," let us be attentive, let us believe, let us look upon him with the eyes of the spirit. For Christ did not give us something sensible; even in the sensible things, all is spiritual. . . . How many there are who still say, "I want to see his shape, his image [Gk. *ton tupon*], his clothing, his sandals." Behold, you do see him, you touch him, you eat him!. . . .

Therefore let everyone be vigilant. No small punishment hangs over him who communicates unworthily. Think of how angry you become against the traitor and against those who crucified Christ. And so beware lest you yourself be guilty of the Body and Blood of Christ.

Rev. James T. O'Connor
The Hidden Manna, A Theology of the Eucharist

The great personal devotion of the Cure himself was his devotion to Jesus in the Blessed Sacrament. He knew that love for the Blessed Sacrament was the most powerful means of renewing the heart of a parish. He inspired his people, mostly by personal example, often to make visits. The school teacher, Mr. Pertinand, testified, "I cannot recollect a single occasion when, on entering the church, I did not find someone or other in adoration." Such was the devotion to the Blessed Sacrament by 1825. Even some men left their farm tools leaning against the wall of the church while they made a visit. One of the men, Mr. Chaffangeon—a dear old man who did not know many prayers—told the Cure one day, "I look at the good God, and He looks at me." His was a simple faith in the Blessed Sacrament like the simple faith of an adoring angel. Perhaps fifty women and maybe a dozen men attended daily Mass. Some families tried to have a representative at Holy Mass each day. Holy Communion, especially frequent Holy Communion, was encouraged in many inventive ways: the people were urged to receive on anniversaries, on the occasion of a Baptism, or a marriage, or on any big feast or holiday.

The climax of the Cure's ardent love for the Eucharist came on Corpus Christi . . .

He had already encouraged as many homes as possible to build altars of repose so that the parish would be blessed by a multiplicity of Benedictions. There were altar boys, flower girls, and a huge procession of all the people . . . Never did he weary of carrying the heavy monstrance. "Why should I be tired?" he questioned a sympathizer. "He whom I carried likewise carried me." The only joy that could approach that of Corpus Christi was the joy of Holy Thursday, when he used to remain all night on his knees in silent adoration.

Fr. Bartholomew O'Brien
The Cure of Ars

Sometimes I think that those who have never been deprived of an opportunity to say or hear Mass do not really appreciate what a treasure the Mass is. I know, in any event, what it came to mean to me and the other priests I met in the Soviet Union; I know the sacrifices we made and the risks we ran in order just to have a chance to say or hear Mass. When we were constantly hungry in the camps, when the food we got each day was just barely enough to keep us going, I have seen priests pass up breakfast and work at hard labor on an empty stomach until noon in order to keep the Eucharistic fast, because the noon break at the work site was the time we could best get together for a hidden Mass. I did that often myself. And sometimes, when the guards were observing us too closely and we couldn't risk saying Mass at the work site, the crusts of bread I had put in my pocket at breakfast remained there uneaten until I could get back to camp and say Mass at night. Or again, during the long arctic summer, when the work days were the longest and our hours of sleep were at a minimum, I have seen priests and prisoners deprive their bodies of needed sleep in order to get up before the rising bell for a secret Mass in a quiet barracks, while everyone else clung to those precious extra moments of sleep. In some ways, we led a catacomb existence with our Masses. We would be severely punished if we were discovered saying Mass, and there were always informers. But the Mass to us was always worth the danger and the sacrifice; we treasured it, we looked forward to it, we would do almost anything in order to say or attend a Mass.

Walter J. Ciszek, SJ
He Leadeth Me

W hen Cyprian (c. 200-258), a pagan rhetorician, was converted to Christianity in 248, who would have thought that within the compass of a decade he would have left so significant a mark on the life not only of the church in Africa but also on that of all subsequent centuries of the Christian Church? For within this short span, which comprised his pastoral ministry as a priest and bishop and, indeed, almost the entire extent of Cyprian's Christian life, his teaching became recognized as a compellingly fascinating witness to and powerful influence on the Universal Church regarding its mission to be a sacrament of unity. His life and teaching offer an inspiring lesson about the spirituality of the Eucharist as the unique sacrifice capable of transforming our personal existence into an offering or gift for others. This teaching is particularly evident in his famous Epistle 63—the earliest work exclusively devoted to the Eucharist. This letter tackles the division of the African Church brought about by the "Aquarian" controversy, which debated the use of water alone or wine mixed with water for the eucharistic celebration. Cyprian insisted, using the most persuasive argument of all, on fidelity to what Christ did, taught, and commanded. Herein is found the Church's unity. More compelling still was his fidelity in deed to Christ, by offering the supreme witness of pouring out his life-blood in martyrdom in imitation of the supreme sacrifice of Christ which he celebrated in the Eucharist. Thus, in this age of martyrs his life itself demonstrated Tertullian's renowned saying: "As frequently as we are bled by you, the more we increase in number; the blood of Christian martyrs waters the seed of faith." (Apology, 50)

Michael L. Gaudoin-Parker
The Real Presence through the Ages

When Ramirus, King of Spain, had been fighting a long time against the Saracens, he retired with his soldiers to a mountain to implore the assistance of Almighty God. While he was at prayer, St. James the Apostle appeared to him and commanded him to make all his soldiers go to Confession and Communion the day following and then to lead them out against their enemies. After all had been done that the Saint commanded, they again had an engagement with the Saracens and gained a complete and brilliant victory.

Fr. Michael Muller, CSSR
The Blessed Eucharist, Our Greatest Treasure

September 18

The efficacy of his prayers is strikingly shown in the conversion to the Catholic faith of a Lutheran prince, John Frederick, Duke of Brunswick. While visiting the principal courts of Europe, in the year 1649, the prince, then twenty-five years of age, came from Rome to Assisi expressly to see Joseph, of whose fame he had heard in Germany. On his arrival at the monastery, he (along with two of his retainers) was given lodging . . . and was led next morning to the door of the chapel, where the servant of God was saying Mass. The saint, who was not informed of their presence, was made aware of it when about to break the sacred host, which he found so hard, that, in spite of all his efforts, he could not break it, but had to replace it on the paten. Fixing his eyes upon the host, he wept and with a loud cry rose in kneeling posture about five paces into the air. With another cry he returned after some time to the altar and broke the sacred host, though with great effort. At the instance of the Duke, the Father Superior asked him why he had wept, and he replied: "My dear compatriot, the persons, whom you sent to my Mass this morning, have a hard heart; for they do not believe all that Holy Mother Church teaches, and therefore the Lamb of God was hardened in my hands so that I could not break the sacred host." The Duke, astonished at this occurrence, deferred his departure in order to consult with the servant of God. This he did after dinner, remaining with the saint till Compline . . . The following year he came to Assisi and, as he had promised, knelt before the Blessed Sacrament, and in the presence of Cardinals Facchinetti and Rapaccioli, made profession of faith in the hands of Father Joseph.

Fr. Angelo Pastrovicchi, OFM CONV.
Saint Joseph of Copertino

It is to be noted that there is no such thing as Communion without a sacrifice. Just as we cannot have the natural communion of eating, unless vegetables have been torn up from their roots and subjected to fire, and animals have been subjected to the knife and slain, and then submitted to purgation, so neither can we have Communion with Christ unless there is first a death. That is why the Mass is not just a Communion service; it is a sacrifice which ends in communion. Communion is the consequence of Calvary; we live by what we slay. Our bodies live by the slaying of the beasts of the field and the plants of the garden; we draw life from their crucifixion; we slay them not to destroy but to have life more abundantly. We immolate them for the sake of communion.

By a beautiful paradox of Divine love, God makes His Cross the very means of our salvation and our life. We have slain Him; we have nailed Him there and crucified Him; but the Love in His eternal Heart could not be extinguished. He *willed* to give us the very life we slew; to give us the very Food we destroyed; to nourish us with the very Bread we buried, and the very Blood we poured forth. He made our very crime into a happy fault; He turned a Crucifixion into a Redemption; a Consecration into a Communion; a death into Life Everlasting.

Bishop Fulton Sheen
This Is the Mass

On another occasion, when she was about to communicate and perceived that many were abstaining from it for different reasons, she rejoiced in spirit and being touched to the heart, said to God: "I give Thee thanks, my most loving Love and my God, that Thou hast placed me in this happy state, in which neither my relations nor any earthly consideration can prevent me from approaching Thy banquet of delights." To which the Lord replied, with His usual sweetness: "Since you have declared that there is nothing which can separate you from Me, know also that there is nothing in heaven or earth, neither judgment nor justice, which can hinder me from doing all the good for you which My Divine Heart desires."

On another occasion, as Gertrude approached Holy Communion and desired ardently that the Lord would prepare her worthily, this sweet and loving Lord consoled her by these tender words: "I will clothe Myself with your person in order that I may be able to extend My Hand to do good to sinners without being wounded by the thorns which surround them. And I will also clothe you with Myself in order that all those whom you remember before Me and even those who are naturally like you, may be raised to this high dignity, that I may do good to them according to My royal munificence."

Monsignor William J. Doheny, csc
The Revelations of Saint Gertrude

His physical life was a mystery. No man could have survived as long as he did, without eating, without taking care of himself, losing a lot of blood every day, and exhausting himself in hard work for many, many years.

It was the eucharistic Bread, on which he fed every day, which gave him health and vigor.

Holy communion was life for Padre Pio, a fusion of hearts, a source of joy and happiness.

The 21st of March, 1912, he wrote to Padre Agostino of San Marco in Lamis: "Only God knows what sweetness I experienced yesterday, the feast of St. Joseph especially after Mass, so much so that I still feel it. My mouth tasted all the sweetness of the immaculate Flesh of the Son of God. How happy Jesus makes me! How sweet is his spirit! But I am confused and can do nothing but weep and repeat: Jesus, my food!" (Letters I, 299)

Padre Alberto D'Apolito
Padre Pio of Pietrelcina

The Lord's Supper, to which the Virgin leads us in order that we may partake of her joy, is renewed every morning. The table is always set, the Bread always offered. The Christian makes his way to eternity from Communion to Communion. At each stage in the journey, Christ is waiting for him in order that he may renew his strength and take heart again.

But let us take care not to allow too much time to elapse between these stages. Long before the grace of a Communion has grown weak in us, long before the silence and peace which emanate from a Communion have been dispelled by nature and the world, we must make our way into the radiant sphere of another Communion. Let there be no opportunity between two Communions for a period of darkness in which we would run the risk of falling into snares. We have nothing to fear if Christ marks our life. Hardly have we had time to lose Him when already we have found Him again.

A contemporary pagan poet speaks of this God with whom no excess is forbidden. How difficult it is to abuse Communion! The only requisite to sit down at that table is the *nuptial garment*, that is to say, the state of grace and love.

Francois Mauriac
Holy Thursday, An Intimate Remembrance

In celebrating the Eucharist, we follow the command of Christ to "do this in *memory*" of him (Luke 22:19), and the way in which we *memorialize* this experience is by "proclaiming the *death* of the Lord until he comes" (I Cor. 11:26).

It is precisely in this *memorialization* of Christ's death that we acknowledge that he has entered into the abode of the dead: "He descended into hell" (Hades—abode of the dead). By his own death he has a special access to the dead to draw them to himself and to lead them to the fullness of the *life* of grace and holiness (I Pet. 3:19 and 4:6).

In participating in the Eucharist we should pray that Jesus who said he has come to give us life more abundantly (John 10:10) may come to the dead, especially our dead family members to give them the *abundance* of eternal life.

In receiving Communion it is helpful sometimes to mention particular names of deceased persons that come to mind so as to receive communion on behalf of that person who does not have access to the abundant life of grace in the Eucharist as we do. In particular there may be a need to pray for this "abundance of life" for aborted babies whose lives have been cut short and who have been rejected from the human race by the aggressive crime of abortion and thus prevented from growing up within the family and participating in the societal benefits of the family tree.

Healing means giving a fuller, richer degree of life. That is precisely what the healing of the family tree is designed to do, for each family member, whether living or dead.

John H. Hampsch, CMF
Healing Your Family Tree

Appearing to St. Margaret Mary Jesus solemnly declares the unspeakable love of his heart, and says, "My divine heart is so passionately in love with men, and with you in particular, that not being able to contain in itself any longer the flames of its ardent charity, it must pour them out through you . . . Behold this heart which has loved men so much, which has spared nothing, going so far as to exhaust itself and consume itself in order to show them its love . . . " Christ is thinking, no doubt, of the multiple proofs, the incomparable signs of his love that he has given us; but very obviously he is thinking as the context shows, of the Eucharist which he calls his sacrament of love. This is evident especially in the last great apparition, for no sooner had the good Master expressed the immensity and intensity of his love, than he complains of the ingratitude he meets with in the Blessed Sacrament of the altar.

In fact, most of the poignant complaints made by our Lord refer to the holy Eucharist. "And instead of thanks, all I get from most men is ingratitude, scorn, irreverence, sacrilege and coldness that they show me in this sacrament of love. What is still harder to endure is that this comes so often from hearts consecrated to me."

"I thirst, I so ardently thirst to be loved by men in the most Blessed Sacrament, that this thirst devours me; and yet I find no one who tries to slake my thirst by giving me some little return of love for love."

Joseph Dargaud
The Eucharist in the Life of St. Margaret Mary

The thought of the presence of God and the spirit of worship will in all my actions have as their immediate object Jesus, God and man, really present in the most holy Eucharist. The spirit of sacrifice, of humiliation, of scorn for self in the eyes of men, will be illuminated, supported and strengthened by the constant thought of Jesus, humiliated and despised in the Blessed Sacrament.

It will be sweet to abase myself and be ashamed, when I am one with the divine Heart, so ill-treated by men; and when the world treats me with indifference and scorn, my greatest joy will be to seek and find comfort only in that Heart which is the source of all consolations.

I impress upon my mind and will two special practices for daily observation: holy communion and the evening visit, besides the continual invocations with which, like St. Aloysius, I shall make a habit of piercing the Heart of the Word. I am determined to give myself no peace until I can truly say I am absorbed into the Heart of Jesus.

Pope John XXIII
Journal of a Soul

The Apostles proclaimed that they were giving the Body and Blood of the Savior at His express command . . . St. Paul wrote (eight years after St. Matthew wrote his Gospel) a letter to the Christian converts at Corinth, 1 Cor 10:16, "The chalice of benediction, which we bless, is it not the communion of the blood of Christ? And the bread, which we break, is it not the partaking of the body of the Lord?" 1 Cor 11:23-29. "For I have received of the Lord that which also I delivered unto you, that the Lord Jesus, the same night in which he was betrayed, took bread, and giving thanks, broke, and said: Take ye, and eat: this is my body, which shall be delivered for you: this do ye, as often as you shall drink, for the commemoration of me. For as often as you shall eat this bread, and drink the chalice, you shall show the death of the Lord, until He come. Therefore whosoever shall eat this bread, or drink the chalice of the Lord unworthily, **shall be guilty of the body and of the blood of the Lord** . . . For he that eateth and drinketh unworthily, eateth and drinketh judgment to himself, **not discerning the body of the Lord**." Here then is fully stated the doctrine of the Apostles and the faith of the Infant Church in the Real Presence of Christ in the Holy Eucharist. Notice the words **Guilty of the Body and of the Blood**—how could a person **be guilty**, if he had merely eaten a little bread and drunk a little wine, as a picture or representation or reminder of the Last Supper? No one is **guilty** of homicide if he merely does violence to the picture or statue of a man without touching the man in person. St. Paul's words are **meaningless** without the dogma of the Real Presence.

Fr. Charles M. Carty and Rev. Dr. L. Rumble, MSC
Q. A. Eucharist, Quizzes to a Street Preacher

Y ou know that you had gone to the church at dawn to hear Mass, and that before that the devil had been tormenting you. You went to stand at the altar of the crucifix, though the priest had come out to Mary's altar. You stood there considering your sinfulness, fearing that you might have offended me while the devil had been troubling you. And you were considering also how great was my charity that I should have made you worthy to hear Mass at all, since you considered yourself unworthy even to enter my temple. When the celebrant reached the consecration you looked up toward him. And at the words of consecration I revealed myself to you. You saw a ray of light coming from my breast, like the ray that comes forth from the sun's circle yet never leaves it. Within this light came a dove, and dove and light were as one and hovered over the host by the power of the words of consecration the celebrant was saying. Your bodily eyes could not endure the light, and only your spiritual vision remained, but there you saw and tasted the depths of the Trinity, wholly God, wholly human, hidden and veiled under that whiteness. Neither the light nor the presence of the Word, whom in spirit you saw in this whiteness, took away the whiteness of the bread. Nor did the one stand in the way of the other. I did not block your sight either of me, God and human, in that bread, or of the bread itself. Neither the whiteness nor the feel nor the taste was taken away from the bread.

Words of God the Father
Catherine of Siena, The Dialogue

The Spirit directed Christ throughout his life. Conceived by the Holy Spirit, Jesus was a "beloved Son" in whom the Father was "well pleased." At Jesus' baptism, the Spirit anointed him, "ordained" him for his redemptive mission. "The Spirit of the Lord is upon me; he has sent me to bring good news to the poor, to proclaim liberty to captives, sight to the blind, and release to prisoners." Christ, "full of the Spirit," reversed the work of Satan by his miracles—casting out devils, healing the sick, raising the dead. Moreover, Christ, "through the eternal Spirit, offered himself unblemished to God" (Heb 9). Finally, the Spirit, "the holy breath of God," brought Jesus through death, alive and indeed glorified.

We approach Jesus in the Eucharist as the bringer of the Holy Spirit. We want the Spirit who abided and worked in Jesus to abide and work in us. Salvation is in the possession of the Holy Spirit.

In a sense, Scripture is the story of the power of the Holy Spirit and what the Spirit did in Jesus in human history. All that is in the church is for the sending of the Holy Spirit. We have no doubt that the power of the Spirit that changes bread and wine into the body and blood of Christ can transform us into the body of Christ, "beloved sons and daughters" in whom God is well pleased.

In the Eucharist the divine Christ descends upon the altar and into our hearts. Jesus, by his gift of the Spirit in the Eucharist, raises us up to be children of God. In Communion Christ enters our heart to transform us, to make us "beautiful."

In truth, "the Eucharist is the sacrament of sacraments, the noblest of them all . . . for it contains the whole mystery of salvation." (Thomas Aquinas).

Fr. Thomas McKeon, sss
Emmanuel Magazine, April 1994

Feast of Archangels Michael, Gabriel and Raphael

As the Feast of St. Michael approached, St. Gertrude prepared herself for Holy Communion by meditating on the
care which the angels had of her, by the Divine command, notwithstanding her unworthiness; and as she desired to render some
return to them, she offered in their honor the life-giving Body
and Blood of Jesus in the Most Holy Sacrament, saying: "I offer Thee this most august Sacrament, O most loving Lord, for
Thy eternal glory, in honor of the princes of Thy kingdom, and
for the increase of their felicity and beatitude. Then our Lord
drew this oblation to Himself in an effable manner, thereby caus-
ing the greatest joy to these angel spirits, who appeared even as
if they had never before experienced such blessedness and
superabounded in delights. Then each of the choirs of angels,
according to their rank, inclined respectfully before St. Gertrude,
saying: "Thou hast indeed honored us by this oblation, and we
will therefore guard thee with special care;" the guardian angels adding: "We will guard thee night and day with ineffable
joy, and will prepare thee for thy Spouse with the utmost vigilance."

Fr. William J. Doheny, CSC
The Revelations of Saint Gertrude

With first Communion, Zoe put aside the things of a child in piety and devotion. From this time on, she went after her spiritual advancement in dead earnest, with order and system. In spite of the mountain of duties piled upon her young shoulders, she set aside certain fixed times for prayer. The most important of these times was the early morning, and her prayer then the greatest of all, the holy Sacrifice of the Mass.

Zoe began to attend Mass daily and to receive Holy Communion frequently. Given the circumstances, these were acts of devotion approaching the heroic. There was no daily Mass in Fain; there was not always Sunday Mass. The only priest in the district said his daily Mass in the chapel of the Hospital de Saint Sauveur in Moutiers-Saint Jean. It was not a question, therefore, of Zoe's rolling out of bed and tumbling into church. The hospital was a good, brisk half-hour's walk from Fain, and the Sisters' Mass was at six o'clock. Daily Mass for this young girl just entering her teens meant an early rising—an earlier rising even than farm life called for, because she had chores to do before she left—and a long walk in all kinds of weather and, half the year, in the dark. The youngster was determined to go, however, and she never faltered. In a sense she had to go, for she went to a daily rendezvous with God, who was her whole life. On certain mornings, frequent but not frequent enough to slake her ardor, she enjoyed complete union with her Beloved in Holy Communion. She could not have this happiness every day, for daily Communion would not be permitted the faithful for a hundred years yet.

Father Joseph I. Dirvin, CM
Saint Catherine Laboure of the Miraculous Medal

October 1

Such tremendous graces had to bear fruit and it was abundant. To be good became natural and pleasant for us. At first my face often betrayed the struggle I was having, but gradually spontaneous self-sacrifice came easily. Jesus said: "If ever a man is rich, gifts will be made to him, and his riches will abound." For every grace I made good use of, He gave me many more. He gave Himself to me in Holy Communion far oftener than I should have dared to hope. I had made it a rule to go very faithfully to every Communion allowed me by my confessor, but never to ask him to allow me more. In those days I hadn't the daring I have now, or I should have behaved quite differently, for I'm absolutely certain that people must tell their confessors of the longing they have to receive God. For He does not come down from heaven every day to lie in a golden ciborium: He comes to find another heaven which is infinitely dearer to Him—the heaven of our souls, created in His image, the living temples of the adorable Trinity!

St. Therese of Lisieux
The Story of a Soul

October 2

Feast of the Holy Guardian Angels

It was during the Mass at 6:30 in the morning, at the moment of Consecration. A dazzling light suddenly shone forth . . . I had the feeling that this adorable splendor was that of the presence of Our Lord Jesus Christ in the Eucharist. Struck to the heart I could only repeat, 'My Lord and My God!'

At the same moment there appeared the outline of angels in prayer before the shining Host. They were kneeling all around the altar in a semi-circle, their backs toward us. There were eight of them . . . They did not have wings, but their bodies were enveloped in sort of a mysterious luminescence which clearly distinguished them from humans.

Amazed, not believing my eyes, I opened and closed them, rubbed them, but nothing changed. All eight were there to adore the Most Blessed Sacrament in an attitude of great devotion. . .

At the moment of Communion, my guardian angel approached me to invite me to advance to the altar. At that moment, I clearly distinguished the guardian angels of each member of the community close to their left shoulders, and of the height a little smaller than each. Like my guardian angel they gave truly the impression of guiding and watching over them with sweetness and affection. This scene in itself opened my eyes to the profound meaning of the guardian angel, better than any theological explanation, even the most detailed. After dinner I gave a complete account of this vision to the Bishop . . . Had they not chosen the Feast of the Guardian Angels to show the example of adoration and to reveal their readiness to lead us to the Lord? (Sister Agnes Sasagawa)

John M. Haffert
Akita, The Tears and Message of Mary

As I was preparing this booklet, I began to see how this same word can apply to the faith crisis people experience concerning the Eucharist. Each and every person must ponder this word concerning Eucharist: **EITHER JESUS IS TRULY PRESENT OR HE IS NOT. IF HE IS PRESENT, THEN HE REALLY IS.** Then in faith affirm this word; *I believe that Jesus is really present in the Eucharist.* In fact this helped my faith in the Eucharist to grow. It is really a simple matter; we need to ask God to increase our faith. Deeper faith will take care of the lukewarmness and unbelief. We need to ponder the truth of Jesus' presence in the Eucharist and affirm it in our lives. It's very simple: Jesus is truly present in the Eucharist or He is not; **I BELIEVE THAT HE IS.**

Think about what a gift it is to know Jesus is truly present in the Eucharist. Do you know what this means? It means Jesus, who sits at the right hand of the Father is present in this wafer of bread. He comes to us daily to nourish us, to heal us, to sustain us. This is incredible! This is awesome! The almighty savior humbles himself to come to us under the appearance of bread and wine at each and every Eucharist. What a precious gift.

Fr. Sam Tiesi, TOR
Remain with Me

Feast of St. Francis of Assisi
1181-1226

Francis considered it an almost unpardonable sin to miss Mass voluntarily; he received Holy Communion very often "and with such devotion that he enkindled the souls of others . . . he was as it were spiritually inebriated, and frequently wrapt in ecstasy." One day a rather worldly friend asked him: "Father what do you do during those long hours before the Blessed Sacrament?" "My son in return I ask you what does the poor man do at the rich man's door, the sick man in presence of his physician, the thirsty man at a limpid stream? What they do, I do before the Eucharistic God. I pray. I adore. I love."

If he were prevented from being present at Mass, he would have the Gospel of the day read to him; in his own words: "If I cannot assist at Mass I adore the Body of Christ in meditation, and with the eyes of the soul, just as if I were present during the Mass."

Nesta de Robeck
The Life of St. Francis of Assisi

Dear Father Martin Lucia,
Perpetual Adoration with exposition needs a great push. People ask me: "What will convert America and save the world?" My answer is prayer.

What we need is for every Parish to come before Jesus in the Blessed Sacrament in holy hours of prayer.

I pray that the Community Missionaries of the Blessed Sacrament dedicated to this purpose of spreading perpetual adoration will flourish . . .

God bless you,
Mother Teresa, MC
Calcutta, August 12th, 1993

"When she was sacristan, she occupied for a time a place in choir from which she could not see the altar, having given hers up to a Sister who was tormented with scruples when she heard Mass without enjoying that consolation. One day as she was watching to ring the bell for the Elevation, she saw the Infant Jesus above the chalice—O how beautiful! She thought herself in heaven. She was about to leap through the grate to get at the Child when suddenly recollecting herself, she exclaimed: 'My God! what am I going to do!'—She succeeded in restraining herself, but forgot to sound the bell, a frequent omission of hers which drew upon her many a reprimand."

Clara Soentgen says: "When Sister Emmerich received Holy Communion her bodily strength increased. She loved, above all, to communicate on Thursday in honor of the Blessed Sacrament; but, as this gave rise to remark, she obtained permission from her confessor to communicate in secret. Sometimes she went to receive a little after midnight, sometimes at three or four o'clock in the morning, her ardent desire rendering it impossible for her to wait longer.

"Once I asked her why she wore her best habit on Thursdays, and she answered that it was in honor of the Blessed Sacrament. She rarely made use of a book before or after Communion."

Very Rev. K. E. Schmoger, CSSR
Life of Anne Catherine Emmerich

October 7

Feast of Our Lady of the Rosary

I had sought and obtained permission from my superior and spiritual director to make a Holy Hour from 11 PM until midnight every Thursday and Friday night. While I was alone one night, I knelt near the altar rail in the middle of the Chapel, and then prostrate, I prayed the Angel's prayers. (Jacinta and Francisco were in heaven ten years at this date.) Feeling tired, I then stood up and continued to say the prayers with my arms in the form of the Cross. The only light was that of the sanctuary lamp. Suddenly, the whole chapel was illuminated by a supernatural light, and above the altar appeared a cross of light reaching to the ceiling. In a brighter light on the upper part of the cross, could be seen the face of a man and his body as far as the waist. Upon his breast was a dove of light. Nailed to the cross was the body of another man. A little below the waist, I could see a chalice and a large host suspended in the air, on which drops of blood were falling from the face of Jesus Crucified and from the wound in His side. These drops ran down on the Host and fell in the Chalice. Beneath the right arm of the cross was Our Lady and in her hand was her Immaculate Heart. It was Our Lady of Fatima with her Immaculate Heart in her left hand, without sword or roses, but with a crown of thorns and flames, the Rosary in her right hand. Under the left arm of the Cross, were large letters, as if the crystal clear water ran down upon the altar forming the words: "Grace and Mercy." I understood that it was the Mystery of the Most Holy Trinity which was shown to me, and I received light about this mystery which I am not permitted to reveal.

Sr. Lucy of Fatima
Padre Pio Gazette
Compiled by Joe Peterson

Although the precise subject of this book is not the sacrifice of the Mass, it is impossible not to speak of the Mass when we speak of the Eucharist as Sacrament. The Sacrament and Sacrifice of the Eucharist are inseparable. The Real Presence of Christ in the Host is the necessary and immediate consequence of transubstantiation. But the purpose of transubstantiation is first of all to make Christ present on the altar in a state of sacrifice or immolation, by the separate consecration of the two species of Bread and Wine. At the same time the sacrifice cannot be completed without these consecrated elements being received in communion at least by the celebrating priest. Finally, the consecrated Host is kept in reserve in the tabernacle in order that the sick and others who cannot receive at the time of Mass may be able to receive the Body of Our Lord at some other time and thus have their share in the sacrifice of Christ. What we adore in our visits to the Blessed Sacrament is therefore Jesus Christ Himself, permanently present in the Host which was consecrated in the Holy Sacrifice and which will eventually be received in Communion.

Thomas Merton
The Living Bread

This is crucial: as long as we pray only when and how we want to, our life of prayer is bound to be unreal. It will run in fits and starts. The slightest upset—even a toothache—will be enough to destroy the whole edifice of our prayer-life.

"You must strip your prayers," the novice-master told me. You must simplify, deintellectualise. Put yourself in front of Jesus as a poor man: not with any big ideas, but with living faith. Remain motionless in an act of love before the Father. Don't try to reach God with your understanding; that is impossible. Reach him in love; that is possible.

The struggle is not easy, because nature will try to get back her own, get her dose of enjoyment; but union with Christ Crucified is something quite different.

After some hours—or some days—of this exercise, the body relaxes. As the will refuses to let it have its own way it gives up the struggle. It becomes passive. The senses go to sleep. Or rather, as St. John of the Cross says, the night of senses is beginning. Then prayer becomes something serious, even if it is painful and dry. So serious that one can no longer do without it. The soul begins to share the redemptive work of Jesus.

Kneeling down on the sand before the simple monstrance which contained Jesus, I used to think of the evils of the world: hate, violence, depravity, impurity, egoism, betrayal, idolatry. Around me the cave had become as large as the world, and inwardly I contemplated Jesus oppressed under the weight of so much wickedness.

Is not the Host in its own form like bread crushed, pounded, baked? And does it not contain the Man of Sorrows, Christ the Victim, the Lamb slain for our sins?

Carlo Carretto
Letters from the Desert

Feast of St. Francis Borgia
1510-1572

S t. Francis Borgia who joined the Jesuit order after the death of his wife, experienced such an ecstatic union of his soul with the Redeemer that frequently he would begin Mass in the morning and conclude it at Vespers (the evening hour of the Divine Office). Because of the length of his Masses, he seldom offered Mass in public.

Joan Carroll Cruz
Eucharistic Miracles

At other times, Father Victor and I would say Mass sitting on the edge of our beds across from one another. We pretended to be reading or talking softly as we said the Mass prayers. We could not use the chalice in the barracks, so our cup became a common drinking glass and our host a piece of leavened bread. If people stopped to chat, we tried to break off conversation as pleasantly and as quickly as we could and so recapture our recollection and continue our secret Eucharist. I worked outside with the lumber gangs, but Father Victor worked as an accountant in the company offices, so he always kept the Blessed Sacrament wrapped in a purificator inside his wallet in the pocket of his coat. That way, we could at least receive Communion each day if Mass became impossible. Later on, after we had made friends with the scrubwoman who took care of the barracks, we would sometimes leave the Blessed Sacrament carefully hidden inside a bundle of clothes in her little private office and living room. She was a Catholic, as we came to know, and she helped us in many ways. It was one of her greatest joys to have the Blessed Sacrament in her room and to know that the Lord she worshiped dwelt under her roof.

Walter J. Ciszek, sj
He Leadeth Me

Just suppose that it was announced that Jesus would be at your parish church next Sunday at 9:30 a.m.! People would be coming from all over the country, clamoring to see Jesus or to get a glimpse of Him. People would come days beforehand and find a place to stay and begin reserving seats in the church. There would be so much commotion that you wouldn't be able to get near your church. Police, television crews, and news media would be everywhere! All to see Jesus. Well, He **IS** there **EVERY SUNDAY**, and in many churches around the world, **EVERY DAY!** How blinded we have become to this reality! How blind we are to SEEING Jesus in the consecrated Host and in the Precious Blood! Are our eyes affixed on Jesus Truly Present in Holy Eucharist? Do we receive Him in Body and Blood with reverence and awe? Do we really want to be in union with God? Do we wish to walk in the Light which is Jesus Christ?

Ann Ross Fitch and Fr. Robert DeGrandis, ssj

Walking in the Light

Just as in the Old Testament the promises were kept in the Ark of the Covenant, and treated with awe and reverence, so in the New Testament the womb of the Blessed Virgin would be the ark of the New Covenant and the first tabernacle of the Most High. That presence of the Messiah in his sacred humanity would continue in the Church, eventually in the tabernacle. That is why Pope John Paul II in the same Eucharistic Congress referred to the Blessed Sacrament as "the beating heart of the Church," as indeed Pope Paul VI had done in his "Credo of the People of God" when referring to the tabernacle as "the living heart of the Church."

This means that the life of Jesus is not just a memory of our Saviour we read about in the Gospels, so that we might say sadly, "If only I had lived then!" As God, the second Person of the Blessed Trinity, he is, of course, everywhere, from the uttermost star of the universe to the depths of the sea, but as God made Man, in his sacred humanity, he is present in the Blessed Sacrament. This means that the very same Jesus who was conceived in the womb of our Blessed Lady, born in the poverty of the manger, who grew up as a young boy "full of grace and truth," who worked in the carpenter's workshop, who preached the gospel to the poor, healed the sick, made the dead to rise again; who suffered and died for us on the cross, who rose again victorious from the dead and ascended in glory and triumph to heaven, is truly present in this mystery of faith and love.

Rev. Edwin Gordon
Homiletic & Pastoral Review
October 1994

Whenever anyone is unavoidably prevented, then so long as he preserves a goodwill and holy desire for Communion, he will not lose the benefits of the Sacrament. For anyone who sincerely desires it may on any day and at any hour make unhindered a Spiritual Communion with Christ to the health of his soul. Nonetheless, on certain Feasts and at certain Seasons he ought to receive the Body of his Redeemer sacramentally with love and reverence, and seek the honour and praise of God before his own consolation. For as often as anyone receives mystic communion and spiritual refreshment, he recalls with devotion the mystery of the Incarnation and Passion of Christ, and is roused anew to love of Him. But he who prepares himself only at the approach of a Festival, or when custom prescribes it, will often be entirely unprepared.

Blessed is the man who, whenever he celebrates the Eucharist or receives Communion, offers himself to Our Lord as a living sacrifice. And when celebrating, be neither too slow nor too hurried, but observe the common usage of those with whom you are living. Be careful not to cause irritation or weariness to others, but observe the customs appointed by the Fathers, and consider the benefit of others before your personal devotion or preference.

Words of Christ
The Imitation of Christ
Thomas à Kempis

Feast of St. Teresa of Jesus
1515-1582

For if what I see is an image it is a living image—not a dead man but the living Christ. And He shows me that He is both Man and God—not as He was in the sepulchre, but as He was when He left it after rising from the dead. Sometimes He comes with such majesty that no one can doubt it is the Lord Himself; this is especially so after Communion, for we know that He is there, since the Faith tells us so. He reveals Himself so completely as the Lord of that inn, the soul, that it feels as though it were wholly dissolved and consumed in Christ. O my Jesus, if one could but describe the majesty with which Thou dost reveal Thyself! How completely art Thou Lord of the whole world, and of the heavens, and of a thousand other worlds, and of countless worlds and heavens that Thou has created! And the majesty with which Thou dost reveal Thyself shows the soul that to be Lord of this is nothing for Thee.

St. Teresa of Avila
The Autobiography of St. Teresa of Avila
E. Allison Peers

October 16

Feast of St. Margaret Mary Alacoque
1647-1690

After encountering various difficulties Margaret Mary entered the convent of the Visitation at Paray-le-Monial in central France in 1671. In the course of eighteen months, beginning in December 1673, she experienced several revelations of the Sacred Heart of Jesus. The purpose of these visions, which took the form of devotions honoring the Sacred Heart, symbol of divine love, consisted essentially in promoting fervent love for the presence of Christ in the Eucharist. The main practices of these devotions included Holy Communion of the First Fridays of each month, Holy Hour of adoration on Thursdays, and institution of the Feast of the Sacred Heart (on the Friday after the octave of Corpus Christi). Despite the encouragement and influence of her confessor, St. Claude de la Colombiere, S.J., these devotions, however, were not officially sanctioned by the Church until seventy-five years after her death. The reason for this divine intervention was to counter the lukewarmness and, particularly, infrequency of Communion, which deprived most of the faithful from access to the consolation of Christ's presence in the Eucharist—an access which the stern and cold teaching of Jansenism played no little part in debarring.

Fr. Michael L. Gaudoin-Parker
The Real Presence through the Ages

Feast of St. Ignatius of Antioch
Disciple of St. John the Evangelist

Of the apostolic men who heard directly from the disciples the truths of faith and transmitted them to us in their writings, we present, in the first place, St. Ignatius the Martyr. He is said to have been one of the fortunate children whom Jesus embraced (Mark 10: 13 ff.), though the Apostles wished to drive them away. It is certain that he was a disciple of the Apostles, and after Evodius succeeded St. Peter in the See of Antioch. Trajan condemned him to be devoured by wild beasts in Rome, where he suffered his most glorious martyrdom 20th December, 108 or 109 of the Christian era.

A guard of ten soldiers escorted him from Antioch to Rome, and he availed of the time to write several letters, which were preserved as precious relics by the faithful, and which fortunately we still possess. In these letters, together with much more that is sacred and wonderful, we possess the most valuable testimonies to the Eucharist. For instance, the Saint, in his very famous letter to the faithful in Rome, declaring his intense desire to die for Jesus Christ, writes: "I care no longer for corruptible food, nor for the pleasures of this life: I desire only the bread of God, the bread of heaven, *which is the flesh of Jesus Christ*, the Son of God, born of the race of David and Abraham; *I desire the drink of God, His blood*, which is love incorruptible and life without end." In this passage the Saint alludes plainly to the Divine words of the great promise: "He that eateth My Flesh and drinketh My Blood hath everlasting life" (John 6: 55).

Cardinal Gaetano De Lai
The Real Presence of Jesus Christ in the Eucharist

On Thursday, when I went to my cell, I saw over me the Sacred Host in great brightness. Then I heard a voice that seemed to be coming from above the Host: "In the Host is your power; it will defend you." After these words, the vision disappeared, but a strange power entered my soul, and a strange light as to what our love for God consists in; namely, in doing His will. (Diary 616)

During this hour of prayer, **Jesus allowed me to enter the Cenacle**, and I was a witness to what happened there. However, I was most deeply moved when, before the Consecration, Jesus raised His eyes to heaven and entered into a mysterious conversation with His Father. **It is only in eternity that we shall really understand that moment.** His eyes were like two flames; His face was radiant, white as snow; His whole personage full of majesty, His soul full of longing. At the moment of Consecration, love rested satiated—the sacrifice fully consummated. Now only the external ceremony of death will be carried out—external destruction; **the essence [of it] is in the Cenacle**. Never in my whole life had I understood this mystery so profoundly as during that hour of adoration. Oh, how ardently I desire that the whole world would come to know this unfathomable mystery! (Diary 684)

Rev. George W. Kosicki, CSB
Tell My Priests,
The Words of Our Lord to Priests About His Mercy
As Revealed to Sr. Faustina Kowalska

Feast of Saint Isaac Jogues
Martyred in 1646

One blessing above all others, Father Jogues desired before he left France. He could not offer the Holy Sacrifice of the Mass canonically. His left thumb had been amputated at the root, and the index finger of that hand was only a stub; the thumb and index finger of the right hand were so shortened and distorted that he could not hold the Sacred Host in the appointed manner. As soon as he reached Paris, in January, he set about seeking a dispensation from the canonical requirements. This dispensation had to be sought from the Pope. Accordingly, he drew up his petition to His Holiness, Pope Urban VIII, instancing the reasons for his mutilated condition and begging for permission, despite that, to offer the Sacrifice of the Mass.

Father Vitelleschi, supported by the French Ambassador to the Papal Court, presented the petition to the Pope. His Holiness inquired with great interest about Father Isaac Jogues, about his missionary endeavors in the New World, about all that he suffered during his captivity among the Iroquois savages. He was deeply moved by the story. "It would be shameful, that a martyr of Christ be not allowed to drink the Blood of Christ." Straightway he granted the petition, and ruled that Father Jogues, despite the mutilation of his canonical fingers, should be permitted to offer the Holy Sacrifice.

The Pope's answer reached Father Jogues in March. It exalted him to Paradise itself. Twenty months had elapsed since he wore the sacred vestments. . . Twenty months since he had pronounced the sacred words of Consecration and lifted the chalice to his lips. Now, once more, he was empowered to ascend as a priest to the altar of his God to offer the Divine Oblation. It seemed to him like his first Mass over again.

Fr. Francis Talbot, SJ
Saint Among Savages
The Life of Isaac Jogues

Covenants, treaties, major contracts are celebrated with exchange of gifts, with banqueting. God, conforming to our nature as He created it, chooses to approach us in accord with our social and business procedures and our psychological makeup. Meeting with Abraham our father in faith, God acted as one head of state approaching another, made a treaty of friendship with him, promising favors beyond Abraham's expectations, asking only that "he keep the way of the Lord by doing righteousness and justice." This covenant God renewed and enriched with Jacob (Israel), then Moses, then David, always with more generous promises of a new and everlasting covenant—the two covenanting parties sealing each treaty with the blood of sacred victims.

Finally God's own Son came and offered a perfect Sacrifice, a pure and holy victim, thereby binding all mankind to Himself in a new and everlasting union or covenant which guarantees forgiveness of sins. It was not just a friendly promise, but a solemn treaty binding under oath; (God's word always has the force of a formal oath). Inaugurating the new Covenant and sealing it with his blood, Jesus declared: "This is my body which will be given up for you. . . .This is my blood, the blood of the new and everlasting covenant. It will be shed for you and for all so that sins maybe forgiven." These are divine words. That we may continually renew this glorious covenant, sealing it again with the blood which earned it for us, and give ourselves to God as loyal covenanters, Jesus added the command: "Do this in memory of me."

Rev. Frank Bittenz, sj
Everlasting Gift

Let us examine more closely the culminating point of Gemma's devotion—Holy Communion—in which precisely the Mystery of the Love of Jesus is accomplished. Would that she who so often disclosed to me the secrets of her soul on this subject would now enable me to relate adequately and exactly what she then told me of the fire that the Divine Spouse enkindled in her heart at the Holy Table. It was her hunger and thirst for Holy Communion that made this young girl hover like a butterfly near the Tabernacle. Her heart longed for this Divine Food only. And we have seen that even when quite a child her ardent desire to make her first Communion almost brought her to death's door. Now I add that this hunger and thirst, far from being satisfied by her daily Communion, kept on increasing until they consumed her whole being. "Every morning," she said to me, "I go to Holy Communion. The greatest and only comfort I have, although I am in no wise provided with what is needed to worthily approach Jesus. The loving treatment that Jesus bestows on me every morning in the Holy Communion excites within me an unutterable sweetness and draws to itself all the weak affections of my miserable heart." And then she exclaimed: "Behold O Lord, my heart and my soul; come Lord, I open my breast to Thee. Send in Thy Divine Fire. Burn me, consume me, come and delay no longer. I would fain be the dwelling of all Thy fires."

Fr. Germanus, CP
The Life of Gemma Galgani

Just at the turn of the century, there was a woman married in Paris, just a good, ordinary Catholic girl to an atheist doctor, Dr. Felix LaSeur. He attempted to break down the faith of his wife who reacted by studying her faith. In 1905 she was taken ill and tossed on a bed of constant pain until August 1914. When she was dying, she said to her husband, "Felix, when I am dead, you will become a Catholic and a Dominican priest."

"Elizabeth, you know my sentiments. I've sworn hatred of God, I shall live in the hatred and I shall die in it." She repeated her words and passed away.

Rummaging through her papers he found her will. "In 1905 I asked almighty God to send me sufficient sufferings to purchase your soul. On the day that I die, the price will have been paid. Greater love than this no woman has than she who lay down her life for her husband."

Dr. LaSeur dismissed it as the fancies of a pious woman. He went to Lourdes to write a book against Our Lady, but as he looked up into the face of the statue, he received the great gift of faith. So total, so complete was it, that he never had to go through the process of juxtaposition and say, "how will I answer this or that difficulty?" He saw it all. At once.

Summoned to Rome by Pope Benedict XV, Dr. LaSeur recounted his conversion and said he wanted to become a Dominican priest. At first, the Holy Father refused, and said he must stay in the world to repair the harm he had done. After speaking to Fr. Jon Vinnea who accompanied Dr. LaSeur, the Holy Father changed his mind.

Lent, 1924. I made my retreat in the Dominican monastery in Belgium, where four times each day, and 45 minutes each time, I listened to Father Felix LaSeur, Catholic Dominican and priest, who told me this story.

Archbishop Fulton J. Sheen

What greater way can a man demonstrate his love than to lay down his life for another? When a woman is pregnant she gives the child in her womb everything she has . . . In a greater way the Lord gives us His very self in the Mass, saying, "I gave my life for you. All I have is available to nourish you and make you healthy and strong."

A powerful story came out in the newspapers about the 1988 Armenian earthquake that killed 50,000 people. In the collapse of an apartment building, Susanna Petrosyana and her four-year-old daughter, Gayaney, fell from the fifth floor to the basement and were pinned under wreckage, barely in reach of each other. Susanna discovered a 1-1/2 pound jar of blackberry jam nearby and on the second day gave the entire jar to Gayaney to eat. After awhile, when the jam was gone, the dehydrated child sobbed, "Mommy, I need to drink." Susanna later told reporters, "I thought my child was going to die of thirst . . . I had no water, no fruit juice, no liquids. It was then I remembered that I had my own blood." She found a piece of broken glass and began cutting her hand, and put it to her child's mouth. She knew she was going to die, but wanted her child to live. She doesn't remember what day she cut open her fingers, or how many times she used the method to feed her daughter. On the eighth day of their captivity they were found by rescue workers. . .

Our lives as Christians involve daily sacrifice. We come to Mass primarily to sacrifice in union with the life and death of Jesus . . . In our repentance, our forgiveness, our renewal of the covenant, we grow in the ability to lay down our lives.

Fr. Robert DeGrandis, ssj
Healing Through the Mass

Now, I am going to let you in on a secret—the secret of my spiritual life. When I travel on the train, I say, ten, twenty "Masses of St. John" — Masses in honor of the Blessed Trinity. There is no prayer like that. I have but three devotions: My Mass, my breviary, my Rosary. The breviary is beautiful, but you cannot compare it with the Mass. There is no prayer like the Mass. As I travel, I offer my Mass on the altar of the holy Will of God, offering it in union with the thousands of priests saying Mass continuously, perpetually. I am tired, I cannot prepare conferences—I offer Mass instead. I said four or five Masses this morning. I do it the whole day. It unites my heart, my will with priests at the altar. When I awake during the night, the first thing I do is to take the shortest form of the Mass of St. John, "Suscipe . . . Offerimus . . . " "Hoc est enim Corpus Meum" . . . "Hic est enim Calix Sanguinis Mei . . . " "Domine, non sum dignus. . . " "Corpus Domini Jesu Christi. . . . Sanguis Domini Jesu Christi, custodiant animam meam in vitam aeternam. Amen!" I hope to die saying Mass—between two consecrations. . .

Learn these prayers by heart and then during the day you can live the wonderful grace of your Mass. You have a few moments free—say a Mass of St. John. You wake up at night—say a Mass . . .

I remember preaching in a big community in California. The Mother Superior said to me one day, "Father, I want to thank you. Yesterday after your conference about Holy Mass I went to the infirmary to see a poor sister who suffers terribly and who cannot sleep at all, especially during the night. She was smiling. 'Mother, I have learned the secret of how to pass the night—the Mass of St. John. Thank Father for me for having told us about it.'"

Fr. Mateo Crawley-Boevey, sscc
Jesus, King of Love

Q. I am afraid of "failing" in my prayer for family healing, since I experience a kind of "spiritual emptiness." I envy those who seem to be bursting with spiritual life.

A. No one is on a constant spiritual "high." And many devout souls are seldom "high." God often serves the cake without the "frosting." But feeling isn't as important as filling—filling yourself with *God's* goodness, not yours.

At Communion time we are in the closest union with Jesus. "He who eats my flesh and drinks my blood abides in me and I in him," the mutual union of "Communion" (John 6: 56). In this *infilling* with the presence of Christ, we have an occasion to fulfill the pleading of Paul in Ephesians 3:19, "that we may be *filled* to the measure of all *fullness* of God." It is only with this *total infilling* with Christ that we have security against contamination or recontamination with the forces of evil. Jesus tells us that after evicting the enemy, the house is "clean but empty" (Luke 11:25)—rather than "clean and full" with the fullness of Christ. This emptiness leaves it open to "seven devils worse than the first."

Pray to appreciate more fully the truth that "you have been given *fullness* in Christ, who is the head over every power and authority" (Phil. 2:10), so as to experience "the *fullness* of him who *fills* everything in every way" (Eph. 1:23). This is the antidote to your "spiritual emptiness."

John H. Hampsch, CMF
Healing Your Family Tree

Tranquil peace and gratitude filled Josefa's heart, and so she went to Mass, then to Holy Communion. On returning to her place, she at once renewed the complete offering of her whole person to her good and beloved Master, definitely abandoning herself into His hands for ever. Jesus ratified the offering:

"It is on account of your nothingness and utter misery that you must let Me kindle your heart's fire, consume and destroy it. You surely know that 'nothing' and 'misery' cannot resist..."

Josefa spent the whole day under the power of "Love that gives"... "and Love that humbles Itself before Its own"... She would hear these words from Our Lord's lips while in the silence and recollection of that day she lived through the ceremonies of religious life, the last actions, the last outpourings of the love of our Saviour among His own.

At about four in the afternoon, Josefa was at prayer in her cell near a statue of Our Blessed Lady and was thinking over the mysterious words of Jesus, when He Himself appeared.

"Yes, Josefa, I did indeed say that Love gives Itself to Its own and it is true . . . Come, draw near My Heart and enter in, and taste and see what its overwhelming emotions are."

"Loves give Itself as food to Its own and this food is the substance which gives them their life and sustains them.

"Love humbles Itself before Its own . . . and in so doing raises them to the highest dignity.

"Love surrenders Itself in totality, It gives in profusion and without reserve. With enthusiasm, with vehemence It is sacrificed, It is immolated, It is given for those It loves . . . The Holy Eucharist is love to the extreme of folly."

Words of Our Lord to Sr. Josefa Menendez
The Way of Divine Love

The well-known story of Widikend, Duke of Saxony, illustrates this. This prince, while yet a pagan, was at war with Charlemagne; having a great curiosity to see what took place among the Christians, he disguised himself as a pilgrim and stole into their camp. It happened to be the Paschal time, and the whole army were making their Easter Communion. The stranger watched the ceremonies of Mass with interest and admiration, but how much was he surprised when the priest administered the Sacrament to see in the Host an Infant of shining beauty! He gazed at the sight with amazement, but his astonishment became yet greater when he saw that this wonderful Child entered the mouths of some of the communicants with joy, while only with great reluctance It allowed Itself to be received by others. This vision was the means of the conversion of Widikend and the submission of his subjects to the Faith, for having sought instruction from the Christians, he understood that Our Lord meant to show him, not only the truth of the Real Presence, but that He comes into our hearts with willingness or unwillingness, as we are well or ill prepared for receiving Him.

Fr. Michael Muller, CSSR
The Blessed Eucharist, Our Greatest Treasure

Before the Blessed Sacrament the devout pilgrim on the journey finds comfort and consolation, for the Savior whispers his secrets to them. They know what the busy people of this world, rushing around, never know; they know Christ better than the busy clergy rushing from meeting to meeting.

With Jesus life makes sense. They are happy of heart; without friendship with him, life is insane and not worth living. They know that he is the gateway to heaven. So the thought of death makes them even more faithful to him. Most pagans think of death and plunge themselves into an even more frenzied hedonistic life. But those devoted to our Eucharistic Lord have hope. Their refuge is Jesus and his love. He awaits us in the tabernacle to give us courage and to lift up our disheartened souls. How obtuse are those who ignore him or are too busy for him. Jesus is joy. They are looking around everywhere, searching desperately for happiness, and they do not see him.

The Blessed Sacrament is where we can find rest for our restless, weary souls. The Eucharist binds us to Christ who said, "Come to me, you who are weary. I will comfort you."

Rev. Rawley Myers
Homiletic & Pastoral Review, June 1994

It was so when more than four thousand followed Him and forgot to eat for three days. As at the wedding feast of Cana, there was in the feeding of the multitude an important message. These kinds of miracles were performed by Jesus to impress upon the minds of the crowd that His power was the power of God. These particular gestures of compassion were wrought as a symbol of something greater to come. Their hearts were prepared to accept a greater mystery that He would reveal before His death—the Mystery of the Eucharist. This Mystery was so great a gift from God that the human mind would never be able to accept such an influx of love without some preparation.

He would one day change bread and wine into His own Body and Blood. The same power would multiply; the same minister would distribute from the same Source of Love—Jesus.

As the steward at Cana and the crowds in the desert did not understand how He did it, they all realized that what He did was done out of love. He nourished their bodies and though all benefitted by the fruit of His Power, none were deprived of His personal attention and love. These two miracles foreshadowed the Eucharist.

He began His life by taking on the flesh of man and ended it by giving that flesh back to man in the form of food. He began His public life by changing water into wine and He ended it by changing bread and wine into His Body and Blood.

He accomplished both miracles with great ease. On both occasions He was surrounded only by His chosen few. Both miracles were accomplished in a quiet conversational tone of voice—as if it were nothing.

Mother Angelica
To Leave and Yet to Stay

In one instance it was possible to confirm the presence, entirely intact at 7 o'clock in the evening, of the small particle of the Host which Resl had received in the morning. Another phenomenon connected with this phase of the stigmatist's life is that as soon as the Sacred Species have dissolved within her, she feels an interior physical pain and her body begins to grow weaker. Her yearning for Holy Communion grows more intense, and she even breaks into loud complaints, saying: "Oh, Saviour, why have You forsaken me? Come, Saviour, come!" St. Teresa of Avila declared that an ardent longing for Holy Communion was a special sign of the mystical life. Therese Neumann expresses this longing often during her ecstasies, and the pain she suffers when the Presence ceases shows its intensity. Sometimes, in the ecstatic state, she can scarcely contain herself when the moment of Communion nears and will in her eagerness stretch out her arms and even tug at the stole or surplice of the priest who is about to place the host on her tongue.

Intimately connected with Resl's abstinence from all natural nourishment and her intense desire to be united with her Eucharistic Redeemer is one of the most extraordinary phenomenon of the Konnersreuth case. This is the ecstatic Communion, minutely described in the lives of earlier mystics, among them St. Catherine of Siena. Its peculiarity is that the host, placed upon the tongue of the ecstatic, disappears immediately.

Albert Paul Schimberg
The Story of Therese Neumann

The founder of the MI (Mission Immaculata) was convinced, as he declared, on December 8, 1937, on Polish National Radio in a broadcast to all Poland, that, "when the spirit of Niepokalanow, the spirit of the MI, penetrates our country and the entire world, when the Immaculate will have become Queen of every heart beating under the sun, then paradise will come on earth, not the paradise of communists and socialists, but—in so far as it is possible on earth—the true paradise. The happiness of this paradise at this moment is the joy of those who dwell at Niepokalanow, where there is but one family, of which God is the Father, the Immaculate is the Mother, the Divine Prisoner of love in the Eucharist the elder Brother, while all the rest are not merely comrades, but younger brothers who love each other.

Jerzy Domanski, OFM CONV.
For the Life of the World,
Saint Maximilian and the Eucharist

During Mass we offer bread and wine which, through the power of God's word, become the Body and Blood of Our Lord, Jesus Christ. We bring a little bread and wine and God transforms them into the Body and Blood of His Son, Our Lord, Jesus Christ. The transformation that takes place is a divine act similar to the first miraculous act of creation. One word was necessary to set off a complete change and transformation in nature. The transformation of the bread and wine takes place invisibly, but in a concrete way. This is an act by which God prepares the food and drink for the road through life on which His people are journeying.

The coming about of the transformation is not only an act, but is also an invitation for every believer to become a new person, day after day. The divine transformation begins to change the individual's life into an *offering*, so that he in turn may be able to offer, to be offered and to receive the offerings of gifts. In this, our immense gratitude for the Eucharistic sacrifice is expressed. We are involved in such a way as to grow into a continuous offering to God and to become new bread so that new words can develop in us and spread from our renewed hearts. This is the beginning of that accomplishment of peace for which we are summoned through the Eucharist.

Fr. Slavko Barbaric, OFM
Celebrate Mass with Your Heart

It was at this period, as we have before remarked, that Jansenism aimed at banishing the Unbloody Sacrifice of the altar and the veneration of Mary, the Mother of God. These abominations filled her soul with anguish as she knelt before the altar and shared with the Heart of Jesus the sorrow occasioned by such outrages. To none other could He turn, since His most cruel enemies were numbered among those whose sacerdotal character gave them unlimited power over this pledge of His love for man. Her ardor led her at night to the church to kneel in the cold before its closed doors, shedding tears of love and desire until daylight gave her admittance, for her only relief was found in the presence of her Savior. Her sufferings were as varied as the sins of that period against the Blessed Sacrament, and she did penance for every affront offered It, from the tepidity and indifference of the faithful in receiving Holy Communion to the sacrilegious insults of Its greatest enemies. She would have sunk under the weight of this terrible mission, had not God effaced its impressions from her soul and inundated her, at times, with consolation. The more lively her intuition of the grandeur and magnificence of this great Sacrament, the more ardent became her devotion toward It, the greater her veneration. Her reverence for It, joined to the deep feeling of her own unworthiness, sometimes filled her with such fear that it was only obedience could make her approach the Holy Table. She believed herself responsible, on account of her own imperfections, for the numerous infractions of charity and the Rule committed by the Sisters, and this fear prevented her approaching Holy Communion as often as she might have done.

Very Rev. K. E. Schmoger, CSSR
Life of Anne Catherine Emmerich

Father Mateo [Crawley-Boevey] had a great appreciation for the value of the Holy Mass. At a talk given in Arizona he said, "Do you know what I am preaching everywhere? I am preaching: *Pay the ransom of souls* with the *Chalice*, with the *Chalice*. The greatest means of converting souls is *one more Mass*, one more Mass during the week, and, with sacrifice, two or three more Masses; if possible, *daily Mass*, to pay for the eternal salvation of souls so dear to you. That is the great thing—the Chalice filled with the Precious Blood."

He spoke of the great value of the Mass in converting sinners. "You are asking for a miracle; I approve. But I tell you that you must pay the ransom for the conversions you make. You have a right to ask for such miracles. Do you know what a conversion is? It is the resurrection of a soul. It is far greater to see the resurrection of a soul than the resurrection of a corpse. Oh, one more Mass! Please—one more Mass! Pay the ransom with the Chalice. One more Mass! If you have anyone at home sick, or dying, oh, pay the ransom with the Chalice—one more Mass!"

Ann Ball
Modern Saints, Their Lives and Faces

Whilst at Lourdes her piety did not seem at all out of the common, so it was said. If we understand by piety exalted reflections on the mysteries of the life of Our Lord or the great truths of the Faith, doubtless it was not. The child herself often said: "I never can make a meditation"; but, on the other hand, she loved prayer and it had a strong attraction for her. She was often to be found in the chapel saying her rosary, and who shall say what ardent love her angelic soul put into every one of the Aves with which she delighted to crown her Heavenly Mother!

She was often known at night, when suffering from one of her attacks of asthma, to refuse a cordial which would have given her relief, but would have deprived her of the privilege of union with Our Lord in Holy Communion on the following day. Love of the Blessed Eucharist was alive in her heart, and if the child was unconscious of her intimate union with Jesus, her simplicity never dreaming of it, we can hardly doubt that the luminous aureole around her head, of which the Cure Peyramale had a fleeting glimpse when she approached the Holy Table, was an outward sign of its existence. The words of the Holy Gospel are as true as ever: "Blessed are the clean of heart, for they shall see God."

J. H. Gregory
Bernadette of Lourdes

In the words of the Holy Father at the Eucharistic Congress, referring to Don Manuel Gonzalez, "the bishop of the abandoned tabernacles; he (Don Manuel) strove to remind everyone of Jesus' presence in the tabernacle, to which we sometimes respond so poorly. By his word and example, he never ceased to repeat that in the tabernacle of each church we possess a shining beacon, through contact with which our lives may be illuminated and transformed. . . . It is important for us to live and teach others how to live the total mystery of the Eucharist: the sacrament of SACRIFICE, of the BANQUET, and of the abiding PRESENCE of Jesus Christ the Savior. . . . It is true that the reservation of the Sacrament was begun in order to take Communion to the sick and those absent from the celebration. However, as the *Catechism of the Catholic Church* says, "to deepen faith in the real presence of Christ in the Eucharist, the Church is aware of the meaning of silent adoration of the Lord present under the Eucharistic species."

This silent adoration of Our Lord in the Holy Eucharist as food for the journey and as abiding presence in the tabernacle is the source of life and of sanctity in the Church. Again in the words of the Holy Father, "His life flows to us as the life-giving sap of the vine flows to its branches to make them live and bear fruit. Without true union with Christ—in whom we believe and who nourished us—there can be neither supernatural life in us, nor fruit." If this is so, then it is essential for the life of the Church that we take to heart the Holy Father's wishes: "If only this form of adoration would continue, so that in all the parishes and Christian communities the custom of some form of adoration of the Eucharist might take root!"

Rev. Edwin Gordon
Homiletic & Pastoral Review
October 1994

I find myself so weak that were it not for Holy Communion I would fall continually. **One thing alone sustains me, and that is Holy Communion.** From it I draw my strength; in it is all my comfort. I fear life on days when I do not receive Holy Communion. I fear my own self. Jesus concealed in the Host is everything to me. From the tabernacle I draw strength, power, courage and light. Here, I seek consolation in time of anguish. I would not know how to give glory to God if I did not have the Eucharist in my heart. (Diary 1037)

September 29, 1937. Today, I have come to understand many of God's mysteries. I have come to know that Holy Communion remains in me until the next Holy Communion. A vivid and clearly felt presence of God continues in my soul. The awareness of this plunges me into deep recollection, without the slightest effort on my part. **My heart is a living tabernacle** in which the living Host is reserved. I have never sought God in some far-off place, but within myself. It is in the depths of my own being that I commune with my God. (Diary 1302)

Rev. George W. Kosicki, csb
Tell My Priests,
The Words of Our Lord to Priests About His Mercy
As Revealed to Sr. Faustina Kowalska

In the time of St. Bernard, a monk of Clairvaux appeared after his death to his brethren in religion to thank them for having delivered him from Purgatory. On being asked what had contributed most to free him from his torments, he led the inquirer to the church, where a priest was saying Mass. "Look," said he, "this is the means by which my deliverance has been effected; this is the power of God's mercy; this is the salutary sacrifice which takes away the sins of the world." Indeed, so great is the efficacy of this sacrifice to obtain relief for the souls in Purgatory that the application of all the good works which have been performed from the beginning of the world would not afford so much assistance to one of these souls as would be imparted by a single Mass.

Fr. Michael Muller, CSSR
The Blessed Eucharist, Our Greatest Treasure

Oh, how high and honorable is the office of priests, to whom is given power to consecrate with sacred words the Lord of majesty, to bless Him with their lips, to hold Him in their hands, to receive Him in their mouths, and to communicate Him to others. How clean should be the hands, how pure the lips, how holy the body, how spotless the heart of a priest, into whom the Author of all purity so often enters. From the mouth of a priest, who so often receives the Sacrament of Christ, nothing should issue but what is holy, true, and edifying. Let his eyes, that so often look on the Body of Christ, be simple and chaste. Let his hands, that handle the Creator of Heaven and Earth, be pure and raised to Heaven (I Tim 2:8). For to priests in particular are addressed the words of the Law, "Be holy, for I the Lord your God am holy" (Lev 19:2).

Almighty God, let Your grace assist us, that we who have undertaken the office of priesthood may be enabled to serve You worthily and devoutly in all purity and with a good conscience. And although we cannot remain in such innocency of life as we ought, yet grant us sincerely to lament our sins, and to serve You henceforward with greater devotion, in the spirit of humility and with good will and intention.

Words of the Disciple
The Imitation of Christ
Thomas à Kempis

Generally, therefore, we preferred to say Mass somewhere at the working site, even though it meant we had to fast all morning and then give up the few moments of rest allowed to prisoners during the luncheon break. Even then, we could not invite many people to attend the Mass lest a daily crowd in the same place might draw attention to our activities. We usually chose a shack or some corner of a foundation far from the current working areas—sometimes it took fifteen minutes or more to reach the shack or building where Mass was to be said—and we had to start on time in order not to return late to our places of work. All of this made it difficult to have many prisoners in attendance, so we would consecrate extra bread and distribute Communion to the other prisoners when we could. Sometimes that meant we would only see them when we returned to the barracks at night before dinner. Yet these men would actually fast all day long and do exhausting physical labor without a bite to eat since dinner the evening before, just to be able to receive the Holy Eucharist—that was how much the sacrament meant to them in this otherwise Godforsaken place.

Walter J. Ciszek, sj
He Leadeth Me

Mary Ann Cortes was healed through the Mass. She spent seventeen years in mental hospitals in the New Orleans, Louisiana area, on every drug treatment program available for manic depressive patients except shock therapy. She encountered the healing Jesus during Mass, and over the course of several months was totally healed. The Lord took away the illness, and took away the fear, so that she could truly say, "I'm not afraid of the morning anymore." The Lord accomplished what no psychiatrist had been able to do. The testimony of her healing has deeply touched hundreds of lives.

"I am coming to know that the Eucharist is the greatest healing sacrament," Mary Ann says, "and that every Mass is a healing service. For seventeen years I was in and out of every mental hospital in the region of New Orleans, Louisiana. I was diagnosed as manic depressive and given almost every treatment available to psychiatric patients. The doctors gave up hope of my recovering my mental health, and doomed me to a life of mood-altering drugs. When I went to bed at night I would pray that I would die in my sleep, I was so afraid of waking up to another day of terror. After I was baptized in the Holy Spirit and began to attend healing Masses, I became mentally, emotionally and physically well. Today I am a new person in Christ. I'm not afraid of the morning anymore.

"In each Mass I unite all that I am with His sacrifice. In that union with Him I receive into my being the risen life of Jesus, which transforms me more and more. I identify with Him and receive His life. The more I actively participate in the Mass, the more real He becomes to me. Jesus Himself enters into me and heals me from the inside."

Fr. Robert DeGrandis, SSJ
Healing Through the Mass

O dearest daughter, open wide your mind's eye and look into the abyss of my charity. There is not a person whose heart would not melt in love to see, among all the other blessings I have given you, the blessing you receive in this sacrament.

And how, dearest daughter, should you and others look upon this mystery and touch it? Not only with your bodily eyes and feeling, for here they would fail you. You know that all your eyes see is this white bit of bread; this is all your hand can touch and all your tongue can taste, so that your dull bodily senses are deceived. But the soul's sensitivity cannot be deceived, unless she so chooses by extinguishing the light of holy faith by infidelity.

What tastes and sees and touches this sacrament? The soul's sensitivity. How does she see it? With her mind's eye, so long as it has the pupil of holy faith. This eye sees in that whiteness the divine nature joined with the human; wholly God, wholly human; the body, soul, and blood of Christ, his soul united with his body and his body and soul united with my divine nature, never straying from me. This, if you remember, is what I revealed to you early in your life and that not only to your mind's eye but to your bodily eyes as well, although because of the great light you soon lost your bodily sight and were left with only your spiritual vision.

Words of God the Father
Catherine of Siena, The Dialogue

The secret lies in a total offering of self, withholding nothing. Jesus was a total oblation on the Cross. There wasn't a cell of his body or sentiment of his heart that he didn't offer to the Father. Anything we withhold for ourselves is lost, because we only possess what we give. St. Francis of Assisi who, because of the elevated fervor of his devotion to the Eucharist can be considered a special guide on the topic, ends his wonderful discourse on the Eucharist with this exhortation: "Look at God's humility, my brothers, and pour out your hearts before him. Humble yourselves that you may be exalted by him. Keep nothing for yourselves, so that he who has given himself wholly to you may receive you wholly. In the *Imitation of Christ,* Jesus says: "Look, I offered myself wholly to the Father for you; I also gave my whole body and blood for you for food, that I might be wholly yours, and you should remain mine. But if you stand upon yourself and do not offer yourself freely to my will, the offering is not fully made, nor will union between us be complete." What we hold back for ourselves to keep a margin of freedom from God pollutes all the rest. It is the little silk thread St. John of the Cross speaks of, which prevents the bird from flying.

Fr. Raniero Cantalamessa
The Eucharist, Our Sanctification

November 13

The Order of the Day for the Missionary Sisters of the Sacred Heart of Jesus begins at five o'clock in the morning. Mother's began an hour earlier. On the night before, she was accustomed to placing her alarm clock under her pillow, so as not to fail in her appointment with Jesus at four o'clock, the hour of her meditation. Frankly speaking, Mother was much too frail to interrupt her sleep so early, but the hour of meditation prescribed by the rule did not satisfy the yearning of her being to enjoy the balm of divine intimacy. When she went to the chapel for the second hour's meditation, her whole attitude (though there was not the slightest sign of affectation) revealed that she was completely immersed in the Divine Presence. One day, during the Exposition of the Blessed Sacrament, a sister brought her a telegram. Observing that Mother made no response, the sister put the telegram on the prie-dieu. Then, perceiving that Mother still did not move, the sister looked into her face. She saw there a seraphic expression, the eyes openly fixed upon the Sacred Heart; but Mother was not able to see nor hear anything that was going on around her.

Mother Saverio De Maria, MSC
Mother Frances Xavier Cabrini

Not only have angels functioned as ministers of the Holy Eucharist, but in at least one incident an angel was assisted by a saint. This occurred to St. Stanislaus Kostka (d. 1568) during the time he was preparing for his admission into the Society of Jesus.

A violent and dangerous sickness overtook Stanislaus while he was on a journey, and he was forced to stay for a time in the home of a Lutheran couple, who would not permit the Eucharist to be brought into their house. Since the physician had abandoned all hope for his recovery, St. Stanislaus was in extreme affliction, not from fear of death, but because he was being denied the reception of the Sacraments. He appealed to St. Barbara, whose confraternity he had joined, as had many of the students of the Jesuit college. St. Barbara was known as the patroness who would insure the reception of the Sacrament of Penance and Holy Communion at the hour of death. For this reason she is depicted in art carrying a chalice and a Host, as well as the palm of martyrdom.

After Stanislaus had prayed to St. Barbara, the saint appeared to him, accompanied by an angel. In answer to his prayers St. Barbara brought him the Holy Eucharist. After communicating, St. Stanislaus slowly recovered his health. Nevertheless, he died at an early age, sometime later, as the result of another ailment.

It is said of St. Stanislaus that he communicated as often as the practice of the time permitted, and that he would fast the day before the reception. He was often found in ecstasy during Holy Mass and after receiving the sacred Host.

Joan Carroll Cruz
Eucharistic Miracles

The manna by which the Chosen People were nourished in the wilderness was a figure of the Eucharist, the spiritual food by which we are sustained and illuminated in the desert of this world.

Jesus, in His discourse on the Bread of Life in the synagogue of Capharnaum (John 6) proclaimed that He was the true manna, the "food that endures for life everlasting," the "Bread of God which came down from heaven and which gives life to the world" (John 6: 27, 33).

. . . Jesus makes clear that the Bread of Life is first of all His own Person, then His communication of Himself to us in two forms: in the Scriptures, the "word of God," and in the Eucharist.

The whole work of man in this life is to find God. We are not to labor for perishing food, but for the food of eternal life, the Logos. "This is the work of God, that you believe in Him Whom He has sent (v. 29). The Jews challenge Him to prove He is the Messiah, by working a miracle. Moses prayed to God and manna was given to feed the people of Israel in the desert. What sign would Jesus give, to prove His claims? Jesus answers that what they need is not more external signs from Him, but faith in the depths of their own hearts. They have already seen a miracle in which He fed five thousand men with a few barley loaves and some little fishes: but that has done nothing to open their eyes: "I am the Bread of Life" says Jesus. "He who comes to me shall not hunger and he who believes in me shall never thirst. But I have told you that you have seen me and do not believe" (v. 35-36).

Thomas Merton
The Living Bread

November 16

Feast of St. Gertrude
d. 1302

After her Communion, as she recollected herself interiorly, our Lord appeared to her under the form of a pelican as it is usually represented, piercing its heart with its beak. Marvelling at this, she said: "My Lord, what wouldst Thou teach me by this vision?" "I wish," replied our Lord, "that you would consider the excess of love which obliges Me to present you with such a gift. After having thus given Myself, I would rather remain dead in the tomb, so to speak, than deprive a soul who loves Me of the fruit of My liberality. Consider also, that even as the blood which comes from the heart of the pelican gives life to its little ones, so also the soul whom I nourish with the Divine Food, which I present to it, receives a life which will never end."

Monsignor Wm. J. Doheny, csc
The Revelations of St. Gertrude

In the year 1453, a fierce war was raging amongst the French, the Savoyards and the Piedmontese. At the sack of the little town of Exilles a robber entered the church, broke open the door of the tabernacle, and took out the ostensorium containing the Host. He hastened away with this and other objects, concealing them in a sack. He loaded the objects on a mule and hastened to Turin to effect the sacrilegious sale of them. But the hand of the Lord was present! Having reached the square of St. Sylvester—it was the 6th of June—the animal stopped suddenly, fell to the ground, and no force could make him move. The cords of the sack were unloosed, then the ostensorium with the Host comes forth, and instead of falling to the earth rises slowly into the air and is visible from all sides. A crowd at once gathers round and cries out "a miracle"; the numbers were so great that even the roofs were filled with people. The Archbishop . . . hastily comes up and awestruck is wrapt in quiet prayer. It is related that the ostensorium fell at once, and the Host remained balanced in the air, flashing forth a most brilliant light. Meanwhile the Archbishop caused a chalice to be brought, and prayed the Lord to deign to descend into it; and the Host, its light growing less and less, descended into the chalice amidst the commotion, the cries and the tears of that immense multitude. It was then brought to the Cathedral, and by order from Rome was consumed . . . a commemoration stone enclosed by an iron railing was afterwards placed where the miracle occurred, and later the municipality of Turin erected there a church, one of the most beautiful in the city, and called it *Corpus Domini*.

Cardinal Gaetano De Lai
The Real Presence of Jesus Christ in the Eucharist

"During the celebration of Holy Mass, I am hanging on the cross together with Jesus, and I suffer all that Jesus suffered on Calvary, as much as is possible for a human nature."

After the Consecration, with tears in his eyes and some sobbing, he slowly continued the Holy Mass.

The Memento for the Dead was also very long.

How many souls, deprived of the full possession of God, did he remember in the infinite mercy of God, offering his blood and his sufferings, united to the blood and sufferings of Christ, for their freedom from Purgatory! At the moment of Holy Communion, the face of Padre Pio became bright and radiant like Jesus transfigured on Tabor. The Communion for Padre Pio was life, a fusion of hearts, a fountain of joy and happiness.

Jesus was his Paradise.

After the Holy Mass he went to the choir, where he stayed until noon before Jesus in the Blessed Sacrament, for thanksgiving and meditation.

Padre Alberto D'Apolito
Padre Pio of Pietrelcina

In a beautiful essay on the Eucharist, written in 1916 during the First World War, Teilhard de Chardin gives us the fruit of a meditation made in front of the Blessed Sacrament. Entitled "The Monstrance," the essay describes how, while kneeling in prayer, a person (probably the author himself) suddenly had the sensation that the Host began "to expand and grow bigger." The white Host soon enveloped not only the one in prayer but all reality as it continued to grow. Soon "through the mysterious expansion of the Host the whole world had become incandescent, had itself become like a single giant Host. . . . It had penetrated, through the channels of matter, into the inmost depths of all hearts and had dilated them to breaking point, only in order to take back into itself the substance of their affections and passions. (*Hymn of the Universe*)

It is truly a magnificent picture, revealing in graphic form the power of the Eucharistic Lord to reach out and embrace and transform all things. It is, moreover, a perception of a great truth and one that corrects the unreflecting accusation made at times by those who have little experience of the true nature of Eucharistic adoration. For it has frequently been said that the Eucharist has been given to us as our food, not (at least not primarily) to be adored, and that adoration in a silent church or before a monstrance is a devotion that flows from a "static" view of the Eucharist, one, that is, that emphasizes the Lord's Presence as opposed to his action of self-giving or sacrificial self-surrender, etc . . . What Teilhard's reflection indicates is that the very Presence of Christ is always dynamic, is indeed the very font of endless, though invisible, activity. Lifted up, he draws all things to himself (cf. Jn 12:32).

Rev. James T. O'Connor
The Hidden Manna, A Theology of the Eucharist

Sometimes—almost habitually, indeed, or at least very frequently—I would find relief after communicating. There were times, in fact, when the very act of approaching the Sacrament would at once make me feel so well, both in soul and in body, that I was astounded. I would feel as if all the darkness in my soul had suddenly been dispersed and the sun had come out and shown me the stupidity of the things I had been saying and doing. At other times, if the Lord spoke only one word to me (if, for example, as on the occasion I have already described, He said no more than "Be not troubled: have no fear"), that one word completely cured me, or, if I were to see some vision, it was as if there had been nothing wrong with me. I rejoiced in God and made my complaint to Him, asking Him how He could allow me to suffer such tortures, but telling Him that I was well rewarded for them, since, when they were over, I almost invariably received favors in great abundance. My soul seemed to emerge from the crucible like gold, both brighter and purer, to find the Lord within it. So trials like these, unbearable as they may seem, eventually become light, and the soul becomes anxious to suffer again if by so doing it can render the Lord greater service. And, however numerous may be our troubles and persecutions, if we endure them without offending the Lord, but rejoice to suffer for His sake, they all work together for our greater gain—though I do not myself bear them as they should be borne, but in a way which is most imperfect.

St. Teresa of Avila
The Autobiography of St. Teresa of Avila
E. Allison Peers

In Europe I have known a poor little peasant girl who like Bernadette used to take care of sheep. I met her through the Archbishop who invited me to talk with her and to give my opinion about her case. He told me he had her case examined by five eminent theologians. They all told him she was a second Margaret Mary. She spoke to me simply, plainly and at great length, for she had confidence in me. She enjoyed an extraordinary privilege, that of seeing what goes on at the altar as you see me sitting here. For her there was no veil during Holy Mass. For her Mass was Calvary, as on Good Friday. And in her simplicity and candor she thought everyone enjoyed the same privilege as she. She was forbidden to speak to anyone about what she saw. There were miracles to prove that she really was what she seemed to be, a Margaret Mary. All this I learned from her.

Fr. Mateo Crawley-Boevey sscc
Jesus, King of Love

"Contemplate Me in the prison where I spent the greater part of the night. The soldiers came and, adding words to injuries, insulted Me, mocked Me, outraged Me, and gave Me blows on My face and on My whole body.

"Tired of their sport, at length they left Me bound and alone in the dark and noisome place, where, seated on a stone, My aching body was cramped with cold.

"Compare the prison with the Tabernacle . . . and especially with the hearts that receive Me. "In the prison I spent only part of one night . . . but in the Tabernacle, how many days and nights?

"In the prison I was insulted and ill-treated by soldiers who were My enemies. In the Tabernacle most often it is they who call Me their Father who treat Me thus, but how unlike that of children is the treatment!

"In the prison I endured cold, sleeplessness, hunger and thirst, pain, shame, solitude, and desertion. And there passed before My mind's eye all the tabernacles where in the course of ages I should lack the shelter of love . . . the icy-cold hearts that would be as hard and unfeeling as the stones of the prison floor were to My numbed and wounded body.

"And how often should I wait for this or that other soul to visit Me in the Blessed Sacrament and receive Me into his heart . . . how many nights should I spend longing for his coming . . . but he would let business or carelessness or anxiety for his health get the better of him . . . and he would not come!

O! if they would thus unite themselves to Me, with what peace would they face difficulties . . . how much fortitude they would win and how they would gladden My Heart!"

Words of Our Lord to Sr. Josefa Menendez
The Way of Divine Love

Multitudes of angels assist at every Mass. St. Gregory: "The heavens open and the multitudes of angels come to assist at the Holy Sacrifice." St. Augustine: "The angels surround and help the priest when he is celebrating Mass." St. John Chrysostom: "When Mass is being celebrated, the Sanctuary is filled with countless angels who adore the Divine Victim immolated on the altar."

The efficacy of the Mass is so wonderful, God's mercy and generosity are then so unlimited that there is no moment so propitious to ask for favors as when Jesus is born on the altar. What we then ask for we shall almost certainly receive, and what we do not obtain in the Mass we may scarcely hope to receive by all other prayers, penances or pilgrimages. The angels know this full well and come in multitudes to adore God and make their petitions at this hour of mercy. What an example for us!

We read in the revelations of St. Bridget: "One day, when I was assisting at the Holy Sacrifice, I saw an immense number of holy angels descend and gather around the altar, contemplating the priest. They sang heavenly canticles that ravished my heart; Heaven itself seemed to be contemplating the great Sacrifice. And yet we poor blind and miserable creatures assist at the Mass with so little love, relish and respect!" Oh, if God would open our eyes, what wonders should we not see!

Fr. Paul O'Sullivan, OP
All About the Angels

Only during the war could Father Kolbe realize his lifelong dream: daily adoration of the most Blessed Sacrament. Brother Benedict Mieczkowski recounts:

Immediately after his return from prison [1939], Father Maximilian introduced adoration of the most Blessed Sacrament throughout the entire day. He regarded this as the most efficacious means for meeting the needs of Niepokalanow and of his country. He announced this in the refectory and ordered me to assign groups of friars from each work sector to take turns adoring for a half-hour each. On each turn, there were several friars. In this way, each, including Father Maximilian, had his own time of adoration each day. Great care and attention were given to this activity. Often, in the early days, he himself would check and remind the brothers of this commitment, so that they would come to realize it as a duty and consider it of vital importance. But above all, he encouraged us with his example, more than once going to the chapel to take the place of someone absent. When he did not feel well, he would get his cane and, leaning on it, would take his place in the chapel for the period of adoration assigned him immediately after the afternoon rest, sometime between 3 and 4 p.m.

Jerzy Domanski, OFM CONV.
For the Life of the World,
Saint Maximilian and the Eucharist

Although this blessed child was always deep in thought, and always found herself in spirit before the sacred Tabernacle, yet she was not fully satisfied unless she could go to church, and there adore her hidden God . . . she contented herself with going to Church only twice a day. In the morning when she went to hear Mass and receive Holy Communion, and in the evening for the public Adoration. "I am going to Jesus," she used to say, "let us go to Jesus. He is all alone and no one thinks of Him. Poor Jesus!" On entering the sacred building she turned her first anxious gaze towards the Tabernacle. Then devoutly recollected and as if quite alone before the Altar of the Blessed Sacrament she remained kneeling motionless in prayer. She never turned her eyes from where they were first fixed, and except for the glow on her face and occasional tears that trickled down her cheeks, you would not have distinguished her from any others attentively engaged in prayer. "Oh ! what immense happiness and joy," she has said, "my heart feels before Jesus in the Blessed Sacrament! And if Jesus would allow me to enter the sacred Tabernacle where He, Soul, Body, Blood and Divinity is present, should I not be in Paradise?" And turning to Our Lord Himself in His Sacrament, "Jesus," she exclaimed, "Soul of my soul, my Paradise, Holy Victim, behold me all Thine. I felt that Thou wert seeking me and I ran." And then with filial confidence she continued to say that she had come to keep Him company, and offer herself wholly to Him, and present Him some little acts of virtue practiced for His love, and to receive any orders He might wish to give her, or at least to listen to some sweet word. But above all, to ask His Love, Love, Love.

Fr. Germanus, CP
The Life of Gemma Galgani

Noel, Noel, the day that Christ was born. His soul sang Noel as he hurried up the road to the monastery church. It was Christmas morning; it was France. He was free, free of the Mohawks, free of the Dutch, free of the English. *Venite adoremus,* throbbed in his brain. The Christmas carols he had sung as a boy pulsed through him. He was before the monastery church. He sought out a gray robed priest and knelt before him to make confession of all the sins he could remember since July 30, a year ago. With bowed head he listened to the priest pronouncing the words of absolution. He knelt on the flagged floor among the people near the altar. The candles, the priest in white vestments, the words he said were blurred and indistinct. It was time for Communion. He felt the Host upon his tongue. It was the Body of Christ. He knelt in adoration. The cloud cleared about him. He came to himself. "It seemed to me that it was at this moment that I began to live once more. It was then that I tasted the sweetness of my deliverance," he said.

Unobtrusively, he slipped out from the church and avoided the knots of villagers who gossiped about. He returned, light-footed with ecstasy, down the road to the cottage of the fishermen.

His hands, they noticed, were knotted and scarred; his fingers were crooked; some were stumps; some had no fingernails; he had no left thumb. They were in pity for him, for his cheeks were sunken and his skin was roughened. With simple curiosity they asked him of himself, of who he was and where he had been. He told them, briefly and modestly. "When they learned how he had suffered that martyrdom, they were at a loss to know what welcome to give him," he related.

Fr. Francis Talbot, sj
Saint Among Savages
The Life of Isaac Jogues

Each day we hear His command, "Do this in remembrance of me." This is the most startling word of the Eucharist—that each Christian is to learn to consecrate, to be drawn into Christ's action so deeply that he becomes a Eucharist! We are to parallel Christ; what He did with His life we are to do with our lives. What a mystery this is, to consecrate ourselves, to become Eucharists! This is what the Christian life is all about; this is the ultimate conclusion and action of following Christ—to be body given, to be blood shed. To consecrate is to sacrifice, to die, to pass over into a new world, a new life, a new level and depth of existence and consciousness. It is easy to offer Christ's sacrifice, to be an innocent bystander and to say, "This is *his* body, this is *his* blood." But when we begin to pray deeply the two-edged real words of consecration, "This is *my* body, this is *my* blood," something begins to happen. Those awesome words of His are stamped deeper and deeper into consciousness. . . . They are a promise and vow committing one's life and presence to another totally until death . . . Only Eucharist enables us to change ourselves into another, giving ourselves into His hands. The Eucharist is a continuum, an ongoing action, of what He and I are doing and becoming. Eucharist is not only His presence with me but my presence with Him. Wherever His is, there I am; wherever He goes, I go with Him. Eucharist is the sign, the visible witness of what we have done, what we are doing and what we will become. In Eucharist we consecrate each day, each person, each event, hallowing it, firing it, filling it with His Spirit, His presence, being taken up with Him.

Rev. Edward J. Farrell
Prayer Is a Hunger

November 28

On Trinity Sunday, June 6, 1830, Sister Laboure was given a special vision of Jesus in the Blessed Sacrament, or more specifically of Christ as King. This time she is precise as to the moment of the vision. Our Lord appeared to her, robed as a king, with a cross at His breast, during the Gospel of the Mass. Suddenly, all His kingly ornaments fell from Him to the ground—even the cross, which tumbled beneath His feet. Immediately her thoughts and her heart fell, too, and were plunged into that chasm of gloom that she had known before, gloom that portended a change in government. This time, however, she understood clearly that the change in government involved the person of the King, and that, just as Christ was divested of His royal trappings before her, so would Charles X be divested of his throne.

Before leaving this vision, we must point out the noteworthy fact that Catherine Laboure was the first saint in modern times to be vouchsafed a vision of Christ as King. In the light of the great present-day devotion to the Kingship of Christ, we would seem justified in questioning whether the vision might not have a mystical meaning. In announcing the end of the oldest of monarchies, might not Christ have meant to point up the passing quality of all earthly authority, and to foretell present-day devotion to His Kingship as the index of the eternal quality of His own Reign?

Father Joseph I. Dirvin, CM
Saint Catherine Laboure of the Miraculous Medal

Moreover, in the Blessed Sacrament our Lord Himself is the light which manifests Him as our model and reveals His beauties to us. He is Himself His light, His means of being known, just as the sun is itself its own proof. To make Himself known, He has only to show Himself. Recognition of Him need not come from its being reasoned out. A child does not have to discourse with himself to recognize his parents. Our Lord reveals Himself through His presence, just as parents do. But as we grow to know His voice better and as our hearts become more sympathetic to Him in emptying themselves of what is not Him, our Lord manifests Himself in a clearer and more intimate manner, which only those know who love Him. He gives the soul a divine conviction which overshadows the light of human reason. Look at Magdalen: one word from Jesus and she recognizes Him. He acts the same way in the Blessed Sacrament: He says one word only, but it rings in our very hearts: "It is I! . . ." We sense His presence; we believe in it more firmly than if we were to see Him with our bodily eyes.

Saint Peter Julian Eymard
In the Light of the Monstrance

November 30

The testimony of the Fathers of the Church also assures us of the Real Presence in the most Holy Eucharist. There is no writer or teacher of the Apostolic times who would doubt, or would fail to affirm that truth.

The first to give such testimony is St. Andrew, the Apostle. Witnesses of his martyrdom tell us that the dying saint thus addressed Edeus, who ordered him to offer sacrifice to the gods: "I offer daily to the Almighty God, the Immaculate Lamb. Though he is really offered, and the faithful eat his flesh, he remains whole and entire and alive."

St. Justin Martyr, about the year 150, wrote, "Let us take unto our hand that blessed bread, not an ordinary bread, but the flesh and blood of Jesus, the Word made Flesh" (Apol. 2 ad Ant.).

St. Irenaeus asks, "How can anyone say that our bodies, which are nourished on the flesh and blood of Christ, are brought to perdition? Our bodies, tasting of the Eucharist, are no longer corruptible, but have the hope of resurrection."

Immaculata Magazine
Special Eucharistic Issue
August 1976

There is no more moving an example of the way contemplation of Christ's love in the Eucharist leads to discernment of his presence and service of him in "the distressing disguises of the poor" than that shown by Mother Teresa of Calcutta. Because of her closeness to Jesus in adoration of the Blessed Sacrament this woman who believes in Love has been able to translate the tenderness of loving into practice, as she simple recalls in the many stories of her "encounters" such as the following:

"I remember when we went to Australia, outside Melbourne—they call it 'a reserve.' People live there and the Sisters and I would go to the poor families and we helped them with their families. So I went to a little house and a man was there. I asked this man whether he would allow me to clean his house, but he said: 'I'm all right.' And I said to him that he would be more all right if he allowed me to do it. And so I started cleaning and washing his clothes. Then I saw a big lamp in that room: it was covered with dust and dirt. And I said to him: 'Do you light this beautiful lamp?' And then he said: 'For whom? For years nobody has visited me,' and then I said to him: 'Will you light the lamp if my Sisters come to you?' 'Yes,' he said. And so I cleaned the lamp and then the Sisters started going every evening to visit him. After two years I had completely forgotten about him. He sent me a message saying: 'Tell my friend the light she lit in my life is still burning.'" *(Address at the 43rd International Eucharistic Congress, Nairobi, August, 1985)*

Fr. Michael L. Gaudoin-Parker
The Real Presence through the Ages

Today there was nocturnal adoration. I could not take part in it because of my poor health, but before I fell asleep I united myself with the sisters who were at adoration. Between four and five o'clock, I was suddenly awakened, and I heard a voice telling me to join those who were adoring at that time. I understood that there was among them a soul who was praying for me. (Diary 1419)

When I steeped myself in prayer, I was transported in spirit to the chapel, where I saw the Lord Jesus, exposed in the monstrance. In place of the monstrance, I saw the glorious face of the Lord, and He said to me, **What you see in reality, these souls see through faith. Oh, how pleasing to Me is living faith! You see, although there appears to be no trace of life in Me, in reality it is present in its fullness in each and every Host. But for Me to be able to act upon a soul, the soul must have faith. O how pleasing to me is living faith!** (Diary 1420)

Sister M. Faustina Kowalska
Divine Mercy in My Soul,
The Diary of Sister M. Faustina Kowalska

On November 18, 1875, the future, modern apostle of devotion to the Sacred Heart of Jesus, Father Mateo Crawley-Boevey, sscc, was born in Arequipa, Peru, in South America.

After joining the religious Congregation of the Sacred Hearts of Jesus and Mary, Fr. Mateo as a young priest, due to ill health, got permission to make a pilgrimage to Rome, and then to Paray-le-Monial in France to prepare for an early death. He was then 32 years old.

In Rome, in a private audience with Pope St. Pius X, Father Mateo begged for his blessing, for permission to devote the remaining days of his life to the promotion of a greater devotion to the Sacred Heart in the homes . . . Kneeling at the feet of His Holiness, Fr. Mateo pleaded: "Holy Father, permit me to be the apostle of the Sacred Heart, to go and work to conquer for Him the entire world, home by home, family by family." What a surprise Fr. Mateo got when Pope St. Pius X replied: "NO!" Looking up at the Pope, Fr. Mateo pleaded his request. Again came the answer: "NO, my son! . . . You ask permission, and I say: "NO! For, not only do I permit you; rather I COMMAND you to give your life for this work of social salvation!"

Proceeding to Paray-le-Monial in France, Fr. Mateo went to pray at the altar where the Sacred Heart had appeared to St. Margaret Mary. As he knelt there during the night of August 24, 1907, Fr. Mateo himself later related what happened to him.

"I saw that altar, the most beautiful, the most holy after that of Calvary. There I prayed and suddenly, I felt within myself a strange shock. I was struck by a blow of grace, at the same time very strong, yet infinitely gentle. When I arose, I was completely cured."

Fr. Albert Kretschmer, svd
Eucharistic Heart Anthology

"From the *Elevation* to the *Agnus Dei*, she prayed for the souls in purgatory, presenting Jesus on the Cross to His Father that He might accomplish what she could not. At this moment, she was often rapt out of herself and, indeed, she sometimes fell into ecstasy even before the Consecration.

"At the *Communion*, she reflected on Christ laid in the tomb, and begged Almighty God to annihilate in us the old man and clothe us with the new.

"If at Mass or any other service, she listened to the music, she would exclaim: 'Ah, how sweet is harmony! Inanimate creatures accord so perfectly, why should not men's hearts do the same! How charming that would be!'— And the thought made her shed tears.

"Once, during the Christmas Midnight Mass, she saw the Infant Jesus above the chalice, and what appeared to her strange was that the celebrant seemed to hold the Infant by the feet, notwithstanding which, she saw the chalice too. She often saw an Infant in the Host, but He was very small."

Very Rev. K. E. Schmoger, CSSR
Life of Anne Catherine Emmerich

When I reached the prison camps of Siberia, I learned to my great joy that it was possible to say Mass daily once again. In every camp, the priests and prisoners would go to great lengths, run risks willingly, just to have the consolation of this sacrament. For those who could not get to Mass, we daily consecrated hosts and arranged for the distribution of Communion to those who wished to receive. Our risk of discovery, of course, was greater in the barracks, because of the lack of privacy and the presence of informers. Most often, therefore, we said our daily Mass somewhere at the work site during the noon break. Despite this added hardship, everyone observed a strict Eucharistic fast from the night before, passing up a chance for breakfast and working all morning on an empty stomach. Yet no one complained. In small groups the prisoners would shuffle into the assigned place, and there the priest would say Mass in his working clothes, unwashed, disheveled, bundled up against the cold. We said Mass in drafty storage shacks, or huddled in mud and slush in the corner of a building site foundation of an underground. The intensity of devotion of both priests and prisoners made up for everything; there were no altars, candles, bells, flowers, music, snow-white linens, stained glass or the warmth that even the simplest parish church could offer. Yet in these primitive conditions, the Mass brought you closer to God than anyone might conceivably imagine. The realization of what was happening on the board, box, or stone used in place of an altar penetrated deep into the soul. Distractions caused by the fear of discovery, which accompanied each saying of the Mass under such conditions, took nothing away from the effect that the tiny bit of bread and few drops of consecrated wine produced upon the soul.

Walter J. Ciszek, sj
He Leadeth Me

The "Miracle of the Eucharist" took place in Betania on the Feast of the Immaculate Conception, December 8, 1991.

Father Otty, a priest from Colombia and the Chaplain for Betania, was celebrating Mass for the vigil of the Feast of the Immaculate Conception. It was a midnight Mass. At the time of the Consecration about fifteen thousand people present saw a bright, rose light over the Host . . . At the time of Communion Fr. Otty broke the Host in half and broke off a small particle to put into the chalice. He had difficulty believing what he saw happening to the remaining part of the Host. It had begun to Bleed. It was truly the Body and Blood of Christ.

For three days the Blood on the Host was fluid, and then it began to dry up. Another small miracle is that the Blood didn't seep through the wafer thin Host. The opposite side of the Host shows no sign whatsoever of Blood.

The Blood on the Host is not a very large spot. The importance of the miracle is that it is a sign. Miracles are signs. The importance is not in the miracle itself, but in the sign. It is a sign that Our Lord is truly present in the Eucharist. In the miracles of the Bible it is not the miracle, but the sign—the sign of our Lord's mercy and love for His Children.

The "Miracle of the Eucharist" has been examined in laboratories and it is human blood.

Again, it is a sign. It is a sign of the Transubstantiation and that is what is important for us today. God is trying to manifest to us that our faith in the consecrated Host as the Body and Blood of Christ is authentic. I intend to construct a special altar in the Cathedral of my diocese of Los Teques for this "Miracle of the Eucharist." (Bishop Pio Bello Ricardo)

Apparitions in Betania, Venezuela
Sister Margaret Catherine Sims, CSJ

Feast of St. Ambrose
c. 340-397

St. Ambrose was born at Trier (today in Germany) between 335 and 340. He became a lawyer and a Roman administrator in Milan. There he was chosen as bishop by popular acclamation, although he was only a catechumen. He thus received all the Sacraments of Initiation and the episcopate within one week. He died in Milan in 397. Ambrose, who may well be the first to refer to the Eucharistic Mystery as the "Mass" (Ambrose, in *Epistola*, 20, 4 (PL, 16, 995), remarks, "I, however, remained at my task and began to offer the Mass" . . . Some would dispute this and say that he is merely speaking of the dismissal of the catechumens. An undisputed reference to the Eucharistic liturgy as "Mass" is found in Gregory of Tours (died 594), who writes of "celebrating daily the solemnity of the Mass," has left us two great works that deal with the Eucharist: the *De Sacramentis* and the *De Mysteriis*, both of them published around 390.

"Now consider which is more excellent, the bread of angels [i.e., the manna] or the Flesh of Christ which is indeed the Body of life. That manna was from heaven, the latter from the Lord of the heavens; the former was subject to corruption if it was preserved for a second day, the latter foreign to all corruption so that whoever shall have piously tasted it will not be able to experience corruption. For the people of Israel water flowed from the rock; for you Blood flows from Christ. The water satisfied them for a while; Blood washes you for eternity. The Jew drinks and is thirsty again; when you drink you will not be able to thirst. The former was given as an image; the latter is given as the reality" (*De Mysteriis no. 48*).

Rev. James T. O'Connor
The Hidden Manna, A Theology of the Eucharist

December 8
Feast of the Immaculate Conception

From early morning, I felt the nearness of the Blessed Mother. During Holy Mass, I saw Her, so lovely and so beautiful that I have no words to express even a small part of this beauty. She was all [in] white, with a blue sash around Her waist. Her cloak was also blue, and there was a crown on Her head. Marvelous light streamed forth from Her whole figure. I am the Queen of heaven and earth, but especially the Mother of your [Congregation]. She pressed me to Her heart and said, I feel constant compassion for you. I felt (202) the force of Her Immaculate Heart which was communicated to my soul. Now I understand why I have been preparing for this feast for two months and have been looking forward to it with such yearning. From today onwards, I am going to strive for the greatest purity of soul, that the rays of God's grace may be reflected in all their brilliance. I long to be a crystal in order to find favor in His eyes. (Diary 805)

Sr. M. Faustina Kowalska
Divine Mercy in My Soul,
The Diary of Sr. M Faustina Kowalska

Concerning the Mass, I will quote a beautiful example given by the Cure of Ars to his parishioners. He told them:

My children, a good priest had the unhappiness to lose a friend he cherished tenderly, and so he prayed very much for the repose of his soul.

One day, God made known to him that his friend was in purgatory and suffered terribly. The holy priest believed that he could do no better than to offer the Holy Sacrifice of the Mass for his dear friend who had died. At the moment of the consecration, he took the host between his fingers and said, 'Holy Eternal Father, let us make an exchange. You hold the soul of my friend who is in purgatory, and I hold the Body of Your Son in my hands. Well, good and merciful Father, deliver my friend and I offer you your Son with all the merits of His death and Passion.'

The request was answered. In fact, at the moment of the elevation, he saw the soul of his friend, shining in glory, rising to heaven; God had accepted the deal.

My children, when we want to deliver from purgatory a soul dear to us, let us do the same: let us offer to God, through the Holy Sacrifice, His Beloved Son with all the merits of His death and Passion. He will not be able to refuse us anything.

Sister Emmanuel of Medjugorje
The Amazing Secret of the Souls in Purgatory
An Interview with Maria Simma

In the Old Testament the Messiah was announced as the "Prince of Peace" (Isaiah 9:5). His birth was proclaimed as the new era of peace "to guide our feet into the way of peace" (Lk 1:79). Jesus himself established his kingdom as a reign of peace. "Peace is my farewell to you, my peace is my gift to you" (Jn 14:27). After his resurrection, his first greeting was, "Peace be with you."

Through the Eucharistic celebration, Jesus continued his work of establishing and implementing his peace in our hearts. Peace comes into our hearts only through our personal intimate relationship with Jesus. At Mass this relationship is deepened and enriched.

At Mass the entire Body of Christ comes together to pray for peace. As his family we pray, "Lord, may this sacrifice, which has made our peace with you, advance the peace and salvation of all the world" (Eucharistic Prayer III). Later we pray for peace as a healing balm: "Deliver us, Lord, from every evil, and grant us peace in our day."

As we become more and more aware of the indwelling of the risen Jesus within us, we are more and more at peace. How appropriately the Church incorporates her prayer for peace just before Holy Communion, when Jesus comes to us to augment our peace by his very presence. "Lord Jesus Christ, you said to your apostles: I leave you peace, my peace I give you. Look not on our sins, but on the faith of your Church and grant us the peace and unity of your kingdom where you live forever and ever. Amen."

David E. Rosage
The Bread of Life

And if Our Lord took such delight in Gemma's Communions, was it possible for His Sweet Mother, who in her turn so tenderly loved this angelic girl, not to take the same delight in them? After the many marvels we have seen up to this, I do not think anyone will be tempted to doubt the veracity of another fact that I am about to relate. It is of the Blessed Virgin, who sometimes joined the Angels of the Eucharist to assist at Gemma's Holy Communion. At the unexpected vision the good child went into ecstasy, palpitating with joy at her Mother's feet. "How delightful it is," she said to me afterwards, "to receive Holy Communion in company with my Mother of Paradise! I did so yesterday, the 8th of May. I had never before received Holy Communion in her company. Do you know, father, in what all the outpourings of my heart consisted during those moments? In these words: O Mother! My Mother!"

Fr. Germanus, CP
The Life of Gemma Galgani

December 12
Feast of Our Lady of Guadalupe

"*I vividly desire that a church be built on this site, so that in it I can be present and give my love, compassion, help and defense, for I am your most devoted mother . . . to hear your laments and to remedy all your miseries, pains and sufferings.*"

Prior to Our Lady of Guadalupe's conversion of millions, the major empires in the Americas were evil, resisting the efforts of the conquistadors to conquer them, or the efforts of the missionaries to convert them. Only the direct intervention of Our Lady of Guadalupe could successfully launch the evangelization of the Americas, which she did 'with the rapidity of light' after revealing herself to the Indian Juan Diego.

These pagans could not resist Our Lady of Guadalupe and they flocked in droves to the waters of Baptism on a scale and with a speed that has no equal in recorded Catholic history. The missionaries were overwhelmed by the crowds requesting Baptism and to be taught the catechism.

The lesson that Our Lady of Guadalupe taught is that whole continents will be converted through her.

Fr. John A. Hardon, SJ
Spoken in Kentucky at 'Church Teaches Forum'

St. John Chrysostom wrote a remarkable passage in which he brought out the intimate connection between the Eucharistic Body of Christ and the Mystical Body which is the Church. Speaking of the precious vessels of the altar and of the other liturgical objects by which we surround the Blessed Sacrament with honor, the Greek Father pointed out that it was even more important to honor the body of Christ by giving alms to the poor. In this way, we are not only doing good to Him in the person of the poor, but we are making our own souls into sacred vessels of gold which give Him great glory:

If you wish to honor the Eucharistic Victim, offer your own soul for which the Victim was immolated. Make your soul all of gold. If your soul remains viler than lead or clay, what good does it do to have a golden chalice . . . ?

Do you wish to honor the Body of Christ? Then do not disdain Him when you see Him in rags. After having honored Him in Church with silken vestments do not leave Him to die of cold outside for lack of clothing. For it is the same Jesus Who says "This is my Body" and Who says "You saw me hungry and did not give me to eat—What you have refused to the least of these my little ones, you have refused it to me." The Body of Christ in the Eucharist demands pure souls, not costly garments . . . Peter thought he was honoring his Master by not letting the Lord wash his feet; and yet it was just the opposite. Give Him then the honor which He Himself has asked for, by giving your money to the poor. Once again, what God wants is not golden chalices, but golden souls (*St. John Chrysostom, Homily 50 on St. Matthew, 3*).

Thomas Merton
The Living Bread

December 14

Feast of St. John of the Cross
1542-1591

S t. John of the Cross, who with St. Teresa of Avila restored the unmitigated rule to the Carmelite Order and founded the Discalced branch of this order, was occasionally irradiated with light. It is claimed that after one of his Masses a student saw him aglow and was so impressed that he eventually entered the religious life.

At the convent of Caravaca, when a new prioress was to be elected, St. John offered holy Mass and prayed that the newly elected would be blessed with the wisdom and grace to fulfill the office to the satisfaction and pleasure of God. During this Mass a heavenly light engulfed the saint. Two of the nuns thought it proceeded from the tabernacle, but when the saint turned around, the rays were seen to originate from his face. Another sister observed the same as she stood by a different grille.

Joan Carroll Cruz
Eucharistic Miracles

Once, when I was about to communicate, I saw, with the eyes of the soul, more clearly than ever I could with those of the body, two devils of most hideous aspect. Their horns seemed to be around the poor priest's throat; and when I saw my Lord, with the Majesty which I have described, in the hands of such a man, in the Host which he was about to give me, I knew for a certainty that those hands had offended Him and realized that there was a soul in mortal sin . . . This upset me so much that I do not know how I was able to communicate, and I was sore afraid, for, I thought, had it been a vision from God, His Majesty would not have allowed me to see the evil that was in that soul. Then the Lord Himself told me to pray for him and said He had allowed me to see this so that I might realize what power there was in the words of consecration, and that, however wicked the priest who pronounces those words may be, God is always present without fail. He wanted me also to appreciate His great goodness in placing Himself in the hands of that enemy of His, and this solely for my good and for the good of all. This showed me clearly how much stricter is the obligation laid upon priests to be virtuous than upon other people, and what a terrible thing it is to take this Most Holy Sacrament unworthily, and how complete is the devil's dominion over the soul that is in mortal sin. It was of the very greatest help to me and gave me the fullest knowledge of what I owe to God. May He be blessed for ever and ever.

St. Teresa of Avila
The Autobiography of St. Teresa of Avila
E. Allison Peers

Q. A Protestant told me that the early Church believed that Jesus was only symbolically present in the Eucharist and that the doctrine of the Real Presence came about eleven centuries later. Is he correct?

A. Not true! Jesus' own words in Scripture tell us: *"Take and eat; this is My Body. Take and drink; this is My Blood of the New Covenant which shall be shed for many"* (cf. Matt. 26:26-27; Mark 14:22, 24; Luke 22: 19-20) and *". . . Whoever eats My flesh and drinks My blood has eternal life"* (John 6:54). The early Church accepted these words literally as she still does today.

Ignatius of Antioch who was a disciple of the Apostle John and who wrote an epistle to the Christians of Smyrna condemned those that *"abstain from the Eucharist and from prayer because they do not confess that the Eucharist is the flesh of Our Savior Jesus Christ."*

And Origen, in a homily given about 244 A.D. attested to belief in the Real Presence and admonished his listeners to take care *"lest a particle of it (the consecrated bread) fall and lest anything of the consecrated gift perish."*

Athanasius of Alexandria, told the newly baptized in 373: *"So long as the prayers of supplication and entreaties have not been made, there is only bread and wine. But after the great and wonderful prayers have been made, then the bread is the Body, and the wine the Blood, of Our Lord Jesus Christ."*

Dozens of testimonies could be given. Suffice it to say that it is certain the early Church took chapter 6 of John literally. There exists no document with a symbolic interpretation.

Perpetual Eucharistic Adoration Newsletter
October 1989

Many priests owe their vocation to a saintly mother's prayers. There can be little doubt that Herbert Cardinal Vaughan (Archbishop of Westminster, England) owed his vocation to the Priesthood to his mother's prayers before the Blessed Sacrament. When he was a young man of twenty-one, he wrote: "During the day my mother was often before the Blessed Sacrament. Every morning before breakfast she was in the chapel for half an hour or three-quarters of an hour. After breakfast an hour in the morning was always spent in meditation in the chapel, which was her real home. I do not remember ever seeing her distracted on these occasions, or looking anywhere than toward the Blessed Sacrament or on her book. She often remained with her eyes fixed on the tabernacle. While her body was kneeling back in the chapel and her face was beautiful and tranquil with the effects of divine love, her heart and soul were within the tabernacle with her dearly beloved Savior."

For nearly twenty years it was Mrs. Vaughan's daily practice to spend an hour in prayer before the Blessed Sacrament, asking that her sons might become priests. In answer to her prayers all her five daughters eventually entered convents, and of her eight sons six became priests. Of the six priests, three became Bishops, and one of these a Cardinal.

Rev. L. G. Lovasik, SVD
Immaculata Magazine
December 1984/January 1985

"Standing in front of the congregation holding the wine cup was not a difficult job, nor did it make me nervous. However, as I held the cup during communion at one Saturday evening Mass, I was given an insight as to what it contained. That little glass cup held the blood of Jesus Christ. Not wine and water, but the same Blood that dripped from Jesus' wounds and crown of thorns some 2,000 years ago. Although it has a different form now, it is, to Catholics, the same Blood that fell from His back after the scourging at the pillar. These few ounces in the small cup also stained the wood of the Cross. The humanity of Jesus became strikingly apparent to me as I stood looking down into the cup.

"I had a true sense of awe as I realized that this is the same blood shared by our Christian ancestors while they hid in the catacombs in Rome; the same blood which all the Popes have raised in offering to God.

"Now, every time I hold the cup, I firmly understand that this is Jesus' Blood. I still feel no sense of worthiness or unworthiness, but I do sense the value and actuality of what is in that cup."

A Eucharistic Minister
Healing Through the Mass
Fr. Robert DeGrandis, ssj

Another healing involving the Eucharist happened in Sydney, Australia. A woman came to a place where Father Kevin and I were speaking. She came up to me in a hallway to ask me to pray with her. She was desperate because she was suffering from stomach cancer. She had a tumor which caused great swelling. The doctors had told her there was little point in operating because it had spread too extensively. I knew there was a Mass that afternoon, so I told her I'd pray with her, but I also told her to go to Mass and to ask Jesus to heal her . . .

That night, when we were having a rally, a woman came running up the aisle of the hall and she threw her arms around me saying, "Sister, it happened! It happened . . . Look at me. I came to you this morning. I went to Mass as you said. When I was walking up to communion, I said to myself, 'In a few minutes, I am going to meet Jesus. I'm going to take him in my hand and I will ask him for his help.'"

While she was a Catholic who received communion often, this time she looked at the sacred Host and said, "I know you are really here. Today when you come into me, take away this fear. Heal me if you want, but please do something for me."

She told me, "I had no sooner put the Host on my tongue and swallowed it than I felt as though something was burning my throat and down into my stomach. I looked down at my stomach and the growth was gone."

That woman was healed. I wonder how many of us come to the Eucharist only physically present, without any expectant faith, any excitement over what we are doing. Perhaps we come to the Eucharist only for what we get out of it and we do not thank God or praise him for giving himself to us.

Sr. Breige McKenna, osc
Miracles Do Happen

From the Consecration to the Communion of the Midnight Mass of 1927 Therese saw the glorified Christ Child, though she was at home and abed because of the extreme weakness following Passion ecstasies. She became ecstatic now when the church bells were heard announcing the Consecration. The infant Saviour as she saw Him measured about 40 centimeters and was dressed in a shirt of dazzling whiteness. He stood on a bright cloud and held out His arms and smiled. His hair was fair and curly, his eyes deeply blue: an apparition of more than earthly loveliness. In the distance there was wondrously sweet music.

Albert Paul Schimberg
The Story of Therese Neumann

In an age of many abuses Francis declared that were he confronted with an angel and an unworthy priest, he would kiss the hand that had touched the Body of Christ before he saluted the angel. He put this into practice one day when he was preaching in a Lombard village. Someone in the crowd pointed to a priest asking, "Tell us, good man, how can he be a shepherd who is living in notorious sin?"

Instantly Francis knelt before the priest, kissing his hands. "I do not know whether or not these hands are clean, but even if unclean the power of the sacraments they administer is not diminished. These hands have touched my Lord, and out of reverence for Him, I honour His vicar. For himself he may be bad; for me he is good."

Clare perforce was deeply impressed by this devotion of Francis; his attitude had been her school. Even before his conversion he sent costly and beautiful gifts to adorn poor churches; nothing was good enough for the dwelling place of Christ. Clare did the same, and even during her long illness she had herself propped up in bed, and made many things of the finest material for churches of Umbria. Sister Francesca told how she had counted some hundred corporals made by Clare, and she had seen a beautiful Child in the Host while It was being brought to Clare in Holy Communion, and on another occasion that same Child was resting on her heart and covering her with luminous wings.

Nesta De Robeck
St. Clare of Assisi

The Holy Eucharist is the continuation of Christ's incarnation on earth. The mystery of the Eucharist gives us the joy of having Christmas everyday. When we come to the Blessed Sacrament we come to Bethlehem, a name which means 'house of bread.' Jesus chose to be born in Bethlehem because He would dwell with us forever as the *"Living Bread"* come down from heaven. When the shepherds and Magi came to adore Him, they brought Him so much joy with their humble visit to Bethlehem that their visit has been praised and retold down through the centuries. God has never stopped honoring them for honoring His Son in Bethlehem.

So, too, your humble visit to Jesus today in the Blessed Sacrament brings Him so much joy that it will be retold for all eternity and bring the world closer to His promise of peace on earth.

We are as privileged in being called to adore Him today as were Mary, Joseph, the shepherds and Magi then, because here Jesus continues His incarnation on earth. Here Jesus loses His Heart to us in love. Love expresses itself to the object of its affection; the Eucharist is the continual expression of God's perfect, unselfish love for man. The Word again becomes flesh and dwells among us, veiled under the Species of the Sacred Host, where the same Jesus born two thousand years ago as a little babe in Bethlehem is truly, really, bodily, and personally present to us in this most Blessed Sacrament.

Fr. Martin Lucia, MSS
Rosary Meditations from Mother Teresa of Calcutta

I am the lover of purity and giver of all holiness. I seek a pure heart, and there will I dwell (Acts 7:49; Isa 66:1). Prepare and make ready for Me a large upper room, and there will I and My disciples eat the Passover (Mark14:15; Luke 22:12) with you. If you wish Me to come and dwell with you, purify the old leaven (1 Cor 5:7), and cleanse the dwelling of your heart. Exclude the whole world and its sinful clamour; sit there alone, like a sparrow on the roof-top (Ps 52:7), and consider your sinfulness in bitterness of soul. (Isa 38:15). For every loving person prepares the best and fairest room for his dear friend, and in doing so, shows his affection.

However, know that even your best efforts cannot make a worthy preparation for Me, although you were to prepare for a whole year and do nothing else beside. It is of My mercy and grace alone that you are allowed to approach My table; as though a beggar were invited to a rich man's supper, and could offer no return for his kindness save humble gratitude (Luke 14:12). Do whatever lies in your power, and do it earnestly, not out of habit or necessity, but with awe and reverent love receive the Body of your Lord and God, who deigns to come to you. It is My invitation and My bidding: I will supply whatever is lacking in you. Come, therefore, and receive Me.

Words of Christ
The Imitation of Christ
Thomas à Kempis

After supper we hurried away to finish our work, and at nine I was able to go to the chapel for adoration. I was allowed to stay up and wait for the Midnight Mass. I was delighted to have free time from nine until midnight. From nine to ten o'clock I offered my adoration for my parents and my whole family. From ten to eleven, I offered it for the intention of my spiritual director, in the first place thanking God for granting me this great visible help here on earth, just as He had promised me, and I also asked God to grant him the necessary light so that he could get to know my soul and guide me according to God's good pleasure. And from eleven to twelve I prayed for the Holy Church and the clergy, for sinners, for the missions and for our houses. I offered the indulgences for the souls in purgatory. (346)

As Holy Mass began, I immediately felt a great interior recollection; joy filled my soul. During the offertory, I saw Jesus on the altar, incomparably beautiful. The whole time the Infant kept looking at everyone, stretching out His little hands. During the elevation, the Child was not looking towards the chapel but up to heaven. After the elevation, He looked at us again, but just for a short while, because he was broken up and eaten by the priest in the usual manner. His pinafore was now white. The next day I saw the same thing, and on the third day as well. It is difficult for me to express the joy of my soul (146). The vision was repeated at the three Masses in the same way as in the first ones. (347)

Sister M. Faustina Kowalska
Divine Mercy in My Soul,
The Diary of Sister M. Faustina Kowalska

What is Holy Mass? It is Christ, the God-Man, the Son of God and the Son of Mary, offering on the calvary of the altar the thanksgiving due to God His Father; making atonement for sin; the only perfect divine atonement and thanksgiving, with you and for you.

What is Holy Mass? It is Christ, the Judge of the living and the dead, the God-Man, Son of God and Son of Mary, imploring, with you and for you, a deluge of graces and blessings, through the power of His wounds, through the power of His cross, through the power of His Blood, and through the power of His sacrifice.

If all this is true, then doctrinally we can say that Holy Mass is a *daily Christmas*. The crib is the altar; the hands of our Lady, the hands of the priest. Yes, in every Mass we can say, "*Puer natus est nobis*," a Child is born, a little Boy is born, the Son of God and of our Lady, far more little than in the crib but still the same Christ. At the altar as in Bethlehem is sung the same *Gloria in excelsis*, for the Savior is born, He is there on the altar; there is but one Jesus . . . Christmas, Incarnation, every day.

Mateo Crawley-Boevey, sscc
Jesus, King of Love

(During Communion)

My dear one, I am now within you. It is in the Eucharist that I am consecrated to you and you to Me.

Many of My people do not realize what it means to receive My Body. My people do not realize the power they receive when they receive the Eucharist.

It is My power . . . the power of Christ!

I, in you, shall grant your heart's desire. It is I, through Eucharist, Who makes your image one in the likeness of God, because you are receiving My Body. I grant you special graces, not by human desire, but my Mine. You become people of God. All you need do is ask.

My people need to be open to this.

Words of Our Lord
I Am Your Jesus of Mercy, Vol I
The Riehle Foundation

December 27

Although the beloved disciple loved much, it was God who first loved him (cf. 1 Jn 4:10). The Father graced him with an unbreakable bond of friendship with his Son. Jesus loved the beloved disciple, called him, ate with him, held him in his gaze, died for him, and rose for him.

This friendship celebrated in Scripture excites a passion in us that causes us to wish that Jesus will rejoice in the Holy Spirit because of us "as he said to them privately, 'Blessed are the eyes that see what you see'" (Lk 10:23). What ecstasy is the intimacy of the Risen Lord!

To be the beloved is to exult in the sweetness of paradisiacal joy. And it is also to be graced with suffering. It is to be one with the crucified and risen Lord, if you are his beloved. It is to see Jesus in the poor, the rich, the miserable, the magnificent—the person closest to us, and the one whose face we have never seen.

On this earthly pilgrimage we know Jesus "in the breaking of the bread." Knowing is not an intellectual exercise but an intimate knowledge of the heart. *Heart speaks to heart!* Knowing and believing in Jesus is saying "Amen" to him and to every member of his mystical body. We are called to a position of privilege, the mystery of election. We are those "who have been chosen beforehand by God to eat and drink with him after he rose from the dead" (Ac 10:14), for every Eucharist is a post-resurrection meal. The exact identity of the beloved disciple is uncertain. We are the beloved disciple!

Michele T. Gallagher
Honey from the Rock

B ut just as He stood quietly among His apostles in the amazing beauty of His resurrection, and said, handle Me and see, so does He abide with us in the Blessed Sacrament, that we may get to know Him, to outlive our tremulous agitation, and the novelty of our surprise, and to grow familiar with Him, if we can, as our life-long Guest. There we can bring our sorrows and cares and necessities at all hours . . . We can choose our own time, and our visit can be as short or as long as duties permit or as love desires. There is an unction and a power in the mere silent companionship of the Blessed Sacrament which is beyond all words. . . . The ways of visiting the Blessed Sacrament must be as various as the souls of men. Some love to go there to listen; some to speak; some to confess to Him as if He were their priest; some to examine their consciences, as before their judge; some to do homage as to their king; some to study Him as their Doctor and Prophet: some to find shelter as with their Creator. Some rejoice in His Divinity, others in His Sacred Humanity, others in the mysteries of the season. Some visit Him on different days by His different titles, as God, Father, Brother, Shepherd, Head of the Church, and the like. Some visit to adore, some to intercede, some to petition, some to return thanks, some to get consolation; but all visit Him to love and, to all who visit Him in love, He is a power of heavenly grace and a fountain of many goods, no single one of which the whole created universe could either merit or confer.

Fr. Frederick William Faber
The Blessed Sacrament

All my life I've been saying the *Kyrie Eleison* at Mass. Finally one day it dawned on me, many years after I was ordained into the priesthood, "Lord, have mercy!" I never heard it so deeply before. We are like sponges floating on an ocean of mercy, crying "Mercy." All we need is the capacity to receive, like the sponge. When a sponge has a capacity to receive, water rushes in and the sponge is filled. As we forgive, and receive His forgiveness, then we can soak up the mercy. Mercy means love and forgiveness in action. Psalm 51:1 says, "Have mercy on me, O God, in Your goodness . . ." The Lord extends His arms to us and says, "Receive my forgiveness, my pardon, my mercy." As you open your heart and say, "Lord, I receive," the dry sponge that has been floating on an ocean of mercy begins to soak up all that waiting grace.

The Lord then holds you up tenderly to His Father, covered in His precious blood, and says, "Mercy." The accuser, the devil, interrupts angrily and asks, "But what about this . . . and this . . . and this?" The Father ignores the accuser, looks down at you and sees someone clean and free and whole, washed in the blood of His Son." His heart overflows with joy as He says, "Come, beloved of my Son." There is no time with God. Because He lives in the eternal now He sees us in glory already, and is so happy with our presence.

Robert DeGrandis, SSJ
Healing through the Mass

A s we consider the wonder of the Eucharist and the enormous value of the Mass in our lives, we must never forget that the Lord, in His extraordinary love for us, has not only given us the Eucharist, but has desired that this Eucharist be maintained as a living and lasting memorial in our tabernacles. In the document *Holy Communion and Worship of the Eucharist Outside Mass,* we read: "The celebration of the Eucharist in the Sacrifice of the Mass, moreover, is truly the origin and purpose of the worship that is shown to the Eucharist outside Mass. Christ the Lord is offered in the Sacrifice of the Mass when He begins to be sacramentally present as the spiritual food of the faithful under the appearance of bread and wine. After the Eucharist has been offered, as long as the Eucharist is reserved in churches and oratories, Christ is truly the Emmanuel, that is, God with us. Day and night He is in our midst, full of grace and truth He dwells among us" (Sacred Congregation for Divine Worship).

The Most Reverend Theodore E. McCarrick
Archbishop of Newark
All Praise and All Thanksgiving,
A Pastoral Letter on the Eucharist

After Holy Mass, we are called upon to live in the Spirit and to continue the struggle against the limitations of the body. In this struggle for life there are both victories and defeats; sins are committed and wounds are received. But, love and the healing of the wounds are active and effective. So, we go to the Mass that Jesus celebrates for us and leave it renewed and ready to go out into the world.

Hence, we can say that at the first step the Church takes, at the moment when Jesus celebrates Mass for us, our own Mass begins, as does our sacrifice for others. Our sacrifice grows as a result of Christ's sacrifice, and it is the highest result we can reach, a point of departure and of arrival.

So our lives can be a Mass, a Eucharist for others. This fulfills us, unites us and becomes something concrete in the world. We are linked with Christ in the true unification of life, and we become a living sacrifice to render glory to the Father. We become His presence in the world, continuing the work of Redemption, having been ourselves the result of this Redemption.

For this reason, in the sense that it is a life of love, the Christian life is essentially Eucharistic, giving itself willingly and joyously to others. In this way, the Eucharist becomes a source of peace. Every path to peace is the way of the Eucharist. The more unselfish the love we show to others, the more easily peace can be made with God and with man.

Fr. Slavko Barbaric, OFM
Celebrate Mass with Your Heart

Copyright Acknowledgements

For permission to reprint copyrighted material, grateful acknowledgment is made to the following publishers and authors. Reasonable care has been taken to trace ownership and, when necessary, obtain permission for each selection included.

Agreda, Mary. *The Mystical City of God*. trans. by Fiscar Marison (Rev. George J. Blatter), Rockford, IL: Tan Books and Publishers, 1978.

Alberone, James, SSP. *Thoughts: Fragments of Apostolic Spirituality from His Writings and Talks*. Boston: St. Paul Editions, 1974.

Angelica, Mother M. *The Mass In My Life*. Birmingham, Alabama: Our Lady of the Angels Monastery, EWTN. 1976.

_____. *To Leave and Yet to Stay*. Birmingham, Alabama: Our Lady of the Angels Monastery, EWTN, 1976.

Thomas Aquinas: Selected Writings. Selected & ed. by M.C. D'Arcy, S.J., Everyman: Dent, London.

The Autobiography of St. Margaret Mary. trans. Sisters of the Visitation. Rockford, IL: Tan Books and Publishers, Inc., 1986.

Ball, Ann. *Modern Saints, Their Lives and Faces*. Books One & Two. Rockford, IL: Tan Books and Publishers, Inc., 1990.

Balthasar, Hans Urs von, *First Glance at Adrienne von Speyr*, trans. by Antje Lawry and Sr. Sergia Englund, O.C. D. San Francisco: Ignatius Press, 1981.

Barbaric, Slavko, OFM. *Celebrate Mass with Your Heart*. Milford, OH: Faith Publishing, 1994.

Barry, A. M. Barry, RSCJ. *Saint Madeleine Sophie Barat*. Newton, MA: Newton College Of The Sacred Heart, 1959.

Bernier, Paul, SSS. *Bread Broken and Shared*. Notre Dame, IN: Ave Maria Press, 1981.

Bertolucci, John. *Healing: God's Work Among Us*. Ann Arbor, MI: Servant Books, 1987.

Bittenz, Frank SJ. *Everlasting Gift, Our Involvement In the Eucharistic Sacrifice*. Boston MA: Daughters of St. Paul, 1987.

Cantalamessa, Raniero. *The Eucharist, Our Sanctification*. trans. Frances Lonergan Villa. Collegeville, Minnesota: The Liturgical Press, 1993. Copyright 1993 by The Order of St. Benedict, Inc. Used with permission.

Carty, Chas M., and Dr. L. Rumble. *Q.A. Eucharist, Quizzes To A Street Preacher*. Rockford, IL: Tan Books and Publishers, 1976.

Carretto, Carlo. *Letters from the Desert*. Maryknoll, NY: Copyright Orbis Books, 1972.

Catherine of Siena, The Dialogue. trans. Suzanne Noffke, O. P. New York: Copyright 1980 by The Missionary Society of St. Paul the Apostle in the State of New York. Used by permission of Paulist Press.

Chesterton, G. K. *Saint Thomas Aquinas, The Dumb Ox*. New York, NY: Doubleday, a division of Bantam Doubleday Dell, 1956.

Ciszek, Walter J, sj. with Daniel L. Flaherty, S.J. *He Leadeth Me*. New York: Copyright 1973 by Walter J. Ciszek. Used by permission of Doubleday, a division of Bantam Dobleday Dell Publishing Group, Inc.

Connell, Francis J. *The Seven Sacraments*. New York: Copyright 1996 by The Missionary Society of St. Paul the Apostle. Used by permission of Paulist Press.

Crawley-Boevey, Mateo, sscc. *Jesus, King of Love*. Pulaski, WI: Franciscan Publishers, 1963.

Cristiani, Leon. *Charles De Foucauld, Life and Spirit*. Derby, NY: St. Paul Publications, 1965.

Cruz, Joan Carroll. *Eucharistic Miracles*. Rockford, IL: Tan Books and Publishers, 1987.

_____, *The Incorruptibles*. Rockford, IL: Tan Books and Publishers, Inc., 1977.

D'Apolito, Alberto. *Padre Pio of Pietrelcina, Memories, Experiences*. trans. Frank J. Ceravolo and his wife Julia with the collaboration of Miss Betsy Ann Spach from the second Italian edition. San Giovanni Rotondo, FG, Italy: Our Lady of Grace Friary, 1983.

Dargaud, Joseph. *The Eucharist in the Life of St. Margaret Mary*. trans. from Sainte Marguerite-Marie et l'Eucharistie Paray-le-Monial, 1921, by Brother Richard Arnandez, FSC. Kenosha, WI: Prow Books, Franciscan Marytown Press, 1979.

Davis, John F. *An Audience with Jesus*. Boston, MA: The Daughters of St. Paul, 1982.

DeGrandis, Robert, SSJ. *Healing through the Mass*. Mineola, New York: Resurrection Press, 1992.

DeGrandis, Robert, SSJ & Ann Ross Fitch. *Walking in the Light,* Scottsdale, AZ: M.A.R.Y. Ministries, 1993.

DeLai, Gaetano. *The Real Presence of Jesus Christ in the Eucharist*. trans. 2nd revised by a Christian Brother, New York: P.J. Kennedy & Sons, 1925.

De Ligouri, Alphonsus. *The Holy Eucharist*. Brooklyn, NY: Redemptorist Fathers, 1934.

De Maria, Mother Saverio,. MSC. *Mother Frances Xavier Cabrini*. ed. Rose Basile Green, Ph.D. Chicago: Missionary Sisters of the Sacred Heart of Jesus, 1984.

DeRobeck, Nesta. *The Life of St. Francis of Assisi*. Italy: Casa Editrice Francescana, 1975.

_____. *St. Clare of Assisi*. Chicago: Franciscan Herald Press, 1980.

De Sales, Francis. *Introduction to the Devout Life*. trans. by Michael Day. London: Cong. Orat., Burns & Oates, 1956.

Desbonnets, P. Theophile. *Assisi, in the Footsteps of Saint Francis*. trans. Nancy Celaschi, O.S.F. Paris: Franciscaines, 1971.

Dirvin, Joseph I. *Saint Catherine Laboure of the Miraculous Medal*. Rockford, IL: Tan Books & Publishers, 1984.

Dollen, Charles. ed. *Prayer Book of the Saints*. Huntington, IN: Our Sunday Visitor, Inc., 1984.

Domanski, Jerzy OFM CONV. *For the Life of the World, Saint Maximilian and the Eucharist*. trans. Peter D. Fehlner, FFI. Libertyville, IL: Academy of the Immaculate, 1993.

Doheny, William J. *The Revelations of Saint Gertrude*. Revised. Private circulation, 1978.

Eudes, John. "What We Must Do to Assist Worthily at the Holy Sacrifice of the Mass," in *Berulle and the French School: Selected Writings*. ed. William M. Thompson. New York: Paulist Press, 1989.

Eymard, Peter Julian. *In the Light of the Monstrance*. ed. Charles DeKeyser, sss. Cleveland, Ohio: Eymard League, Blessed Sacrament Fathers and Brothers, 1947.

Faber, Frederick William. *The Blessed Sacrament*. Rockford, IL: Tan Book & Publishers, Inc., 1978.

Fabing, Robert sj. *Real Food, A Spirituality of the Eucharist*. Copyright 1994 by Robert Fabing, S.J. Used by permission of Paulist Press.

Farrell, Edward J. *Prayer is a Hunger*. Denville, NJ: Copyright 1972 Dimension Books, P O Box 811, Denville NJ, 07834

Gallagher, Michele T. *Honey from the Rock*. Staten Island, NY: Alba House, Society of St. Paul, 1991.

Gaudoin-Parker, Michael L. ed. *The Real Presence through the Ages*. Staten Island, NY: Alba House, Society of St. Paul, 1993.

Germanus, Rev., CP. *The Life of Gemma Galgani*. trans. A. M. O'Sullivan. Pittsburgh, PA: St. Gemma Publications, 1992.

Gobbi, Don Stefano. *Our Lady Speaks to Her Beloved Priests*. St. Francis, ME: National Headquarters of the Marian Movement of Priests, 1986.

Gregory, J. H., trans. *Bernadette of Lourdes*. Nevers, France: St. Gildard, 1926.

Grimm, Eugene, ed. *"The Holy Eucharist"* in *The Complete Works*. Vol VI. Brooklyn, NY: Redemptorist Fathers, 1934.

Haffert, John M. *The World's Greatest Secret*. Washington, NJ: Ave Maria Institute, 1966.

_____. *Akita, The Tears and Message of Mary*. Asbury, N.J. 101 Foundation, Inc., 1989.

_____.*The Meaning Of Akita*. Asbury, NJ: 101 Foundation, Inc., 1989.

Hahn, Scott and Kimberly. *Rome Sweet Home, Our Journey to Catholicism*. San Francisco: Ignatius Press, 1993. All rights reserved; reprinted with permission of Ignatius Press. Pages: 50, 87, 88, 142, 158, 162.

Hampsch, John H, CMF. *Healing Your Family Tree*. Huntington, IN: Our Sunday Visitor, 1986.

Hardon, John A., SJ. *The Catholic Catechism*. New York: Doubleday, a division of Bantam Doubleday Dell publishing group, Inc. Copyright 1975 by John A. Hardon. Used by permission of Doubleday.

Homiletic & Pastoral Review. Kenneth Baker, S.J. ed. New York: Catholic Polls, Inc.

Immaculata, Conventual Franciscan Friars of Marytown. Libertyville, IL. December 1984/January 1985.

_____. *Special Adoration Issue*. Conventual Franciscan Friars of Marytown. Libertyville, IL.

John XXIII. *Journal of a Soul*. trans. Dorothy White. New York: McGraw Hill. Complete Engish trans. copyright © 1965 Geoffrey Chapman Ltd.

Kaczmarek, Louis. *Hidden Treasure, The Riches of the Eucharist,* Manassas, Virginia: Trinity Communications, 1990.

Kempis, Thomas à. *The Imitation of Christ*. trans. Leo Sherley-Price. Middlesex, England: Penguin Classics, 1952. Copyright © Leo Sherley-Price, 1952.

Kosicki, George W., CSB. *Living Eucharist, Counter-Sign to Our Age and Answer to Crisis*. Milford, OH: Faith Publishing, 1991.

_____.*Tell My Priests, The Words of Our Lord to Priests About His Mercy As Revealed to Sr. Faustina Kowalska*. Stockbridge, MA: Marian Helpers, 1992.

Kowalska, Sister M. Faustina. *Divine Mercy in My Soul, the Diary of Sister M. Faustina Kowalska*. Stockbridge, MA: Congregation of Marians, Copyright 1987. Reprinted with permission. All rights reserved.

The Link, Eucharistic Union for the Life of the World. ed. Roland Huot, sss Drumcondra, Dublin: Blessed Sacrament Community, No. 44, July, 1994.

LaVerdiere, Eugene, sss. *Dining in the Kingdom of God.* Chicago, IL: Liturgy Training Publications, 1800 North Hermitage Avenue, Chicago IL 60622-1101. Copyright 1994. Archdiocese of Chicago. All rights reserved. Used with permission.

Lisieux, Therese. *The Autobiography of St. Therese of Lisieux, The Story of a Soul,* trans. by John Beevers. Translation copyright 1957 by Doubleday, a division of Bantam Doubleday Dell Publishing Group, Inc. Used by permission of Doubleday, a division of Bantam Doubleday Dell Publishing Group, Inc.

Lucia, Martin, sscc. *Rosary Meditations from Mother Teresa of Calcutta.* Mt. Clemens, MI: Apostolate of Perpetual Adoration, 1984.

Manelli, Stefano OFM CONV. *Jesus Our Eucharistic Love.* Brookings, S.D: Our Blessed Lady of Victory Mission, 1973.

Mauriac, Francois. *Holy Thursday, An Intimate Remembrance.* Manchester, NH: Sophia Institute Press, 1991.

McCarrick, Theodore E. *All Praise and All Thanksgiving, A Pastoral Letter on the Eucharist.* Newark, NJ: Archdiocese of Newark, 1993.

McKenna, Briege OSC. *Miracles Do Happen.* Ann Arbor, MI: Servant Books, 1987.

McKeon, Thomas, sss. ed. *Emmanual Magazine.* Cleveland, Ohio: Congregation of the Blessed Sacrament.

Menendez, Josefa. *The Way of Divine Love.* Rockford, IL: Tan Books and Publishers, 1981.

Merton, Thomas. *The Living Bread* © 1955 by the Abbey of Our Lady of Gethsemane. © renewed 1984 by the Trustees of the Thomas Merton Legacy Trust. Reprinted by permission of Farrar, Straus & Giroux, Inc.

_____. *The Seven Storey Mountain.* Copyright 1948 by Harcourt Brace & Company and renewed 1976 by the Trustees of The Merton Legacy Trust, reprinted by permission of the publisher.

Muller, Michael, CSSR *The Blessed Eucharist, Our Greatest Treasure.* Rockford, IL: Tan Books and Publishers, 1994.

Newman, John Henry. *An Essay on the Development of Christian Doctrine,* Longmans, Green & Co., London, 1914.

Nouwen, Henri J. M. *With Burning Hearts, A Meditation on the Eucharistic Life.* Maryknoll, NY: Orbis Books, 1994. Copyright 1994 by Henri J. M. Nouwen.

O'Brien, Bartholomew J. *The Cure of Ars, Patron Saint of Parish Priests.* Rockford, IL: Tan Books and Publishers, 1987.

O'Brien, John A. ed. *Roads to Rome, The Intimate Personal Stories of Converts to the Catholic Faith.* New York: All Saints Press, 1960.

O'Connor, James T. *The Hidden Manna, A Theology of the Eucharist.* San Francisco: Ignatius Press, 1988. All rights reserved; reprinted with permission of Ignatius Press. Pages: 13, 14, 18, 19, 38, 46, 47, 80, 81, 281, 282.

Olin, John C. ed. *The Autobiography of St. Ignatius Loyola.* New York: Harper & Row, Publishers, Inc., 1974.

O'Sullivan, Paul O.P. *All About the Angels.* Rockford, IL: Tan Books & Publishers Inc., 1990.

Padre Pio Gazette VII. Cromwell, CT: Padre Pio Foundation.

Pastrovicchi, Angelo, OFM CONV. *Saint Joseph of Copertino.* Rockford, IL: Tan Books & Publishers Inc, 1980.

Peers, E. Allison. *The Autobiography of St. Teresa of Avila.* Kansas City, MO 64141: Sheed & Ward, 115 East Armour Blvd, P. O. Box 419492,. To order call (800) 333-7373. Reprinted with permission.

Perpetual Eucharistic Adoration Newsletter. Vol. 4, No. 1, Los Angeles, CA: Perpetual Eucharistic Adoration, Inc., March 1991.

_____. "Eucharistic meditations from the writings of St. John Vianney, Christ Present in the Eucharist. " Vol. 1, No. 3. Los Angeles, CA: Perpetual Eucharistic Adoration, October 1988.

_____. *"Pastoral Letter on the Holy Eucharist"* by Thomas V. Daily, D.D. Bishop of Brooklyn. Vol. 6, No. 1. Los Angeles, CA: Perpetual Eucharistic Adoration, March 1993.

Rahner, Karl. *The Christian Commitment.* Sheed and Ward, 1963.

The Riehle Foundation, *I Am Your Jesus of Mercy.* Vol 1 & 2. Milford, OH: The Riehle Foundation, 1990.

Rolfus, H. *An Explanation of the Holy Sacraments.* New York: Benziger Brothers, 1907.

Rosage, David E. *The Bread of Life.* Ann Arbor, MI: Servant Books, 1979.

Schimberg, Albert Paul. *The Story of Therese Neumann.* Milwaukee, WI: The Bruce Publishing Co, 1947.

Schmoger, K.E., CSSR. *Life of Anne Catherine Emmerich.* Los Angeles: Maria Regina Guild, 1968.

Shea, Mark P. *This Is My Body: An Evangelical Discovers the Real Presence.* Front Royal, VA: Christendom Press, 1993.

Sheen, Fulton J. *Life of Christ.* New York, NY: Doubleday, a division of Bantam Doubleday Dell Publishing Group, Inc., Copyright © 1958, 1977 by Fulten J. Sheen. Used by permission of Doubleday.

Sims, Margaret Catherine CSJ. *Apparitions in Betania, Venezuela.* Framingham, MA: Medugorje Messengers, 1992.

Talbot, John Michael. *The Fire of God.* New York, NY: The Crossroad Publishling Co., 1988.

Talbot, Francis. *Saint Among Savages, The Life of Isaac Jogues.* New York: Copyright Harper & Brothers Publishers, 1935

Teresa, Mother. *Words To Love By.* Notre Dame, IN: Ave Maria Press, 1983.

Tiesi, Sam, TOR. *Remain with Me.* Steubenville, Ohio: Franciscan University Press, 1990.

To Jesus through Mary. Los Angeles, CA: Perpetual Eucharistic Adoration, 1989.

Young, William J. trans. *The Spiritual Journal of St. Ignatius of Loyola:* Feb 2, 1544 to Feb 27, 1545, (Roma Centrum Ignatianum Spiritualitatis, 1979). Reprinted from Woodstock Letters (1958).